MAKING SCHOOLS
MATTER

MAKING SCHOOLS MATTER

Good Teachers at Work

**Edited by
Satu Repo**

An Our Schools/Our Selves Series Title

James Lorimer & Company Ltd., Publishers
Toronto, 1998

James Lorimer & Company Ltd. acknowledges the support of the Department of Canadian Heritage and the Ontario Arts Council in the development of writing and publishing in Canada. We acknowledge the support of the Canada Council for the Arts for our publishing program.

Canadian Cataloguing in Publication Data

Main entry under title:

Making schools matter: good teachers at work

(Our schools/our selves, ISSN 0840–7339 ; no. 25)
Includes bibliographical references.
ISBN   1–55028–624–2

1. Teaching – Canada.   2. Education – Canada.
I. Repo Satu.   II. Series.

LA412.M228 1998   371.1'020971   C98–931145–7

Design and typesetting: Tobin MacIntosh.

Cover Design: Nancy Reid.

Front cover photo illustration: Vincenzo Pietropaolo

James Lorimer & Company Ltd., Publishers
35 Britain Street
Toronto M5A 1R7

Distributed in the United States by:
Orca Book Publishers
P.O. Box 468
Custer, WA
USA 98240-0468

Printed and bound in Canada

Contents

MAKING SCHOOLS MATTER
Good Teachers at Work

Part IV – Science Teaching: On Having Wonderful Ideas

Introduction

There are two competing reform movements in Canadian education today. One is driven by cost–cutting governments, flanked by business advisory councils. It is centralized, top–down, geared towards accountability and testing. This "official" reform movement is preoccupied with how to produce students that fit the needs of what it refers to as "the global market–place." The other reform movement is not oriented towards testing, surveillance, global competition. It is rooted in a solid curriculum and inspired classroom teaching. It is teacher–driven, grassroots, bottom–up, a democratic movement which believes that schools should help to develop well–rounded individuals, good citizens and a just society.

Since it was founded in 1988, *Our Schools/Our Selves* has reflected these grassroots concerns of teachers and parents and friends of public education across the country. This anthology brings together a selection of our best writings on curriculum, classroom teaching and equity issues, with a couple of new additions. It also celebrates our 10th anniversary as a forum for discussion, debate and reflection on education by Canadian education activists.

"Why are we here?" asks the editorial in our debut issue in 1988, and goes on to offer as a "short answer" a desire to help to create a practical alternative to "the corporate vision of public education," which views schools both as a lucrative market and as an assembly–line for producing avid consumers and cheerful, "flexible" workers.

When it comes to curriculum, the editorial speaks of the need to develop an alternative moral vision which links school work with popular struggles for justice and equity: the union movement, the women's movement, the anti–racist movement, the struggles for peace and a clean environment. These struggles, we argue, must increasingly be woven into the core of our school curriculum, as they are already woven into the fabric of the lives of so many of us.

From the beginning *Our Schools/Our Selves* has also taken seriously the feminist imperative that we must link the personal and political. Reflecting this spirit, the first editorial speaks of encouraging classroom work where students are taught to examine their own lives: "We must encourage kids to be open about their own lives, to work at imagining the lives of others, and to think about how they can make the world a better place for everyone. We must protect them when they do this. And we must persuade other parents and teachers that this is how kids get strong and smart."

Many of the features in this first issue reflect this alternative moral vision. It is expressed with particular eloquence by Jane Gaskell in "A Feminist Agenda for Canadian Education" and by the students and staff of the Saskatoon Native Survival School talking about their school. Gaskell stresses that a feminist agenda is not just about equal access and the removal of gender stereotyping, but involves a radical rethinking of curriculum and schools. It does not take away from issues of curriculum reform, racism, teachers' rights and teacher education, but is intrinsic to all of them. Likewise the students and teachers at the Saskatoon Native Survival school stress that the personal not only leads to the political, but is essential to it. As an example, they offer their school drama program in which they not only learn to act well, to write more effectively and to develop better self–knowledge, but also to "take care of people" both in and out of school.

Our Schools/Our Selves began with a decentralized structure, with editorial groups across the country which participated in decision making and contributed to the content. While all these groups have not survived the decade, they have each produced a lively array of writers, contributors and critics. They have done their best to make sure that we reflect education struggles across the country and don't become too Ontario-centered, just because the editorial office happens to be in Toronto.

Today the battle lines between the two reform movements are drawn even more clearly than a decade ago. We hope that this anthology will help to strengthen the resolve of the grass-roots movement for public education and promote the view that all our children deserve the best education schools can offer.

Satu Repo
Toronto
June 1998

Part I

A Canadian Curriculum

NATIONAL IDENTITY has always been a difficult issue for English Canadians, caught between the powerful economic and cultural pull of two empires, first the British, then the American. Robin Mathews speaks of the "missing centre" in Canadian school curriculum, asking some hard questions: Why is the Canadian education system almost alone in the world in refusing to begin its curriculum with the history, experience and accomplishments of its own people? Why can't we take pride in who we are?

He describes his own experience, teaching English to under-graduates, and their delight and enthusiasm when exposed to writers who helped them to clarify their own experience as Canadians. Students discovered that the writers of their own tradition wrote good works, led exciting lives and thought imaginatively about society. They often wanted to know why their high schools had deprived them of that knowledge.

Mathews ascribes the reluctance to deal with Canadian content to the colonized consciousness of many Canadians in positions of authority. He urges Canadian teachers to begin to reverse this process. Canadian teachers alone could begin a major decolonization process, he argues. He urges them to perceive their task from an anti-imperialist perspective by insisting, quietly and firmly, upon a Canadian-centred treat-ment of Canadian affairs and that of the world around us.

Ken Osborne examines the issue of a Canadian national curriculum from a socialist perspective. He reminds us that socialists have historically been leery of using the public school system to promote nationalism among the young. Instead they have argued that schools should be used to teach international and global awareness and solidarity. Most of the Canadian left, nevertheless, has been favourably disposed to nationalism. As they see it, given Canada's geopolitical realities, the alternative to Canadian nationalism is not internationalism, but the cultural domination of the United States.

There are still major dilemmas of what should be taught, as Osborne makes clear: How can a Canadian national education policy be *national* in any meaningful sense while at the same time acknowledging the rights of both official languages, the multicultural reality of Canada, native rights, not to mention regionalism, and the political reality that education is under provincial control?

While Osborne has many helpful suggestions about what should be included in a Canadian nationalist curriculum, he emphasizes a particular approach to the subject. He insists that we should not attempt to impose on students this or that version of Canadian reality. Instead, we should introduce them to the continuing Canadian debate on the subject, teaching them the various versions of what Canada is or should be, and give them the knowledge and skills to make up their own mind.

John Willinsky focuses on the "multicultural" dimension of Canadian curriculum. Making his contribution to the ongoing Canadian debate on national identity and national curriculum, he offers a "post-colonial supplement." What we need, he argues, is to create space in the curriculum for thinking about the implications of five centuries of imperialism on Canadian mainstream views. He reminds us that in the last century Canada emerged as one of the "white colonies," given to colonizing its aboriginal peoples and those immigrants who did not fall within what we know as the country's founding peoples, the English and the French. He argues that racist legacies still linger in unspoken assumptions that need to be dealt with. For instance, there is still a sense in which students from Vietnam, Taiwan or Hong Kong must first learn how it is they are "Asian" on their way to learning how they might become citizens of their new country.

As an example of the lingering "colonial gaze" he points to the persistent problems with the often acknowledged shallowness of multicultural school programs. These programs often continue to treat cultures other than the dominant ones as either exotic or monolithic; they represent these cultures through food–and–festival events; and they regard racism as solely an isolated matter of individual ignorance.

At issue in all this, Willinsky reminds us, is the continual search for an effective starting point in "decolonizing" the Canadian curriculum. In this search and debate on what it means to be a Canadian, he urges us to remember Paulo Freire's admonition that the true focus of revolutionary change is never merely the oppressive situation we want to escape, but the piece of the oppressor which is planted deep within us.

Chapter One

CURRICULUM AND TEACHING IN CANADA
The Missing Centre

Robin Mathews

Those of us who have cared about the meaning of humanity in our place and time have had to care about how we've been educated. When we awaken to the knowledge that both the forms education takes and the content which makes it up are unconnected to our daily experience of life, we think about what has been offered to us as 'primary' knowledge. What is it, when we become teachers, we are being asked to pass on?

I awakened, first, to the realization that Canada is almost alone among the countries of the world in teaching other peoples' central knowledge as primary, and our own as secondary. Because I'm a writer of 'imaginative' work I found myself getting to know other Canadian poetry and fiction writers and delving into the Canadian literary tradition, though I was never offered a Canadian literature course in my educational formation. I became alarmed at the Canadian 'knowledge' denied Canadian students.

Even when Canadian materials would have been relevant and interesting, they weren't brought in to courses on foreign literatures. For instance, Oliver Goldsmith, famous English author of *The Deserted Village* (1770), had a grand nephew who was born in Saint Andrews, New Brunswick. This nephew was taken with the new society forming and wrote *The Rising Village* (1825) about society forming in Canada, using the same form and style as his uncle had used. An English woman writer, Frances Brooke, in the circle of Samuel Richardson, came to Canada around the time of the Conquest in 1760. Richardson (one of the creators of the novel) had written the famous epistolary novel, *Pamela* (1740). Brooke published a very fine epistolary novel about Quebec in 1769. It is the first novel about and at least partly written in North America. Those works weren't mentioned to classes full of Canadian students when the related British works were being taught. (The Canadian works are probably still ignored when the "English" literature authors and works are discussed).

Later, after the influx of U.S. professors to Canada, first-year university and college courses almost all had *Huckleberry Finn* included. Almost none had *The Mountain and the Valley* or *Who Has Seen the Wind* — both better novels and more relevant to young Canadians than the U.S. novel.

A "Quality" Decision

I realized that quality often didn't decide what we studied (or later taught). In literary studies, of course, the argument for choice of texts is almost always quality. When it became clear to me that I was being asked to study British and U.S. materials that were not as good as absent Canadian materials, I had to ponder. I came to the realization that Canadians, often, were not so much learning a basis of excellence as being unconsciously conditioned to adopt a colonial-minded view of the world.

The first part of my awakening was proof the formal educational system, happily, only does part of 'educating' (or I never would have awakened). The second part was more painful. I realized that structural alienation is very difficult to overcome. Tinkering inside the structure may have some good effect, but liberation can only come from a renewed structure. A renewed structure, I suspect, only comes about when a large part of the population is determined to repossess its culture and traditions.

What has happened in Canadian education over the last 25 years — to use literary studies as a representative example — is an improvement. Canadian courses have increased in number, and Canadian literary artists are valued more highly. Young Canadians have greater opportunity than 25 years ago to meet excellent aspects of their own culture. But the touchstone of value is still overwhelmingly foreign. Canadian materials are, in most humanities and social science disciplines in colleges and universities, largely pressed through critical and theoretical screens formed in metropolitan society to explain metropolitan experience. Postmodernism, for instance, serves to destroy the metanarratives (the broad, socially useful concepts) that provide a basis for Canadian resistance to absorption into the United States. Post–colonialism, a theoretical mode used frequently in Canada, is quite evidently a misnomer. It permits a patina of vanguardist terminology on work that often utterly ignores the Canadian condition. Both theoretical structures are willing to treat Canadian materials. They do so, however, with colonial-mindedness that assumes we have no worthwhile traditions, that we are not in a colonized state and that metropolitan reality is still the basis of legitimacy. We have broken some bonds; but we have tied ourselves up with others because we haven't restructured learning in Canada.

A Canadian Core

During the 1970s I used to draw a new map of Canadian curriculum for audiences at educators conferences. At the core was Canadian knowledge: that would mean knowledge of anglophone Canada, francophone Canada and aboriginal Canada, and would embrace immigration and all our smaller contributing groups. The starting point (for pedagogy) might be chosen at a number of points. But why not use, as the example, the Conquest of New France? Histories exist, as do novels, poems, stories and paintings.

What was the state of the native peoples at that time? Of the French in New France, and away from it? Of the English at the gates of Quebec, in the rest of North America and England? What was being fought over? Why would it be a short 16 years before the Thirteen Colonies to the south would decide to set up a separate country? In Canadian terms — in the terms set up by a a Canadian-centred approach to the subject — the U.S. view of the beginnings of the United States could be demystified, deconstructed. The beginnings of U.S. imperialism could be signalled early in U.S. life. Then the attack upon Montreal in 1775 by U.S. forces makes perfect sense. What was it that both French and English at the time appeared to want to protect from U.S. invasion and conquest? What was the dilemma of the native peoples? How were they treated?

Out of a Canadian-centred treatment of Canadian and other experience young Canadians would be invited to consider the legitimacy of all the contributors to our history and the legitimacy of themselves as products of the process. The essential pedagogical shift would be in the minds of the teachers, of textbook writers and of administrators. Assume the primacy and centrality for Canadians of the peoples of Canada, and the rest follows.

Extending Our Experience

The circle drawn immediately around that centre would involve the world of parallel experience. Briefly, that world would be made up of what might be called the anglophone and francophone 'commonwealths' and parallel native experience in North and South America. It, too, would engage literature, history, politics, economics, religion, etc., but of other white settler colonies and native-race colonies. Canadians would see our experience as part of a structure of colonialism.

The third circle would involve study related to metropolitan centres of influence: Britain, France, and the United States. Needless to say, those centres would have had to come earlier, but in a different, decolonised perspective than is presently the case. As part of the third circle the subject of metropolitan centres in history could be opened up: China, Russia, Europe, Greece, Rome, for instance.

"Modified Colonialism"

The idea of a newly constructed Canadian curriculum was called bizarre by those who hold power in Canada, and so the gains made were fought for and won piecemeal — tinkering within the alienated structure. Canadian materials, Canadian courses, Canadian Studies programs all increased, but were pressed into corners and niches of the already constructed colonial curriculum. The idea of a reconstructed curriculum was, of course, not bizarre. It simply suggested that Canada follow a structure being followed in most other educational systems in the world. We got, instead, what I might call 'the modified colonial curriculum.' By that I mean the curriculum structure which effectively keeps large numbers of Canadians responding to the world as people who understand that certain events and 'knowledge' of primary importance to their lives always originate somewhere else than in their own community.

A number of forces were present to assure that Canadians would not get a reconstructed system, a decolonized system. Canadian personnel in place with strongly formed attitudes often did not believe Canadian-centred education was legitimate. The colonial structure of teacher training and support materials had no opening for a Canadian-centred approach. At the university level, where initiatives had to begin, imperial interests were expressed and reinforced by both British and U.S. concentrations of personnel. They often resisted the expansion of Canadian courses and the legitimacy of Canadian knowledge. The students, who would normally take Canadian materials to the schools as newly-hired teachers, were denied the opportunity to get knowledge and materials they had to get at university if they were going to be able to open up new courses in the schools.

Behind those forces was a larger one — a force that legit-imized the others. It could be called the Ruling Class, Estab-lishment Interests, North American Corporate Capitalism, or several other names. Its effect was and is ubiquitous. Let me give three examples.

Battles on the Ground

A number of years ago, we discovered that the NATO tax agreement was being applied in Canada in such a way that especially British and an enormous number of U.S. immi-grant professors were, in fact, defrauding the tax department. They arrived in Canada, signed a contract leading to perma-nency but signified to the tax department that they were only staying for 23 months. That way they got their first two years in Canada tax free, although the majority of them intended to stay, and did stay. The tax department needed only to ask for their contract of employment to know they were not temporary. The department didn't even need that for those who were already over 23 months in Canada. Mil-lions of dollars in taxes were being filched from the Canadian taxpayer and, in effect, the immigrant professors were being paid significantly more than Canadians in their first two years. We presented the case to the government minister in charge and to the tax department. They refused to act — even to regain the lost revenue — and years passed before they moved to close the loopholes.

Conducting studies, interviewing Canadian applicants, sur-veying foreign hirings, we became convinced, as well, that Canadian applicants of quality were being discriminated against in hiring for college and university positions on behalf of foreign, especially U.S. applicants. We not only fought in the media and at public meetings, we also gained an interview with the Minister of Manpower and Immigra-tion, as he was then called. He flatly refused to act in any way, even to make sure departmental regulations provided fairness for Canadians. (He was a man who flew in nannies directly from England to look after his Canadian children.) The larger matter eventually became publicly recognized as an ongoing, genuine injustice. Several years passed before the present two-tier hiring process was introduced. It is and has been so badly administered that it is breached as often as it is observed.

Finally, I spoke all over Canada on the kinds of problems described here and on the idea of a Canadian-centred curriculum. I think I spoke in every university in Canada and many, many colleges, over a number of years. I do not remember once being invited by a university or college administration. I was certainly never invited to speak to its top administrators and consider the ideas with them. Indeed, at the University of British Columbia (UBC), student council representatives had to force the American chair of the English Department to hold a consultation with me during one visit there. The English department at UBC hired almost as if Canada didn't exist. The U.S. chairman told me gravely that his department hoped at some time in the future to arrive at a point where it would hire 50 per cent Canadians at each time of hiring.

Wins and Losses

The media made a great deal of the general issue over some years. Two provinces conducted commission inquiries into the matter. A few private organizations did serious study into Canadian curriculum. The university presidents' organization, the AUCC (Association of Universities and Colleges of Canada), created the Commission on Canadian Studies, a nearly million-dollar commission that had surprisingly little effect and refused to look at the most pressing problems: discrimination against Canadians and immigration procedures admitting foreign professors. The AUCC searched widely for a commissioner and settled on a former university president of impeccable Establishment bias. No federal/provincial policy was put into place that would have any serious effect on curriculum and teaching focus. Indeed, in the middle of the struggle the Ontario Ministry of Education cut French as a required course in high schools. Canadian youth were being denied their own information, information they needed to be fully functioning citizens in an independent nation. Canadians of excellence were being widely discriminated against in hiring. The Canadian taxpayer was being bilked and Canadians newly hired were, in effect, being paid less than most foreigners newly hired.

Accident or conspiracy? Both, of course.

Just think what would go on in the minds of young Canadians if they began (using literature again as a representative study) with English Canadian and Quebec literatures; then African, Australian, Central American, and Indian literatures; and then, thirdly, British, French, and U.S. literatures.

Such an idea for curriculum was destroyed before it could take hold. Ironically, the chief argument used against it came from a completely colonial-minded position. The important knowledge, great events and significant literature, it was argued, would be sacrificed for narrow, navel-gazing, parochial material and concerns. The curriculum I proposed, of course, did not neglect non-Canadian material and concerns, but it did place the material of imperial powers in a decolonised perspective; off-centre if you like. That was not to be allowed.

The Student Response

It was not to be allowed because the role for Canada in a North American imperialist structure as envisioned by the Canadian Ruling Class did not envision a Canadian population rooted in and determined to defend the excellences and the cultural uniquenesses Canada possessed. Indeed, the more Canadian-centred information Canadians had about their history, their institutions, their cultural flexibility, their potential to build a good society, the less they would accept Ruling Class plans for Canadian integration into U.S. policies for North America. Ironically, students brought face to face with the idea of reconstructed curriculum responded enthusiastically. They formed a part of the next phase of my awakening.

It is harder to describe. Certainly it cannot be presented diagrammatically. I came to believe that — taught as central — Canadian materials could excite and liberate students not given to excitement about study. I proved that to myself in classroom after classroom. Students discovered that the writers of their tradition wrote astonishingly good works, lived exciting lives and thought imaginatively about society. The students discovered something that they had not known before when the literature was taught from a confidently Canadian-centred approach. They told me that repeatedly. They discovered that all literature opens the reader to deeply significant human experience, but that the literature of their own people and country has an extra relevance and power. For instance, I well remember a red-headed male of about 20 from the prairies (with a French last name) coming to my desk after a lecture about Susanna Moodie. "She's not an English woman," he said. "She's Canadian. She's writing about me."

That was their discovery. They discovered a literature that not only concerned the universal human heart, but that universal heart as it beat in their own breasts. That discovery gave them knowledge and confidence no one could take away. Their discovery is one made by all people reading the writers of their own culture. Consider, for instance, the Canadianness of Margaret Laurence's *The Diviners*. Consider that it is an internationally successful novel. It has universal power, but it has extra relevance and power for many Canadians. Maybe that's why Laurence wrote, not long before she died, that she loved having an international audience but her Canadian readers kept her honest. A part of my awakening, then, was that Canadian knowledge could have extraordinary power in the lives of young Canadians.

The Teacher Response

But even as that was happening I had to face the insurmountable reality we all like to ignore when discussing curriculum — the bearers of curriculum, the teachers. I was hearing on all sides the old clichés: Canadian history is dull;

Canadian literature is second rate; no one's really interested in the structure of Canadian politics, or the struggle for Canadian trade unions, or the varieties of religion in Canada, or the foundation of Canadian philosophy, or the story of sport in Canada or the economics of Canadian dependence.

An eternal truth that runs through all pedagogical literature since Plato was thrust upon me. Students who find themselves with a teacher who knows and loves his or her subject and loves his or her students will be excited and liberated. Equally as eternal a truth became clear to me. Teachers with colonized minds are almost incapable of exciting and liberating students into knowledge about themselves and their primary community. They are almost incapable of doing anything else but alienating students from the knowledge that should be primary to them. Not only were many Canadian teachers failing to take young Canadians to their own — their most relevant materials — they were also attempting to tell them that the most relevant materials were those of another country.

It would be easy to attack Canadian teachers for failing to teach in a Canadian-centred way. But they have long been prepared to do otherwise. As British intellectual domination receded in Canada, U.S. intellectual domination moved in to take its place. That would seem strange, except that a condition Americans were happy to encourage was, indeed, promoted by the Canadian Ruling Class. The examples I gave of government refusal to act and the attempt by university and college administrations to ignore the issue of discrimination against Canadians make that clear. Informed of striking irregularities, ministers of federal departments didn't move to assure Canadian rights and opportunities. Rather, they maintained systems that assured U.S. intellectual leadership in Canada. Ruling Class attitudes, of course, are mirrored all through the society. When the issue of Canadian rights in educational hiring, curriculum and administration were first presented, the *Globe and Mail* published nothing. Only after other media forced the paper's hand did it begin to cover the issue. The point, very simply, is that teachers in Canada, like everybody else, spend their lives being told that Canadian sovereignty, Canadian rights and Canadian culture are not really things Canadians should be deeply interested in. To be interested in them is to be extremist, narrow, parochial, illiberal, even (for some strange reason) 'racist.'

The Freire Method

A brief illustration of the process of alienation of students is readily available. I use an example from *A Pedagogy For Liberation* purposefully. Many more Canadians will have read it than a relevant Canadian text. Apparently dealing with a subject quite unrelated to Canada and Canadian curriculum, it makes dramatically the point I want to make. The book is a series of dialogues between Paulo Freire and U.S. educationist Ira Shor. Throughout the book, Freire is at ease, urbane, sophisticated, open, loving. Shor has trouble fixing and defining the resistance and obstructions plainly evident to him in U.S. classrooms.

The two discuss student response to (putting it briefly) the Freire method. Shor reports two responses he's experienced. To sum up the unsympathetic response, he says:

> Then, there was also anger and anxiety. Students might ask out loud, what the hell do you want? Why don't you just fill the hour with teacher–talk and let me copy down the answers silently, staring at you with glassy eyes, making believe I am listening to your words flying through the air while in fact I am dreaming about beer or dope or sex or Florida or the big football game or the party this weekend.[1]

The statement gives Shor away; it doesn't record communication but excommunication. Students who are unsympathetic to a method different to the ones they are used to may be very intelligent and responsible. They may, however, in tension blurt out stock phrases of resistance. To stereotype them as the brain–dead speaks volumes. Another factor complicates the very strange statement Shor makes. Shor may — with complete confidence and ease — be trying to impose on students a method that is quite foreign to their culture and sensibility — however good it may be in South America. The method Shor wishes to introduce may simply not be effective for dealing with reality as it exists in the United States.

In the Canadian case, teachers who don't believe in the importance of Canadian materials, who believe deeply that such materials represent second-rate knowledge, will have difficulty teaching. When those same teachers really believe foreign materials are the important materials, they will produce students who claim Canadian history is dull, Canadian literature second rate — students who will repeat the litany of clichés.

I am not saying simply that teachers can kill the possibility of learning. I am saying that the conscious and unconscious ideology of teachers permits them to say that, 'objectively speaking,' perfectly good and important material is unsuitable. With the power they have — throughout the Canadian educational system — the place of Canadian knowledge and legitimacy could be returned to Canadian education. Indeed, I hold it to be true that Canadian teachers alone could begin a major decolonization process among the population merely by perceiving their task, quietly and firmly, from an anti–imperialist perspective — from a perspective that insists upon a Canadian–centred treatment of Canadian and other experience.

Consciously or unconsciously colonized teachers are a very special kind. They are frequently unsympathetic not only to the materials of their own people but to their own people themselves. To those teachers, the good is elsewhere; it can't be sitting in this room.

Teaching in Canada

If what I awakened to in that regard is true, teaching in Canada has a special set of obstructions. But the teachers, as many have already observed, are products of the society in which they live. Forces that denigrate Canadian independence, initiative, and self-respect have dominant power in the society. One need only think of a few obvious things. Most Canadian teachers are members of unions which have done a great deal to establish teachers' securities and economic status. But most schools (colleges and universities) don't teach the story of Canadian unionism or union-related relevant materials in disciplines. Where 'labour/management relations' are taught, they are rarely taught with genuine sympathy for labour. Indeed, my experience tells me that teachers as a body at all levels within the educational system convey a negative impression of unionism in Canada.

A leading Canadian feminist (to use another example) wrote to me recently to say that Canadians care a great deal more about U.S. feminists, however irrelevant, than Canadian feminists. She went on to say that the people who very often invite the U.S. feminists to Canada instead of calling upon Canadian feminists are people in Canadian educational institutions.

In the production of musical entertainments by schools all over Canada, to use a final example, Canadian teachers responsible invariably produce tired old Broadway musicals. They pay very high royalties to (usually) New York, and they provide for their audiences materials that are very often racist, imperialist, and ethnocentric.

Many of the people involved with the productions are wonderfully talented people who write shows themselves. But they have no national organization, no policy to produce Canadian materials, no touring circuit to send successful new shows on, no central repository and clearinghouse for new Canadian materials they originate. They don't have the self-respect to believe they might be the basis for a national development in Canadian music.

Those examples reveal a special aspect of Canadian colonialism as it appears in education. Stated broadly, it is that many, many Canadian educators look South for ideas and do not recognize ideas when they originate in Canada. I am willing to state categorically that if unionism was taught seriously and sympathetically in U.S. schools, it would be taught that way in Canada. The U.S. dominates the Canadian economy and culture, forcing them to serve the interests of large corporations and their pursuit of profit. Even though Canadian teachers are in unions of real significance, their pedagogy mirrors U.S. corporate interests, not the interests of most Canadians.

Very briefly, U.S. imperialism as it affects Canada is neither faced squarely nor taught seriously in any significant way in Canadian education. Consider only books, films, and electronic teaching aids in schools. If the more than half million teachers at all levels in Canada — through their organizations — had firm, collaboratively-drawn, ongoing policies demanding a viable Canadian film industry, they could influence public policy significantly. Production of texts wholly produced from Canadian sources, and the development of Canadian software and hardware for Canadian education would significantly influence policy, increase employment and help centre the focus of education reasonably on the Canadian community of the learners.

Canadian teachers, in the vast majority, do none of those things. Indeed, Canadian teachers, in a majority, happily attend U.S. films, for instance, which contribute to the consolidation of U.S. imperial power in Canada. They return to their classrooms and, formally or informally, discuss with their students the films as Canadian events.

Canada and Columbus

Finally, a contentious point. The discussion and examination of 500 years of oppression in the New World since the arrival of Christopher Columbus have sparked vital debate. All other things being equal, the subject provides many avenues of interest for Canadian teachers and students. But all other things are never equal in Canada.... We discover in the best Canadian articles on the subject discussion of Eurocentrism, Eurocolonization, racism, non-white immigration, decolonization of native peoples, the guilt and shame of the 'West,' and imperialism as a Eurocentric manifestation. Those are aspects of the subject blessed by progressive forces in the metropolitan centre.

What we don't see is Columbus and Eurocolonization in

relation to Canada, specifically. We don't see discussed the effect of Eurocolonization transforming into U.S. economic, military and cultural domination of the hemisphere and the effects that domination has on Canadian responses to native existence. We don't see, in short, any discussion of the U.S.-centrism in human evaluation that is a palpably obvious fact of life in the New World — a very real extension of the Euro-centrism of original European expansionism into this hemisphere. We don't see discussion of the relation between imperialism and racism historically, and the effects of U.S. racism, particularly, throughout the hemisphere.

Our critics and commentators act as if 'Christopher Columbus discovered America,' and from that day on a solid, monolithic force was created to promote 'Eurocentred' exploitation of any difference from itself. I have insisted elsewhere, and I insist again, that Canadian racism exists, is lamentable, and must be faced. But it is not U.S. racism. The pressure from the metropolitan centre is to treat racism, always, from the point of view of U.S. experience and to practice U.S.-centrism in human evaluation.

The Missing Centre

Canadians who go along with that world view help to create the missing centre in Canadian curriculum. The first part of the missing centre is, quite simply, absence of the rich and special experience of Canada and its people. The second part is — in our time — directly linked and imperiously important. It is the lack of pedagogical, curricular confrontation with the forces that warp, displace, dominate and oppress the reasonable desire of Canadians to talk to themselves about themselves. The forces are cultural, economic, political and psychological, and have very largely to do with U.S. imperialism.

By failing to make those two aspects of the centre battle-grounds of curriculum and pedagogy in Canada, we, as teachers, are simply failing in communication. We are actively engaged in excommunication of our students and, by extension, all other Canadians.

NOTE:

1. Ira Shor and Paulo Freire, *A Pedagogy For Liberation*, Massachusetts: Bergin and Garvey Publishers, 1987, pp. 24–25.

Chapter Two

NATIONALISM, CITIZENSHIP AND CURRICULUM

Ken Osborne

Democratic Socialism and National Education

Socialists have been historically opposed to the use of education to promote nationalism in the young. With others, they have long argued that the schools should teach international and global awareness and solidarity. Thus it would seem contradictory for Canadian socialists to press for Canadian schools to cultivate Canadian national sentiment, were it not for three important considerations. First, there is a realization that, as things currently stand in Canada, the alternative to Canadian nationalism is not a spirit of internationalism, but domination by the United States. Second, Canadian socialists insist that Canadian society is worth preserving; that, with all its imperfections, it constitutes a basis for the nurturing of socialist values; and that, however gravely it may be threatened, it makes possible a way of life that is different from and preferable to the one found, for example, in the United States. Third, their view of Canadian nationalism is neither aggressive nor exclusive, but quite compatible with internationalism and indeed a necessary step towards it.

More fundamentally, Canadian socialists cannot work in a

vacuum. We must begin somewhere and the most obvious and practical place is our own society. It should be self-evident that Canadian students must learn about the society of which they are a part. It is of little use to teach them about utopian fantasies of future global interdependence if it means ignoring the problems of the here and now. The task is, of course, to link the two, so that today's utopian fantasies cease to be either fantastic or utopian. For all these reasons, any attempt to see Canadian education in a socialist framework, and especially one that is centrally concerned with citizenship, must take into account the national question.

In 1968 a bombshell hit Canadian educational circles. At first sight, it looked harmless enough: a slim volume bearing the title *What Culture? What Heritage?* and the subtitle "a study of civic education in Canada." Very quickly, however, the book gained national attention. It proved to be far more than a report on education, since it raised fundamental questions of national identity and even of the possible disappearance of Canada. So far as the strictly educational aspects of the report were concerned, it described itself as presenting "a very strong indictment of the way Canadian studies are now being taught in our schools." More broadly, the report argued that the teaching of Canadian studies in the schools was, with a few exceptions, worse than useless, producing in students a boredom and a cynicism that were a threat to national existence.

What Hodgetts did for the schools in 1968, T.H.B. Symons did for the universities in 1975. Symons investigated the university thoroughly and reported a startling absence of Canadian content and Canadian materials in the university curriculum. Even more disturbing, "there was a tremendous doubt about whether it was academically appropriate or worthwhile or legitimate or dignified for schools and teachers to pay attention to Canadian questions. Also there was down right hostility or disdain...." (Symons, 1975, p. 13)

In all the discussion and activity that followed the publication of these and other documents, a number of questions recurred frequently: just what should be the connection between education, whatever the level, and nationalism? To what extent should education be placed at the service of the nation–state? Who was to define what the national interest was? Should there be a national policy, not to mention a national department of government, for education? In educational terms, what should be the balance between national and regional interests.

With some exceptions, the idea that education should promote and strengthen any one particular conception of national unity was rejected. The very diversity of Canadian society, it was argued, made such concepts divisive. As Hodgetts put it in *What Culture? What Heritage?*: "Programs based on our concept of Canadianism would make it impossible to teach national unity, but they could help our young people to develop an intelligent, knowledgeable affection for their country and a critically responsible interest in it" (Hodgetts, 1968 p. 121). Symons agreed: "Patriotic appeals to preserve and develop Canadian identity do not constitute, in practice or in principle, an adequate rationale for Canadian studies at any level of education" (Symons, 1975, p. 12). This was partly because the very concepts of unity and identity were themselves contested; they were matters of debate rather than of consensus; and part of the reality of the Canadian experience was and is that they are open–ended questions for continuing discussion rather than truths that have been decided once and for all. It also arose from a conviction that education, at all levels, should be a matter of opening minds, not closing them, of teaching students to think and to deal with issues critically and independently. Thus, the key words were knowledge, understanding, awareness.

The debate that began in the late 1960s continues into the present and, indeed, is the contemporary version of something that is as old as Canada itself. Here, for example, is Vincent Massey in 1926:

> In a country with so scattered a population as ours and a vast frontier exposed to alien influences, the task of creating a truly national feeling must inevitably be arduous, but this

is the undertaking to which our education systems must address themselves, for by true education alone will the problems be solved. To our schools we must look for the good Canadian (Milburn, 1972, p. 100).

The key questions are all here: what does it mean to be a "good Canadian?" What is a "truly national feeling?" For that matter, what is "true education?" And how can education cope with the "alien influences" that come from the United States as well as with the regionalism that derives from Canada's history and from its scattered population? In broad terms, what should and can the schools do to maintain and strengthen the existence of Canada as an independent state?

As early as the 1890s there had been attempts to answer these questions by providing a truly national history textbook which would be acceptable to all groups in all regions of the country. Although such a book was produced, it proved to be far from universally acceptable. The fundamental problem lay in the lack of any agreement on how to define the Canadian nation. Then, as now, for most anglophone Canadians Canada is a nation, or, if it is not, it should be. For many francophone Québécois, Canada is a state, a political entity; but it is not a nation, not a cultural unit. In the latter view, Quebec represents a nation, while Canada does not. Given this basic disagreement, fundamental problems arise for any attempt to create a national education policy. Indeed, in the 1980s such a policy has become even more problematic as Canada's native peoples lay claim to the right of nationhood and as multicultural policies are entrenched in much of Canada, thereby reducing even further the possibility of one universally acceptable version of Canadian history.

The question may then be phrased as: How can a national education policy be national in any meaningful sense while at the same time acknowledging the rights of both official language groups, of regionalism, of multiculturalism, of native rights, and the political reality of provincial/territorial control of curricula and programmes?

A useful distinction here is that made by Ramsay Cook

between the concepts of the nation–state and the nationalist-state. The former is primarily a legal and political unit in which individual and group rights are respected and protected and in which diversity is not only tolerated but encouraged, with no attempt being made to propagate any one official ideology or culture, except to insist upon the observation of consonant broad principles such as tolerance, respect for human rights and obedience to the law. The latter, the nationalist–state, is one which, by contrast, does propagate an official culture and which sees itself as far more than a legal and political unit, since it is committed to certain fundamental values. In Ramsay Cook's words, "The nationalist–state is one in which the ideological demands of one cultural group or nation are forced upon all other groups within its borders" (Cook, 1987, p. 5). If Canada is to survive, and if it is to encourage the diversity that is its very essence, it is the ideal of the nation–state, not the nationalist–state, that must pervade the curriculum. In the words of the Royal Commission on Bilingualism and Biculturalism (1963–69):

> An understanding of contemporary society is made inadequate if it is based on narrow exclusiveness. Even if one thinks solely in terms of French Canadian or English Canadian society, the social purpose of history is best achieved by a conscious effort to explain the different values and aspirations of the two societies when controversies arise. But if any textbook lays claim to being a history of Canada, it must go much further. It must be the history of both societies…. The establishment and survival of French Canada is a significant aspect of Canadian history and so is the establishment and survival of Canada as a political union in North America. Any Canadian history textbook should present both these themes (Milburn, 1972, pp. 173–8).

We must not so much teach students this or that version of the Canadian reality, and even less should we pretend that there is one official or objectively correct version, but rather we should introduce students to the continuing Canadian debate by teaching them about the various interpretations of what Canada is and should be, and by giving them the knowledge and the skills to make up their own minds. It is not so much teaching them to understand *the* Canadian identity as teaching them what the various interpretations of Canadian identity (or identities) are.

We must then abandon the practice of using conventional definitions of nationality and nationhood with their emphases upon uniformity and officially approved values. We must learn to see these definitions not as timeless and objective realities, but rather as historical constructions of the European Nationalist movements of the nineteenth century with their insistence that each "nation" should have its own unique geographical boundaries and political state. This nineteenth century nationalist dogma is, in fact, a fundamental interruption in a much older tradition of multiethnic, multilingual, multiracial political units, of which the Roman Empire is a classic example, with its willingness to confer citizenship upon all who were willing to undertake the accompanying obligations, regardless of their ethnic or racial background. The nineteenth century concept of nationalism, which continues to exert a powerful influence in our own time, does not apply to Canada and, when it is so applied, Canada must inevitably be found defective. Canada, with its French–English duality, its multiculturalism, its diversity, can never be a nation–state in the conventional sense, and any attempt to make it so will be as destructive as it is unrealistic.

Paradoxically, Canadian schools will best serve their national purpose by de–nationalizing students, that is to say, by showing them that the conventionally accepted notion of the nation–state is an historical, time–bound, ideological construct that should not be allowed to stand unchallenged and that is neither desirable nor appropriate when applied to Canada. We must see questions of Canadian identity, of national unity, of what it means to be Canadian, precisely as questions, that can be explored and investigated and that will yield a variety of answers, not as dogmas placed beyond question and accepted undisturbed. To return to Ramsay

Cook's distinction, we must show students the difference between the concepts of the nation–state and the nationalist-state and their implications for Canada. This means also abandoning the tradition of using the schools as an instrument for assimilating children into some officially approved version of Canadianism.

What Should Students Know About Canada?

Some years ago Hodgetts and Gallagher worried aloud that the discipline of Canadian studies was galloping off in all directions and argued that "what is needed now ... is a common framework of ideas that educators in all provinces should use in the development of Canada studies that will be country–wide in perspectives and objectives." They certainly addressed themselves to the right questions, though their answers are open to challenge. They insisted that the crucial question was (and is): "What should young Canadians understand about their country?" Their answer was that any curriculum or programme that addressed this question must be based on "the analysis of Canada as a political community," with the concept of political community being understood as "simply a convenient, value–free term ... to describe any group of people living within recognized, dearly defined geographic boundaries, having a system of government and other shared institutions, and possibly a minimum set of goals." Hodgetts and Gallagher acknowledged that a political community, and especially the Canadian version, contains many groups "based on such factors as family, neighbourhood, region, ethnic origin, religion, language, occupation, and economic status" (the closest they came to mentioning social class) and that "controversy and tension ... are inevitable in society." Indeed, it is precisely these controversies and tensions that should lie at the heart of the curriculum and that make Canadian studies so important. "A political community also requires a minimum ability among its citizens to resolve conflict with tolerance, knowledge, and understanding of opposing viewpoints. Without this ability, the tensions may cease to be beneficial and become debilitating or destructive." On this basis, Hodgetts and Gallagher proposed that Canadian studies programmes should encompass these "four separate but inter-related components":

1. the Canadian environment;
2. the structure and functioning of government;
3. the essential characteristics and functioning of the Canadian economic system;
4. public issues in Canada.

These four components, in turn, were designed to illustrate the "readily identifiable characteristics or basic features that collectively make Canada a unique country," and were described as follows:

1. Canada is a northern, vast and regionally divided country.
2. Canada has a broad natural resource base composed of both renewable and non-renewable resources.
3. Canada is an industrial, technological and urbanized society.
4. Canada is a culturally diverse, multiethnic country with two historically predominant linguistic and cultural groups.
5. Canada is exposed to a multitude of external economic, political and cultural influences (Hodgetts & Gallagher, 1978, *passim*).

Here, then, is an attempt to see Canada whole and to teach students what makes it tick. One can applaud the attempt without accepting it in every detail. Hodgetts and Gallagher were right to insist that careful thought had to be given to the purpose of teaching students about Canada, and to insist that it was not good enough simply to bundle more Canadian subject matter into the curriculum. Their idea of providing some kind of model also has much to commend it, and it should be stressed that they were speaking not of any one course but rather of a framework that would guide curriculum planning from kindergarten to the end of high school.

Fundamentally, the question is this: What should students have learned about Canada by the time they finish high school? How this is done can be decided at the local level: the choice of grade levels and subjects, the sequencing of subject-matter, the formulating of objectives and all such technical questions cannot be settled in one simple formula. Rather, what is needed is a grid that can be placed over a curriculum in order to see what it includes and what it omits, and to provide some basis for analysis and revision. At the same time, it must be emphasized that no such grid can ever be fully satisfactory: it is itself a basis for discussion, analysis and revision. But discussion has to begin somewhere and the grid can provide a useful starting point, even if it is totally scrapped and replaced by something different. For what is needed is really very simple. Those of us who see the Canadian context of school curricula as important must engage in a continuing debate over what precisely schools should be teaching and work to ensure that it be taught — and learned. Here, then, is such a formulation:

1. Canada is a country in which national unity cannot be taken for granted. It is officially bilingual, culturally diverse and subject to often severe centrifugal forces. Many of its various cultural groups are experiencing a new sense of identity.

Students should:

(a) know the variety of cultural groups that comprise Canada;

(b) know the major issues between Anglophone and Francophone Canada;

(c) know the history of English–French relations in Canada;

(d) be able to compare Canada with other multilingual countries (e.g. Switzerland, Belgium);

(e) know about cultural/ethnic/racial antagonisms in Canada past and present;

(f) know about the situation of native peoples in Canada;

(g) know the pros and cons of the various ideals of Canada (e.g. unitary, bi–national, multicultural, bilingual).

2. Canada is characterized by strong feelings of regional, a result of history, geography and economic relationships.

Students should:

(a) know about the major regions of Canada: their terrain, climate, economy, lifestyle;

(b) know about the different perceptions of Canada characteristically held in each region;

(c) know how regionalism has affected Canada historically;

(d) assess the varying interpretations and assessments of the role of regionalism in Canada;

3. Canada is exposed to strong external influences, especially from the United States.

Students should:

(a) know why there are such strong external influences;

(b) know the advantages/disadvantages derived by Canada from its proximity to the U.S.A.;

(c) know the current issues and relationships between Canada and the U.S.A.;

(d) evaluate different solutions proposed for Canadian U.S. tensions;

(e) understand similarities and differences between Canadian and American society.

4. Canada is an industrialized, technological and urbanized society, although to varying degrees in different regions. This creates both benefits and problems.

Students should:

(a) know the geography of Canada and its regions;

(b) know the history of technology, urbanization, labour and industrial development in Canada;

(c) know about regional disparities in Canada and attempts to overcome them;

(d) know the different theories concerning the impact of modem industry, technology, urban growth and population settlement;

(e) assess the pros and cons of various forms of urban and rural life;

(f) assess the various prognoses of and solutions to the problems of urban, technological society.

5. Canada 's political system is that of a liberal parliamentary democracy. Canada is federally organized, with consequent federal/provincial tensions.

Students should:

(a) know how "political systems" operate at different levels (e.g. classroom, school, municipality, etc.);

(b) know the structure of Canada's political system — with special reference to how it works in practice rather than in theory (e.g. the role of pressure groups, decision–making processes, etc.);

(c) know the federal–provincial government structuring of Canada;

(d) compare the Canadian political system with others;

(e) evaluate the different solutions proposed for problems of federal–provincial relations;

(f) understand the major problems facing Canada.

6. Canada is undergoing a trend towards larger and larger institutions — both governmental and non–governmental — against which individuals feel that they have little or no power.

Students should:

(a) identify the larger institutions;

(b) know that a trend to larger institutions is taking place (e.g. in workplace, government, etc.) and know the reasons for this;

(c) determine the pros and cons of the phenomenon;

(d) assess the various solutions/suggestions to overcome its impact.

7. Canada is experiencing a serious ecological crisis, exemplified by industrial pollution in some parts of the country, and generally, by the dilemma that pits the demand for energy against the demand to preserve natural environments and to respect the rights of particular groups of people.

Students should:

(a) be familiar with current ecological problems;

(b) be familiar with the cause of the ecological dilemma locally, regionally, and globally);

(c) be familiar with various points of view (no growth, limited growth, laissez-faire, etc.);

(d) evaluate the implications of the "ecological dilemma."

8. Canada has one of the highest material standards of living in the world, although poverty still exists in specific areas or among specific groups of people.

Students should:

(a) know the extent and impact of poverty in Canada;

(b) compare the Canadian standard of living with others around the world;

(c) examine some of the possible causes of poverty;

(d) know and evaluate efforts to alleviate/abolish poverty, both governmental and non-governmental.

9. Canada has a mixed economy with inequities in the distribution of wealth and power. This produces considerable debate and disagreement on the role of the state vis–à–vis the role of private business.

Students should:

(a) know basically how economic systems work;

(b) know the main features of the Canadian economic system;

(c) be familiar with the distribution of wealth and power in Canada, and its intersection with social class;

(d) examine the dominant forms of economic systems in the world (planned/market/mixed);

(e) examine current economic problems in Canada;

(f) evaluate proposals for economic change in Canada.

10. Canada is an economically developed middle–power with various aims and responsibilities.

Students should:

(a) know the nature of Canada's world position;

(b) know the historical background of Canada's world position;

(c) know what involvement Canada has with international trade and investment;

(d) know Canada's relationships with the Third World;

(e) assess the position of Canada in world affairs and the possible directions Canada should take in the future.

11. Canada is a society based upon a commitment to human and constitutional rights.

Students should:

(a) know the main elements of the Constitution and the Charter of Rights and Freedoms;

(b) assess the strengths and weaknesses of the existing for-

mulation of human rights, and of alternative formulations;

(c) know how human rights are protected;

(d) know the violations of human rights past and present;

(e) be familiar with current issues of racism and sexism;

(f) be personally committed to human rights.

12. Canada has a rich artistic and cultural tradition.

Students should:

(a) know the main elements of the history of the arts in
Canada;

(b) understand the role of the arts in society;

(c) understand the issues facing the arts in Canada today;

(d) acquire an adequate knowledge of and an interest in/
taste for the arts.

13. Canada is a society characterized by low rates of political social involvement.

Students should:

(a) know the data concerning political participation in
Canada;

(b) understand the relationship between participation,
power and class;

(c) acquire the skills and dispositions necessary for participation

14. Canada is a society that frequently debates what kind
of society it should be.

Students should:

(a) know the main elements of this debate, e.g. concerning
the role of regionalism, federalism, language, the
nature of government;

(b) assess the various proposals put forward from time to
time concerning the future of Canada;

(c) form a personal assessment of the kind of society Canada should be;

(d) assess the various philosophies of society, e.g. conservatism, liberalism, socialism, anarchism, etc.

It bears repeating that these fourteen statements are not intended to form the basis of a course of study, but rather to describe what students should be learning about Canada during their twelve or so years of public schooling and from whatever combination of subjects. Nothing is said here about how this might best be accomplished, for such decisions can only be made in light of local circumstances. The list is intended to be neither exhaustive nor definitive. It is offered simply as a starting-point for discussion and as a way to give concrete form to an otherwise abstract issue. It deals mainly with content; it describes what students should know. As it stands, it could obviously be arid and boring, though every attempt has been made to link what is to be known with the world in which students find themselves. Nonetheless, if it is to come to life in the classroom, much will obviously depend upon how it is taught. It should also be emphasized that more than armchair, theoretical knowledge is intended. We will not have accomplished very much if students only learn what is suggested here in order to pass a test or get a mark. What the philosopher A.N. Whitehead once called "inert ideas" are not enough. The reason for teaching students about Canada, after all, is to enable them to take part in the continuing debate about what kind of society Canada is and should be, to give them the tools to take more control of their own lives and of the direction of Canadian society. As described elsewhere, knowledge must be linked to commitment and action, in a framework of respect for democratic values.

Canadian Studies and World Studies

In devoting so much attention to Canada, we should not forget that it is important to devote adequate time and attention to the rest of the world. There is a danger that in our concern to make sure that students learn about their own country, we might forget how important it is for them to learn about others. In an age when international problems are of obviously increasing importance, and when they inevitably impinge upon Canadians' lives, it seems self-defeating to ignore the rest of the world, or to leave students to discover it through the vagaries of chance and television — which usually means they see it through U.S. eyes. As things now stand, however, most students leave high school with little more than the most basic knowledge of, say, Russia, communism, Africa, the Middle East, the arms race, problems of development and so on. And, even then, their knowledge is often drawn, directly or indirectly, from U.S. sources, so that they see the world through American rather than Canadian (and never through French, or Russian, Chinese, or Algerian) eyes.

There are useful courses in world affairs in most high school curricula (though it is not at all certain that taking one course will accomplish the kind of global literacy that is needed in the modern world) but they are elective courses, taken by only a minority of students. Perhaps one of the worst features of the Americanization of Canadian children's view of the world is its failure to treat the world seriously on its own terms, but to see it only as a vehicle for American policy interests. Canadian students by and large know little or nothing even of Canada's role in the past Cold War, in the United Nations, in Southern Africa, in disarmament negotiations, let alone of the history and current status of China, the Soviet Union and other major countries. In their understandable concern to ensure that Canada was dealt with adequately in the curriculum, Canadian nationalists failed to ask themselves what was the best balance between national and global concerns. The challenge now facing Canadian studies in the schools is to find a way of combining these two emphases that will do justice to both.

This is more than simply a question of establishing a proper balance between the attention given in the curriculum to Canadian and non-Canadian topics. The reality is that we now live in a world fundamentally different from that of a generation or so ago and students must be properly equipped for living in it, both for its sake and for theirs, for, as has been often pointed out, we continue to live by old assumptions and conceptions which can be positively dangerous in the changed circumstances of today. Einstein said it best when he observed in 1946 that "the unleashed power of the atom has changed everything save our modes of thinking, and thus we drift toward unparalleled catastrophe." Einstein was speaking specifically of atomic power and nuclear weapons but his words can be applied equally to the issues of environmental exploitation, of international economic development, of north–south relations and of social justice, all of which might prove to be as dangerous and disastrous as nuclear war itself. The world is no longer a collection of autonomous states that can all act independently, doing whatever they think is best for their own interests, without concerning themselves unduly with the consequences for others. The world has become an interlocking system in which, as in any system, movement in one part sets up reaction in others, often in unforeseen and unpredictable ways. The old liberal assumption that the greatest good of the greatest number can be achieved by everyone acting in their own particular interests was always shaky: in today's world it is a recipe for disaster. In a superficial way we have accepted this new reality as we have become familiar with new ways of describing the world: global village, spaceship earth, north–south dialogue, interdependence — such phrases have almost become clichés devoid of the power to make us think.

Increasingly, the major problems that face the world can be solved only by international action. This is certainly true of such problems as economic development, refugees, population growth, distribution of goods and resources, environmental damage and, above all, disarmament. For the first time, the planet itself is in danger.

Running through all these issues is a question not so much of survival or prudence, but of simple justice. Can we live comfortably and with easy consciences in a world where so many people live so miserably? Even more, can we face the fact that our prosperity is itself partly based on the poverty and exploitation of other parts of the world? Are we prepared to consider that foreign aid in its present forms is often exploitation in polite disguise? These are not at all abstract, far–away problems beyond the scope of the ordinary person. We live in an age where even eating a hamburger may have entailed raising beef on land torn from rainforest whose depletion is likely to have serious climatic and environmental consequences. In such a context, the phrase "think globally, act locally," has profound consequences for personal living and education.

What then should students learn about the world in their schools, whether through a distinct course of study or as a body of knowledge distributed across the curriculum and throughout their school lives? As with the preceding list of Canadian topics, it should be remembered that what follows is intended as a basis for discussion rather than as a definitive programme. It is offered as a framework either for designing a new programme or for examining an existing programme, and it is intended to describe what students should have learnt not in any given year but as the cumulative result of all their school work. It should be noted also that this list describes only what students should know. It says nothing about the skills and values that should accompany this knowledge, and without which it is nothing more than armchair theory, as is explained in the following section of this chapter. The knowledge that students acquire in school should familiarize them with the main features that characterize the world in which they will spend their lives and with the issues to which they give rise. They are as follows:

1. The great and increasing disparity between the developed and the developing countries.

Students should:

(a) know the main differences between the developed and developing worlds and explore the meanings of the concept of "development";

(b) know the connections that exist between the developed and developing worlds (e.g. through aid, development programmes, trade, tourism, and so on);

(c) examine the political and other problems that exist between the developed and developing worlds;

(d) evaluate the different diagnoses of the problems and the different proposed solutions to these problems;

(e) formulate a personal position on the whole issue of development.

2. The impact of science and technology.

Students should:

(a) be familiar with scientific methods, principles and knowledge;

(b) know the ways in which science and technology have an impact on modern society;

(c) compare this impact with that of other features of modern society;

(d) evaluate the different positions advanced concerning the impact of science and technological development (i.e. the "curse or blessing" arguments).

3. The threat of war, especially in view of the existence of nuclear weapons, great power strategies and international alliance systems.

Students should:

(a) know the effects and risks of nuclear war, and about the various theories and policies advocated to prevent it (i.e. from pacifism to deterrence);

(b) be familiar with the history of the arms race and super power strategies and policies;

(c) know something about current crises, e.g. Central America, Middle East, Africa.

4. The urgency of the ecological question and the growing pressure on resources.

Students should:

(a) know the main principles of ecology;

(b) evaluate the different positions advanced concerning the present danger (or lack of danger) to the environment;

(c) analyze, via particular examples, the dilemma of the need for resources versus the need to preserve ecological balance on both the global and local levels.

5. The lack of basic human rights in many parts of the world, especially where racist regimes are in power.

Students should:

(a) decide what are human rights;

(b) evaluate the different conceptions of human rights and how to protect them;

(c) examine what is like to live under a regime that denies human rights;

(d) know about different regimes, past and present, and their policies on human rights.

6. The importance of ideology as a way of organizing a world-view and of organizing society.

Students should:

(a) know the salient features of the major ideologies that have affected twentieth century life (e.g. anarchism, fascism, marxism, liberal–democracy, capitalism, socialism);

(b) analyze and evaluate these ideologies;

(c) know about the role that ideologies play in human affairs, especially as reflected in the history of the twentieth century.

7. The growing trend towards larger and larger institutions against which the individual feels increasingly powerless (e.g. big government, the trans–national corpora-

tion).

Students should:

(a) know about the historical development of large institutions (e.g. the growth of government, of labour unions, of corporations, of communities) and the reasons for this;

(b) evaluate the pros and cons of this development;

(c) understand the phenomenon of alienation, evaluate its validity and assess its origins.

8. The revolution of rising expectations, by which most people wish, and indeed expect, their living conditions to improve steadily.

Students should:

(a) compare the way of life today with that in other historical eras;

(b) know about the phenomenon of rising expectations and the unforeseen problems it has produced;

(c) evaluate the ways in which people are attempting to deal with these problems;

(d) examine the relationship between quality of life and material prosperity.

9. The interconnectedness of the world.

Students should:

(a) know how the different regions and people of the world are interconnected (trade, investment, alliances, etc.);

(b) know how these interconnections affect the world;

(c) know and assess the impact of such phenomena as modem communications, international trade patterns, increasing contact between governments and people, transnational corporations;

(d) know the work of key international organizations,

especially the United Nations.

10. The demographic phenomena of the "population explosion" and of large-scale movements of people.

Students should:

(a) know about the population explosion, its causes and its effects;

(b) evaluate the different positions advanced concerning population growth;

(c) evaluate the different policies in force around the world that are attempting to deal with demographic problems.

11. The rapidity and pervasiveness of change, so that the ten previous items may well become obsolete.

Students should:

(a) know how change has occurred in different eras;

(b) know how change is occurring today;

(c) evaluate the different arguments advanced concerning the impact of contemporary social change;

(d) examine possible future trends in the world;

(e) give some thought to the kind of world they would prefer to see come into existence.

Active Citizenship and Democratic Socialist Education

To describe those aspects of Canada and the world with which students should have some familiarity is necessarily to talk in terms of knowledge, but it cannot be repeated too often that knowledge alone is not enough unless it is linked with commitment and action. To adapt a well-known maxim: it is one thing to understand the world, but the important task is to change it. To repeat an earlier argument, the task of education, from a democratic socialist perspective, is:

1. to help students to see the world as it is;
2. to help them see it as it might be; and
3. to give them the skills and dispositions to transform one into the other.

This involves a shift in values and assumptions and a rethinking of long-accepted and conventional ways of thinking and acting. This has best been described by the physicist Frijthof Capra and those socialists who have taken to heart the arguments of feminism and contemporary environmentalists. Briefly put, it means leading students to rethink their assumptions in the following ways:

From	*To*
A view of the universe as a collection of separate pieces that can be dealt with in isolation or a linear way.	An integrated view of the universe as a system in which everything is connected.
An individualistic view that sees self-interest as the guiding principle in life and sees individuals as separate one from another.	An emphasis upon connections and interdependence.
An emphasis upon competition.	An emphasis upon cooperation.
An emphasis upon expansion and growth; taking resources and the environment for granted.	An emphasis upon conservation, and the wise use of resources.
An emphasis upon control, domination, exploitation.	An emphasis upon integration, stewardship.
A preoccupation with the	A concern for the future and

here and now and the short-   the long-term.
term.

As Capra himself summed it up, this new way of looking at and acting in the world "recognizes the unjust and destructive dynamics of patriarchy; it calls for social responsibility and a sound sustainable economic system; it rejects all forms of exploitation, of nature as well as of people; and it includes a commitment to non-violence at all levels" (Capra, 1982, *passim*).

There is much that schools can do to facilitate this transformation, both formally and informally. Above all, we can operate our classrooms in this spirit so that we teach as much by example as by any direct message. In Toronto, for example, the Parents for Peace group has emphasized the importance of the peaceful classroom," one that helps children "to decrease competition and increase cooperation, to still aggression and promote helpfulness to divert ostracism and encourage acceptance." Such classrooms are based upon three foundations:

1. students must have a sense that the classroom is theirs;
2. there must be problem-solving approaches in which the teachers and students work together,
3. there must be mutual respect among the students and between them and their teachers.

The Parents for Peace also suggest six criteria for organizing school work in order to promote appropriate values:

1. work must allow for student choice;
2. self-expression must be encouraged;
3. cooperative activities must be stressed;
4. activities that promote a sense of self-worth must be emphasized;
5. students must engage in the exploration of social values;

6. learning must connect with the real world through current events, at local and world levels.

Teaching methods also should reflect and promote the outlooks and values that the new way of looking at the world entails. In this connection, the Club of Rome makes an important distinction between what it calls "maintenance learning" and "innovative learning." The former is what we do now and consists of "fixed outlooks, methods and rules for dealing with known and recurring situations" (Botkin, 1979, p. 43). To use a more familiar term, it is education as problem-solving. It assumes, however, that the problems are identifiable or at least unlikely to differ much from those that have arisen in the past, and that traditional methods will be adequate. While necessary, such a learning style is inadequate in today's world and must be accompanied by an emphasis upon innovative learning, which stresses not the learning of known skills for dealing with known problems, but the ability to anticipate the unknown. In the words of the Club of Rome, it is "a necessary means of preparing individuals and societies to act in concert in new situations." In summary form, it involves the following changes:

Maintenance Learning	*Innovative Learning*
Problem-solving	Problem-formulating
Value-conserving	Value-creating
Adaptation	Anticipation
Following leaders	Participation
Emphasis on the past	Focus on the future
Conformity	Autonomy
Learning facts	Critical judgment
Analysis	Integration
Emphasis on the national	Global orientation

It should be emphasized that what is suggested here is not a diametrically opposed shift of direction from one of the above modes of learning to the other but rather a blending of the two, with a reduced emphasis upon the former, which still receives pride of place in most classrooms. How this might reflect itself in actual lessons and teaching techniques is illustrated elsewhere in this book. Whatever is done, the fundamental point is that, in examining what students learn, we should not ignore how they are learned and are taught. Active, participating citizenship depends upon active, participating schools and both must become part of the democratic socialist agenda.

REFERENCES

Botkin, J.W. et al. (1979). *No Limits to Learning: Bridging the Human Gap*. Pergamon, Oxford.

Capra, F. (1982). *The Turning Point: Science, Society and the Rising Culture*. Simon & Schuster, New York.

Cook, R. (1977). *The Maple Leaf Forever: Essays on Nationalism and Politics in Canada*.

Hodgetts, A.B. (1968). *What Culture? What Heritage?* O.I.S.E. Press, Toronto.

Hodgetts, A.B. & Gallagher, P. (1978). *Teaching Canada for the '80s*. O.I.S.E. Press, Toronto.

Millburn, G. (ed.) (1972). *The State in Capitalist Society*. Weiden-feld & Nicolson, London.

Symons, T.H.B. (1975). *To Know Ourselves*. A.U.C.C., Toronto.

Chapter Three

AFTER 1492–1992
A Post-Colonial Supplement for the Canadian Curriculum

John Willinsky

> This thing of darkness I
> acknowledge mine.
>
> *The Tempest*

For all that has been celebrated and challenged with the quincentenary anniversary of Columbus' landfall, we have tended to overlook the educational imperative that drove the European age of discovery.

On October 12, 1492, the day Columbus first set eyes on the Arawak natives, he recorded in his journal his intention to "carry off six of them at my departure to Your Highness." He had immediately seen the possibility of converting them to Christianity ("it seemed to me that they belonged to no religion"), teaching them Spanish ("that they may learn to speak"), and exhibiting them at Court. This was to become the educational pattern. Europeans treated other lands and peoples as, among other things, adventures in learning out of which they undertook to construct an encyclopedic mastery of the globe. At their most benevolent, Spain, Portugal, England, and the other European nations mounted extended inquiry–centred field–trips. With a decidedly biblical turn to it, they sought to make the world over in their own image, and they saw that it was good.

Soldiers of fortune and men of God, equipped with pen, chart, and collecting jar, were accompanied by gentlemen scholars, writers, and naturalists. They re–named all that they beheld, species by species; they re–moved samples and artifacts to the museums, universities, zoos, and circuses of Europe. One can only imagine the excitement that stirred them at the thought of narrating, collecting, and classifying the wonders of this seeming *terra incognita*. As early as 1557, the Spanish physician Nicolas Monrades was given to claiming that the medicinal properties discovered in the 'new' plants outranked the value (for Europeans) of the pillaged gold and silver.

The Educational Imperative

The educational imperative may have contributed as much to the European sense of superiority, of being invested with a civilizing mission, as did the sword and the cross. Certainly, this new–found learning gave rise to a good deal of speculation among the Europeans about the origins of life, language, and society based on the discovery of this 'primitive' world that was carefully constructed out of racial differences. Columbus' journal entries are marked by a reading of their character, habits, and physical features with an eye to capturing the Adam–and–Eve–like nature of this simpler state of humanity, even as he conveyed to his Queen their considerable potential as slaves. It amounted to a convolution of knowledge and power that incorporated educational interests within an assumed mandate for global domination.

The Europeans were certainly not reluctant to visit the benefits of these interests on those whom they colonized. The lessons gained from these voyages of discovery were all too readily returned in kind to the colonized. Johann Herder, the eighteenth–century German scholar, reminded his fellow

Europeans that "the barbarian rules by force; the cultivated conqueror teaches." The colonial powers' government and mission schools proved an especially effective force, sometimes cultivated, sometimes barbaric, with this global system of schooling forming its own special variation on the educational legacy of colonialism. Although I have done little more here than suggest the scope of the conquest's curriculum project, I suspect that it has taken possession of the colonies in a far more lasting manner than those who commanded the European ships and soldiers.

It would be surprising, after five centuries of this educational imperative, if imperialism had *not* left a mark on schooling in both former colonies and colonial powers alike. Precisely what traces of the imperial past remain in the modern curriculum of the schools, especially in the West, and how these traces might now be turned to educational advantage form the subject of my post–commemoration inquiry. In what ways are educators asking the young to look at the world through Columbus' eyes, to treat it as their "marvelous possession," in Stephen Greenblatt's characterization of the European regard for the New World (1991)? To what degree, I want to ask, does the current curriculum still operate from within an imperial project that was determined to learn about the *other* — the one who is not us — in a process of subordination that was principally constructed around a concept of 'race'?

The issue takes on a certain urgency not simply with the Columbus commemoration but amid the continuing resolution of the colonial legacy worldwide and the related growth of a multicultural classroom in the West. The multicultural classroom manages to confound the traditional self/other distinctions that formed the curriculum project of this earlier imperialism, with its easy equation of race with nation and colony.

Interrupting the Colonial Gaze

During the five centuries of this imperial project, the formulations have changed and are continuing to evolve in ways that can teach us about how we introduce the world to the young. In particular, distinct educational benefits are to be realized, I argue in this chapter, from calling the lingering elements of this colonial viewpoint into question, from asking about the colonial contexts of Western ways of looking at the world. As one of a number of ways of testing these ideas, I want to introduce the pedagogical device of a *post-colonial supplement* designed to create a little space in the curriculum for thinking about the implications of five centuries of a global imperialism. The idea of a supplement is to take hold of the opportunities within the curriculum for asking after, and learning more about, the long-standing colonial gaze of the inveterate educational tourist who is inspired to take in the world without reflecting on what this disposition has come to mean after five centuries of inquiry. In this chapter, I consider the possibilities arising from interrupting that gaze, from turning it inward, to its manner of representing self and other. The instances I briefly consider in the application of this supplement include a community project, a popular educational magazine, a Shakespearean play or two, and a pair of social studies texts.

In using the Columbus quincentenary as a starting point, I am taking my lead from Roger Simon's (1992a) insightful investigations of the counter-commemoration that staged 'decolonizing' events in 1992. These events amounted to, in the words of performance artist Guillermo Gómez-Peña, "a dance on the wound of history," and to which he and Coco Fusco contributed *The Year of the White Bear: Take One — Two Undiscovered Aborigines Visit Irvine*. In this work 'exhibited' at the University of California, they posed as mock-natives in a cage in an effort to make explicit the "voyeuristic" relationship, as they name it, that is endemic to the "imperialist classification and the fetishizing of the exotic body."

The fetishized body of the native also came under scrutiny in Gerald McMaster's 1992 exhibit, *Savage Graces*, at the University of British Columbia's Museum of Anthropology. Amid the museum's regular collection of West Coast Native totem poles and artifacts, McMaster invited visitors to bring in any of their toys, games, souvenirs, and other objects that bear stereotyped images of Amerindians. In return for placing old Washington Redskins caps and Lone Ranger comics in a large Plexiglass bin, this Plains Cree artist graciously offered the donors what he termed "cultural amnesty." How then are we to take these supplementary lessons posed from within this commemoration to an educational curriculum that faces the young?

The Native on Display

Before turning specifically to the Canadian context, it might be helpful to work with perhaps the most familiar example of both the educational staying power and evolution of this colonizing vision, the *National Geographic* magazine. Founded in 1888 during what were still the early days of American imperialism, it has grown into the largest scientific-educational organization in the world. Its dramatic colour portrayal of the world has long been a source of delightful instruction for young and old. What I am asking, by way of a post-colonial supplement, is to imagine the line that runs from the Arawak native that Columbus exhibited at the Spanish court to the photograph of the Kurdish soldier on the August, 1992 cover of *National Geographic*. The primitive nobility of the native-on-display is offered for the consumption of the arm-chair traveller; the world gives up one of its truths to the imperial gaze. The soldier is able to walk away from the camera (but not from our gaze), perhaps with a little extra money to boot. The photograph, however, still represents a dislocation, as the soldier becomes a symbol; you are not expected or invited to participate in the knowing afforded the viewer.

In asking how this process works with the *National Geographic's* treatment of the Kurds, I am not asking for the abandonment of a magazine to which so many happily subscribe. That is not the way of a supplement. The magazine may perpetuate a colonizing of the other which we may now seek to avoid, but perhaps we can begin to do so by also watching ourselves in this process, by attending to the points of our fascination, our wonder, our pity.

Decolonizing Canada

Turning specifically to the Canadian setting, we find a country that forms an excellent educational backdrop for developing this theme of a post-colonial supplement, even as it tends to think of itself as removed from such questions. In the last century, Canada emerged as one of the 'white colonies,' given to colonizing its aboriginal peoples and those immigrants who did not fall within what are known as the country's two founding peoples, British and French. The express need for 'decolonizing' the Canadian school curriculum was first heard in the midst of an emerging nationhood in the nineteenth century. The target then was, among other things, the British imposition of the *Irish Readers*, a colonial text preaching an English and Anglican centre to the human race, which had been field-tested much closer to home. Although Canadian teaching materials were soon developed locally, it was not until the 1960s that a full-scale Canadian studies movement took root, displacing an Anglo-centric focus with a greater nationalist concern in such areas as social studies and literature.

The decolonization process in Canada continues on other fronts, most visibly with Québecois and First Nations efforts to take charge of their association within or apart from this nation as part of constitutional struggle, although they are often at odds with each other in this struggle. The First Nation peoples, especially, do not hesitate to speak in 1992 of a 'colonialism on trial' when speaking of unsettled land claims, taking the issue to the courts and to the highways (Monet and Skanu'u 1992).

A post-colonial supplement in Canadian schools would seek to connect lessons about the country's recurring constitutional crisis with the global phenomenon of self-definition and self-determination that is often caught within concepts and units of a nationalism that are the direct product of the European imperial project, especially in its late nineteenth century guise. It would address issues of a 'neo-racism' and continuing xenophobia that are being experienced in the new Europe in the face of reversed patterns of colonial immigration and economic development.

Even if the incidents of racism in a Vancouver or Montreal neighbourhood are far less incendiary than those that took place in the united Germany, the citizens of this placid country have still indicated in a recent national survey that a third of those surveyed felt it was important to "keep out people who are different from most Canadians" with a majority "really worried that they may become a minority if immigration is unchecked" (*Poll Showed Hostility To Immigrants* 1992). The government's response, the newspaper article goes on to point out, has been to toughen entry laws. Amid a world that is caught between rising forces of economic globalization and ethnic nationalism, there is a need for students to consider their own education and the extent to which the schools are engaged in what Homi Bhabha (1990: 292) terms "the cultural construction of nationness as a form of social and textual affiliation."

Points of Struggle

What I have come to realize in considering the cultural construction of difference is the points at which Canadian schools can be far less accepting of some students, than the students have been of the schools. At least so it seemed as I heard Ted Aoki recently explain to the commencement audience at the University of British Columbia, after receiving an honorary doctorate, how in 1942 he had been unceremoniously stripped of his uniform in the Canadian officer training program at the university before being interned as a Japanese enemy alien during the war. Reflecting on my own post-war education, I have had cause to wonder at the anti-Semitism of my English-class literary heroes — Pound, Eliot, and Lawrence — that went undiscussed, as I gladly learned to celebrate the irrevocable truth of their words. Who was it we were studying to be, I am now given to ask, as students, as Canadians?

I was struck by the question among the current generation of students while recently working in a high school research project in which a student was typing an electronic mail message to a student in another country:

> First let me tell you about myself. My parents came here from Hong Kong (I'm Chinese) about twenty years ago and I was born here in Vancouver. I have never lived anywhere else but I have travelled a lot....

Her simple act of self-presentation at once reminds us of how identity still raises complex questions of race and nationality that is born of colonial days.

Do we have a curriculum that is prepared to address questions of identity as this historical conflation of nationality and race, questions that take on a certain poignancy within the history of British Columbia, a west coast province that is consistently marred by elements of a xenophobic regard for Asian immigrants? To take only the most basic of rights, East Indian and Chinese Canadians were not granted the right to vote in Canada until 1947, with the Japanese permitted to participate two years later (while the First Nations people had to wait until 1960). There remains a sense in which students from Vietnam, Taiwan, and Hong Kong must first learn how it is that they are Asian, in that sense of being apart from the dominant culture, on their way to learning how they might become citizens of this country. They need to consider the degree to which *Asia* is an ongoing invention of the West, and the degree to which this increased study of things Asian can become its own form of neo-colonialism, as the economic tide of opportunities shifts across the Pacific.

Multicultural Concerns

I am not suggesting that these issues are ignored by those responsible for schooling in our country. For some time, Canadian Ministries of Education have been issuing policy statements on the multicultural classroom. Among the multicultural initiatives across the Canadian landscape, the struggle to establish 'heritage language' programs in some jurisdictions has been noted by Jim Cummins (1984), while Marni Price (1992: 31) has described the promising work of Ontario educators who are "beginning to see the possibilities of introducing segments on non-European inventors, scientists and mathematicians."

The study of literature from other cultures has been a particularly strong aspect of the multicultural curriculum in both schools and colleges, and yet one expert in the area, Diana Brydon (1989: 91), has identified the danger of a patronizing regard that amounts to its own colonialism:

> We face the danger that the new vogue for 'third world', 'minority' or 'marginalized literatures', as they have variously been called, will merely introduce more subtle versions of 'incorporated disparity' instead of challenging an organization of discourse that justifies the status quo.

Lee Maracle (1992:14) adds her concerns as 'the most published Native author in the country,' over the way in which "Canadian writers still hover about the gates of the old forts, peek through the cracks of their protective ideological walls." She (1992:15) advises that "in order to resolve this colonial condition in literature we need to have Canada recognize that, first it is our condition and, second, Canada needs to view this condition as unacceptable."

The post–colonial supplement is about inquiring into these incorporating tendencies, as it attends to the legacy these marginalized works are writing both against and within, a legacy that includes this very colonial schooling in English literature.

Imperialism and Racism

More recently, Ministries of Education have taken a more aggressive stand against the racism that has not subsided in the face of multicultural policies. The British Columbia Ministry of Education (1992a: 47) has proposed in its latest guidelines for the senior high school years that teachers seek ways of "explicitly addressing and providing intervention strategies to eliminate stereotyping, prejudice, discrimination, and racism." One of the suggestions, taking the form of an anti–racist initiative, is to expose students to a form of assertiveness training meant to enable them "to intervene in cases of racial and cultural harassment." But whether teachers introduce the literature of other lands or stories by those who have recently arrived in this country, or whether they assist students in checking schoolyard expressions of hate, the historical context that is being played out in the multicultural classroom goes missing, as does some part of its educational promise, I would argue. The post-colonial supplement to multiculturalism would mean realizing that these admirable programs are a response to the colonial legacy.

In yet another form of response to a changing world, British Columbia (1992b) has undertaken a series of Pacific-Rim Education Initiatives which stress the importance of making a positive educational connection with the 'Asia Pacific': "This friendship and understanding are important to B.C.'s future. The countries of the Asia Pacific region are strong economic and technological forces in the world today." Here the post-colonial supplement would need to explore the alterations and continuities in how we are now asked to imagine Asia. It would seek to introduce into the classroom the concepts and methods of analysis helpful to positioning prejudices that are driven, not so much by malice, but by a history of Eurocentric representations of the other as an object of exotic and economic interest.

As much as multiculturalism forms a valuable starting point for a global process of decolonization, it has suffered from tendencies to (a) treat cultures other than the dominant one as both exotic and monolithic, (b) represent these cultures through food-and-festival events, and (c) regard racism as an isolated matter of individual ignorance among certain segments of the population. Anti-racist programs, as a second generation response to the increasing cultural diversity of communities and classrooms, have tended to focus more pointedly on aspects of systemic racism present in immigration, curriculum, housing, and employment policies. Again, these are measures which would be further supported by post-colonial initiatives concerned with the understanding of how difference has been historically constructed on a national and racial basis.

Both multicultural and anti–racist programs have recently come under criticism for their failure to move beyond replacing materials that are selectively prejudiced with another set that are equally selective in their positive images. That is, these programs are failing to provide an education that addresses the whole question of how cultures have come to be represented. By all means, teachers need to confront expressions of racism. But to locate racism in the animosity and ignorance of a small number of people in the community is to ignore how racial difference continues to be constructed in a pattern that was advanced by the colonial project, although it was by no means its point of origin. Despite considerable progress having been made in overcoming the worst indignities of the West's regard for the other, we still tend to accept the basic construct of race as signifying difference.

Creating "The Other"

These additional lessons on the influences of colonialism can be introduced not only into the obvious instances provided by discussions of Christopher Columbus, Southeast Asia, or *The Tempest*. They need to be added to work with *The Merchant of Venice*, as a study in the constitution of a colonizing difference that both sets the Jew apart and brings him under the spell of a desired conversion, or *The Taming of the Shrew* that takes something of the same turn with a defiant young woman. The subjection of the other, after establishing the clear failings of that otherness, to the educative project of the dominant Christian and patriarchal culture proves a common literary theme. Although the humanities form a natural starting point for inserting a post–colonial supplement into the curriculum, imperialism also provides a backdrop for developments in the sciences, especially in biology and the study of genetics and evolution, all of which were bolstered by colonial exploration (Gould 1981).

This rethinking of the disciplines, not as static bodies of perfect knowledge, but as arising out of an intellectual history, adds its own educational motif of discovery to this supplementary work. The points of insertion and supplement are matters of opportunity and potential, as I would demonstrate in a final instance using two social studies textbooks that help Canadian students in the middle grades imagine *their* nation and world.

In *Exploring Our Country*, Daniel Wood (1983) tells the story of a young person's visits to six Canadian communities, focusing on their linked contributions to the nation. Through this familiar genre that establishes the student as interested tourist, the book poses such questions as, "How Does Weyburn Help Feed Canadians?" and "What Do Cape Dorset's Artists Teach Canadians?" The Cape Dorset chapter sets the Inuit prints on the same level as the wheat and oil contributed by other communities; it respects the Inuktitut language, allowing for translation in the discussion with the artist Kenojuak. While the economics of the art work are presented in a realistic manner, from the artists' co-op to the city gallery, the meaning or significance of Kenojuak's beautiful prints are given something of a short shrift. They are referred to as simply 'pictures of spirits' (Wood 1983: 100).

At such points, we need to ask about Kenojuak's participation in this framing of these pictures. How much of this is a reflection of an urbane market for these works that desires, once again, to possess the *primitive* vitality, *unspoiled* freshness, the *spiritual* quality, all of which native art has long represented for the colonizer? As it turns out, one finds in turning to other sources, that Kenojuak has very deliberately distanced herself from such primitivist ascriptions: "I stay away from trying to use the old–fashioned stories from the oral tradition," she says pointedly. "And, rather, what I do is try to make things which satisfy my eye, which satisfy my sense of form and colour" (cited in Blodgett 1983: 34, 37). Spoken like a true artist, one might say, an artist who is all–too–aware of ascriptions of primitive spiritualism. Kenojuak was introduced to Western print–making techniques by James Houston in the late 1950s: "At the time, I was frightened, or nervous, about the idea of trying to express myself in that way but I ended up doing it because he requested, or in our culture, he formally requested, that I try this" (cited in Blodgett 1983: 33).

The colonial framework here is one of the invented or constructed discovery. This is not to condemn either party, but the pattern does add another layer of meaning in understanding Cape Dorset's contribution to our country. In a collection of art and essays presenting Native perspectives on the quincentenary of Columbus, Loretta Todd (1992: 71) addresses the 'discovery' theme in the West's treatment of First Nation cultures: "Everything about us — from our languages to our philosophies, from our stories to our dances — has become material in a quest for further discovery, for new treasures." These colonial themes haunt the educational system, from school to museum: "We are caught in the grasp of neo-colonialism, in the gaze of the connoisseur or consumer, forever trapped in a process that divides and conquers" (Todd 1992: 75).

Something of a neo-colonial gaze also prevails in *Communities Around Our World* by Donald Massey (1984). In this middle-school textbook, students are invited to learn about life in nine communities through a familiar motif: "The best way to learn about any community is to make a visit to it" (Massey 1984: 8). The text presents a series of colourful snapshots of the land and life at each site, accompanied by a story of a family in the community and a series of exercises on reading charts, stories, and pictures. In their 'travels', the students accumulate an appreciation of the breadth of difference, most often marked by poverty, religion, and race, that must in some way speak to Canada's development and bountifulness out of its history as a white colony.

This is not an issue, of course, which the captions and exercises of the text address. Nor do I want to challenge the students' inevitable perceptions of difference. The questions I seek to raise with teachers and students concern the contribution which these books make to the sense of difference without examining how these differences are the product, in part, of an imperial past with which people are struggling all over the globe. Even the visit to the northern community in Labrador insures an appreciation of the distance that exists between what is assumed as a familiar Canada and its indigenous population. As much as this and many similar social studies textbooks eschew stereotypes and depict a gender balance, the books do not begin to deal with the sense of affiliations engendered by such a text's organization of the globe as Our World.

The "Right" to Intrude

The text's striking and vibrant images are a form of educational technology designed to dissolve the distance, to instill the sense of being there. But it does so in order to the make differences known and felt in what was once called living colour. The books ensure the students' understanding of their world is informed by this matrix of difference to which they, like Columbus, have a right to intrude, to possess. This sense, otherwise invisible, can on occasion interrupt the picture if you look closely.

At one point in *Communities Around Our World*, while 'visiting' Zaire, the reader finds a photograph of a small collection of beans, corn, and vegetables, surrounded by a circle of men somewhat out of focus, sitting at the edges of the open hut in which the photo is taken. The caption states that "these people are meeting to give thanks for a good harvest" (Massey 1984: 93). One of the men, however, is looking directly at the camera, attending to the intrusiveness of the photographer which the photo renders invisible. He is clearly expressing something other than thanks, something that I find closer to capturing the very sense of the photographer's intrusion.

If the students could pause over this aspect of the photograph — look into those questioning eyes before turning the page — they would begin to understand what the post–colonial moment holds in store for them. The photographs become a richer source of meaning, a more demanding exercise in reading. Through the insights that come of catching the imperial camera intent on capturing the *colourfulness* of the other, the colonial hold on the imagination begins to break down through a self-conscious questioning of intent and position. Whether the students might then engage in further exercises, perhaps to fill in missing aspects of these depictions or to construct alternative visual and verbal representations — historical, economic, literary — to supplement the text, has still to be worked out and tested with interested educators.

Less Than They Are

I think it is fair to ask whether children in middle school can be expected to find these disruptive moments in the photographs and exercises with which they work. If that seems unlikely, consider how perfectly reasonable it is to assume that the young in our schools will understand, with little help from the text accompanying the picture, that the people depicted are somehow less than they are, less fortunate, less civilized, even as these people are said to form part of the students' world. The students' resolution of the material and cultural differences they confront in class might well take on a form of social Darwinism that blames or pities those represented in their apparent failure to evolve. The post–colonial supplement is in a position to interrupt the pattern, if only by calling into question the temptation to make judgments apart from the otherwise masked colonial relations that define the picture.

There is also the question of what such gazing on the other means to a student with roots in one of these seemingly unconnected communities around our world. The people depicted are both the student and not the student as they represent a part of what keeps this child from what is proposed as Canadian. It does not seem too much, then, to ask for this critical reading in light of post–colonial theories of representation. The incentive here, for interrupting what amounts to an imperial gaze, is primarily educational in its encouragement of a certain reflectiveness. But it also offers, for the students especially, the pleasure of interrupting the authoritative text, if only momentarily. It is to take a critical stance with regard to the uses of representation and the authority of the text. Ultimately, the irreverence of this disruption has as its purpose an understanding of the degree to which the world of difference is often organized as *out there* in other lands, when it already exists *here* in our community and has for some time, to return to an educational theme of the multicultural curriculum.

A Second Look

In taking a second look at this picturing of the other, the post-colonial supplement raises the symbolic benevolence and violence in this manner of studying the world. The privilege of taking in the surface features of others' lives, of witnessing this life-so-removed-from-our-own, risks turning the student into a consumer of others' experiences; an educational tourist. It can only add to the scope of students' education to learn about the ways in which their culture tends to picture the larger world as, on the one hand, exotic and remote, and, on the other within easy reach of understanding, travel, and economic advantage.

This will mark only the smallest progress down the long road out of that colonial era; it does not absolve the West of its responsibilities for finding ways to share with others in what may still seem to be either paternal acts of aid or reparation payments. But raising the post-colonial question does seem to hold some promise of advancing educational objectives in an intellectually disquieting and provocative manner. Whether a few students work up this supplement into their own commentary on the textbook's pictures, or the teacher draws attention to how one of the pictures actually tips the photographer's or writer's hand, is still to be explored by educators who are drawn to addressing these issues in their teaching. The starting point makes a sufficiently compelling case for the educational benefits of introducing, when opportunity arises, some form of post-colonial supplement.

Such pauses will complicate lessons, raising issues that are still undoubtedly difficult to articulate. It can be a rough getting of wisdom. There has been considerable controversy over *A Curriculum of Inclusion* that came out of the Task Force on Minorities (1989) in New York State which boldly proposed the development of American and world history programs that were other than Eurocentric. More has yet to be done, I fully realize, in bringing forward curriculum materials that will support these alternative viewpoints while bearing critical scrutiny. In terms of specific pedagogies for the Canadian English-language context, Simon, Brown, Lee and Young (1988) have created curricula which deal with national incidents of racism in ways that prompt students to expand their sense of social responsibility and democratic participation.

In working with the somewhat more modest prospects of the curriculum supplement proposed in this paper, I recognize that there is still much to be done in making readily available to educators this additional layer of historical meaning in the arts, humanities, and sciences; setting their development, where relevant, within the history of the European colonial empires. At this point, I am clearly depending on the interests of educators in finding the supplementary and enriching moments of interruption, reflection, and anecdote. By no small coincidence, this struggle with the significance of difference has its parallels with current efforts at a redefinition of gender, from its critiques of a less-than-objective science to its reading of the social construction of difference. A second concern is that the proposal at this point of a *supplement* may well strike some as a half-measure that leaves the core texts and dispositions in place. I agree that it is not the only form of response to the continuing state of racism and sexism, but it does offer a degree of intellectual integrity and engagement that may earn it a place in more classrooms than would a less supplementary approach.

A Place to Start?

At issue in all of this is the continual search for an effective starting point. As Audre Lorde (1990: 287), drawing in turn on Paulo Freire, points out, "the true focus of revolutionary change is never merely the oppressive situations which we seek to escape, but that piece of the oppressor which is planted deep within each of us, and which knows only the oppressor's tactics, the oppressor's relationships." After centuries of using blackness to define white, native to define European, woman to define man, Jew to define Christian, French to define English, we need to question how it is we want to be known and how it is that we come to know others. The structuring of difference has been at the heart of the colonial enterprise since the beginning. It can no longer be assumed, as Claude Lévi-Strauss (1961: 391) does in reflecting on his 'study of primitive societies in Brazil', that "knowing them better does none the less help us to detach ourselves from our own society."

This anthem of detachment, that has long served the caus-es of anthropology, social studies, and a good deal of travel, is due for post–Quincentenary reconsideration. One might want to think about the ways in which our coming to know 'them' has, since before the time of Columbus, been about affixing ourselves to, not detaching ourselves from, 'our own society', as we seek to take them in, fix them in a curious, superior gaze, that is blind to the history out of which it peers. For a maker of 'anti–anthropological' films, Trinh Minh-ha (1991: 20), the educational process must now begin by naming the full and often forgotten extent of a colonialism that has long operated in the name of humanism and education:

> Maintaining the intuitive, emotional Other under the scien-tistic tutelage of the rational, all-knowing Western Subject is an everlasting aim of the dominant which keeps on renew-ing itself through a wide range of humanistic discourses … Decolonization often means dewesternization as taught by the White man.

Fortunately, through a burgeoning body of research into these questions, it has become easier to appreciate how the schools continue to work through this historical process that contributes to lessons of difference, of privileged centre and margin, for such a long list of markers that include gender, ethnicity, class, religion, sexual orientation, ability, and others. In this instance, I have proposed that we consider it in order to pause in planning units and working with texts over the legacy of this westernization, to consider what it has come to mean in the curriculum's depiction of the Other, in the curriculum's rendering of the world as the fascinating, educational object of our interested vision.

Given these concerns, it may seem too little to interrupt this long history with a supplement that inquires into how we continue to make the world over in these earlier images. It may seem ill-advised to proceed without a fully realized vision for an alternative program, without yet understanding how we are to make a clean break in seeing beyond this history. Yet, decolonization for educators in what is known as the West may well begin with one of the traditional heroes of the literature curriculum, Prospero, who, toward the conclusion of *The Tempest*, owns that "this thing of darkness" is his. For the ways in which the schools continue to participate in the organization and production of difference bear traces of a colonial legacy that we have still to address in seeking to improve the educational prospects of the next millennium.

REFERENCES

Bhabha, H. K. "DissemiNation: Time narrative, and the margins of the modern nation," in H. Bhabha (ed.) *Nation and Narration* (New York: Routledge, 1990), 291–322.

Blodgett, J. *Kenojuak* (Toronto: Firefly Books, 1983).

Brydon, D. "New approaches to the new literatures in English: Are we in danger of incorporating disparity?", in H. Maes-Jelinek, K. H. Petersen, and A. Rutherford (eds.) *A Shaping of Connections: Commonwealth Literature Studies — Then and Now* (Sydney, AU: Dangaroo, 1989), 88–99.

British Columbia Ministry of Education. *Pacific Rim Education Initiatives* (Victoria: British Columbia Ministry of Education, 1992a).

British Columbia Ministry of Education. *The Graduation Pro-*

gram Working Paper: Partnerships for Learners (Victoria: British Columbia Ministry of Education, 1992b).

Cummins, J. "Heritage language teaching and the student: Fact and friction," in J. H. Esling (ed.) *Multicultural Education and Policy: ESL in the 1990s: A Tribute to Mary Ashwoth* (Toronto: O.I.S.E. Press, 1989), 3–17.

The Globe and Mail. "Poll Showed Hostility to Immigrants," (Toronto: September 14, 1992), A4.

Greenblatt, S. I. *Marvelous Possessions: The Wonder of the New World* (Chicago: University of Chicago Press, 1991).

Gould, S. T. *The Mismeasure of Man* (New York: Norton, 1981).

Lévi–Strauss, C. *Tristes tropiques: An anthropological study of primitive societies in Brazil* (J. Russell, trans.) (New York: Atheneum, 1961).

Lorde, A. "Age, race, class, and sex: Women redefining difference," in R. Ferguson, M. Gever, T. T. Minh–Ha, and C. West (eds.) *Out there: Marginalization and Contemporary Cultures* (Cambridge, MA: M.I.T. Press, 1990), 281–287.

Maracle, L. "The 'post–colonial' imagination," *Fuse*, 16: 12–15, 1992.

Massey, D. L. *Communities Around our World* (Scarborough, ON: Ginn, 1984).

Minh–ha, T. T. *When the Moon Waxes Red: Representation, Gender and Cultural Politics* (New York: Routledge, 1991).

Monet, D., and Skanu'u (Argthe Wilson). *Colonialism of Trial: Indigenous Land Rights and the Gitksan and Wet'suwet'er Sovereignty Case* (Gabriola Island, BC: New Society Publications, 1992).

Price, M. "An anti–racist generation: A challenge for education," *Education Today*, 4: 8–11, 30–31, 1992.

Said, E. W. *Orientalism* (New York: Random House, 1978).

Said, E. W. "Yeats and decolonization," in T. Eagleton, F. Jameson, and E. W. Said (eds.) *Nationalism, Colonialism, and Literature* (Minneapolis: University of Minnesota Press, 1990a), 69–98.

Said, E. W. "In the shadow of the West: Edward Said," in R. Ferguson, W. Olander, M. Tucker, and K. Fiss (eds.) *Discourses: Conversations in Postmodern Art and Culture* (P. Mariani and J. Crary, interviewers) (Cambridge, MA: MIT Press, 1990b), 93–104.

Simon, R. *"Forms of Insurgency in the Production of Popular Memories: The Columbus Quincentenary and the Pedagogy of Counter-Commemoration,"* (unpublished paper) (Toronto: O.I.S.E., 1992a).

Simon, R., Brown, J., Lee, E., and Young, J. *Decoding Discrimination: A Student-based Approach to Anti-racist Education Using Film* (London, ON: Althouse, 1988).

Task Force on Minorities. *A Curriculum of Inclusion* (Albany, NY: State Education Department, 1989).

Todd, L. "What more do they want?", in G. McMaster and L. A. Martin (eds.) *Indigena: Contemporary Native Perspectives* (Vancouver: Douglas and McIntyre, 1992), 71–79.

Wood, D. *Exploring Our Country In Explorations: A Canadian Social Studies Program for Elementary School*, [Kit] Pt. 3 (Vancouver: Douglas and McIntyre, 1983).

Part II

Teaching for
Social Justice

"**THE UNDERLYING THEME** in my classroom is that the quest for social justice is a never-ending struggle in our nation and the world and that we each have to decide whether we want to participate in it," writes Bob Peterson in "Teaching for Social Justice." He describes an array of his own classroom activities with primary school students, based on this premise. In outlining an effective pedagogy for this task, Peterson stresses the importance of taking seriously the lives of our students by making their viewpoints part of the curriculum. He insists, however, that this is not enough, if you aspire to be a "critical," rather than a "progressive," teacher. Students also need help in probing the ways their lives are both connected to and limited by society. Drawing on a 15-year career as an inner-city classroom teacher, Peterson sums up what for him are the five essential features in teaching for social justice: a curriculum grounded in the lives of our students; dialogue; a questionig/problem-posing approach; an emphasis on critiquing bias and attitudes; the teaching of activism for social justice.

Streaming or "tracking" is one unfortunate way schools deal with the fact that many students from working class backgrounds are not motivated to learn the standard academic program. Memory Olympics just isn't their game. These students often end up in dead-end lower streams — "dummy classes," to go by their schoolyard name — which means that they fail to fully develop their potential and are, in addition, handicapped when it comes to future educational opportuni-

ties. In "Getting Off the Track," Bill Bigelow, a high school history and social science teacher, offers examples of how to
develop an anti-tracking pedagogy that will keep all students,
irrespective of their class background, engaged and interested
in learning.

Like Peterson, Bigelow stresses that an effective curriculum
must constantly draw on students' lives as a way of delving
into broader social themes. He also insists that the whole process of tracking needs to be demystified as part of learning
how society works. While all students need to understand
this, it is particularly valuable for working class students to
examine the history and practice of tracking in order to
become aware of and expel doubts about their capacity to
think and achieve.

While sharing Peterson's and Bigelow's basic critique of
tracking/streaming, Bob Davis decided that a major focus of his
teaching life would be with so-called "G[eneral]-level" students.
In "Teaching Streamed Students," he describes a unit on History
and Work which he developed while teaching grade nine students in this lower-level stream. Underpinning this program is
his conviction that traditional history courses neglect the conflicts between social classes which are an important part of all
history: conflicts between slaves and owners, peasants and
lords, soldiers and officers, workers and management, tenants
and landlords, rich and poor. He argues that while all students
need to learn about these class conflicts, they are of particular
importance to working class students, who are denied knowledge of both their history and their heroes in conventional
high school history courses.

The unit gets students engaged in learning about working-
class jobs and the politics of work, both in the past and the
present. It draws not only on written material but also on
folk songs, documentary films, personal interviews and large
field projects. The most spectacular project is a giant Bean
Bake where proud "G-level" grade nine students, while
exploring the history of Ontario lumberjacks, cook a mess of
beans and pork overnight outdoors, in three giant iron pots,

and feed the whole school of 1300 students a lunch of beans and freshly baked bread, topped off with an old-fashioned country hoe-down to the music of an accomplished fiddle band.

Davis is careful in specifying that he is not advocating a special history program for working class students that side-steps knowing about broader political developments, nationally and internationally. He is not looking for a "feel-good" alternative for these students. If extensive changes were to take place in the regular courses, these kind of experimental units might cease to be needed. He insists that they should not be thought of as models for a whole program, but are meant to only highlight elements missing in the regular history curriculum.

How does one engage students, in a meaningful way, in discussions, debates and activities dealing with issues of war and peace? And from a social justice perspective: how can such a topic encourage a younger generation to help build a world with less violence and armed conflict? Chris Searle works as a head teacher and classroom English teacher in a comprehensive school in a working class neighbourhood in Sheffield, England. He gives an account of how his students, many of them children of immigrants from the Middle East, learned to make sense of the Gulf War in 1991.

Searle describes the jingoistic atmosphere in Great Britain during this war and the national-chauvinist and anti-Arab sentiments expressed not only on TV and the tabloid press, but also by the government, opposition parties and respectable local community newspapers. The presence of a large number of students from countries like Yemen, Syria and Jordan at the school, as well as a sizeable community of Yemeni in the area, meant that it was possible for all students and teachers in his school to get more actual information about these countries, the cost of this conflict, and the moral dilemma it represented for England.

Searle — who had been actively involved in making sure the school had access to this wider information — describes how his own students wrote about their feelings, conflicts and confusions about the war. He also had them stretch their capacity for empathy by such tasks as writing down the "last thoughts" of an incinerated Iraqi soldier whose picture had been published in an anti-war newspaper under the headline "the real face of war."

Racism and imperialism are other topics that inevitably emerge in dealing with a war like this one. Because of the atmosphere created in the classroom through writing, shared feelings and experiences, and debate without acrimony, a bond of friendship, mutual respect and affection was developed between white local students and those with immigrant parents from the Middle East. As a result, the frankness about these painful issues was not divisive. The students learned to broaden their horizons and increase their empathy for each other, at the same time as they became more critical of knee-jerk nationalism and racist stereotyping.

Chapter Four

TEACHING FOR SOCIAL JUSTICE

Bob Peterson

I t's November and a student brings in a flyer about a canned food drive during the upcoming holiday season. The traditional teacher affirms the student's interest — "That's nice and I'm glad you care about other people" — but doesn't view the food drive as a potential classroom activity.

The progressive teacher sees the food drive as an opportunity to build on students' seemingly innate sympathy for the down-trodden and after a class discussion has children bring in cans of food. They count them, categorize them, and write about how they feel.

The critical teacher does the same as the progressive teacher — but more. The teacher also uses the food drive as the basis for a discussion about poverty and hunger. How much poverty and hunger is there in our neighbourhood? Our country? Our world? Why is there poverty and hunger? What is the role of the government in making sure people have enough to eat? Why isn't it doing more? What can we do in addition to giving some food?

Participating in a food drive isn't the litmus test of whether one is a critical teacher. But engaging children in reflective dialogue is.

Unfortunately, lack of reflective dialogue is all too commonplace in North American schools. Less than 1% of instructional time in high school is devoted to discussion that requires some kind of response involving reasoning or an opinion from students, according to researcher John Goodlad in his study of American schooling. A similar atmosphere dominates all too many elementary classrooms, where worksheets and mindless tasks fill up children's time.

Divisions between traditional, progressive, and critical teaching are often artificial and many teachers use techniques common to all three. As I attempt to improve my teaching and build what I call a "social justice classroom," however, I have found it essential to draw less on traditional methods and more on the other two.

Lots of literature has been written on progressive methods — the process approach to writing, whole language, activity-based mathematics, and so forth. But there is little written about critical/social justice approaches to teaching, especially for elementary teachers. What follows is an outline of lessons that I have learned as I have tried, sometimes more successfully than others, to incorporate my goal of critical/social justice teaching into my classroom practice over the last 15 years.

There are five characteristics that I think are essential to teaching critical/social justice:

- A curriculum grounded in the lives of our students.
- Dialogue.
- A questioning/problem-posing approach.
- An emphasis on critiquing bias and attitudes.
- The teaching of activism for social justice.

A well-organized class based on collaboration and student participation is a prerequisite for implementing such a program. I'd also like to add that such "characteristics" are actually goals — never quite reached by even the best teachers, but always sought by all good teachers.

Curriculum Grounded in the Lives of Our Students

A teacher cannot build a community of learners unless the voices and lives of the students are an integral part of the curriculum. Children, of course, talk about their lives constantly. The challenge is for teachers to make connections between what the students talk about, and the curriculum and broader society.

I start the year with a six-week unit on the children's family and background. To begin the unit I have students place their birthdate on the class time line — which covers nearly 600 years (an inch representing a year), and which runs above the blackboard and stretches around two walls. Students write their names and birthdates on 3x5 cards and tie the cards with yarn to the hole in the timeline that corresponds to their year of birth. On the second day we place their parents' birthdates on the timeline, on the third day those of their grandparents or great-grandparents. Throughout the year, students add dates that come up in our study of history, literature, science, and current events. The timeline provides students with a visual representation of time, history, and sequence, while fostering the understanding that everything is interrelated.

The weekly writing homework assignment during this family background unit consists of children collecting information about their families — how they were named, stories of family trips, favourite jokes, an incident when they were young, a description of their neighbourhood. Students share these writings with each other and at times with the whole class. They use these assignments as rough drafts for autobiographies which are eventually bound and published. They also inspire classroom discussion and further study. For example, one of my students, Faviola Perez, wrote a poem about her neighbourhood which led to discussions about violence and what we might do about it. The poem goes:

My mom says, "Time to go to bed."
The streets at night
are horrible

I can't sleep!
Cars are passing
making noise
sirens screaming
people fighting
suffering!
Suddenly the noise goes away
I go to sleep
I start dreaming
I dream about people
shaking hands
caring
caring about our planet
I wake up
and say
Will the world be
like this some day?

In the discussion that followed, many students shared similar fears and gave examples of how family members or friends had been victims of violence. Others offered ways to prevent violence.

"We shouldn't buy team jackets," said one student.

"The police should keep all the criminals in jail forever," was another suggestion. Needless to say the students don't have a uniform response, and I use such comments to foster discussion. When necessary or appropriate, I also interject important questions that might help the students deepen or reconsider their views. I also try to draw connections between such problems and issues of conflict that I witness daily in the class. When a student talks about a killing over a mundane argument or a piece of clothing, for instance, I ask how that differs from some of the conflicts in our school and on our playground, and how we might solve them.

Focusing on such problems in writing and discussion acknowledges the seriousness of a child's problem; it also fosters community because the students recognize that we share common concerns. Ultimately, it can help students to re-examine some of their own attitudes that may in fact be a part, albeit a small part, of the problem.

Throughout the rest of the year I try to integrate an examination of children's lives and their community into all sections of the curriculum. In reading groups, children relate both contemporary and classic children's books to their own lives. For example, in one activity I have students divide their paper vertically: on one side they copy an interesting sentence from a book they are reading; on the other side they write how that reminds them of something in their own lives. The students then share and discuss such reflections.

In math we learn about percentages, fractions, graphing, and basic math through using numbers to examine their own lives. For example, my fifth grade class keeps logs of the time that they spend watching TV, graph it, and analyze it in terms of fractions and percentages. As part of our school's communication theme [a nine-week, schoolwide theme on "We Send Messages When We Communicate"], they surveyed all the classes in the school to see how many households had various communication equipment, from telephones to computers to VCRs.

Such activities are interesting and worthwhile, but not necessarily critical. I thus tried to take the activity a step further — to not only affirm what's going on in the children's lives, but to help them question if it is always in their best interest. As we looked at television viewing, for instance, we found that some of our students could save over 1000 hours a year by moderating their TV watching.

"I can't believe I waste so much time watching TV," one girl stated during one discussion.

"You're not wasting it," replied another. "You're learning what they want you to buy!" he said sarcastically.

Similar discussions helped children become more conscious of the impact of TV on their lives and minds, and even led a few to reduce the number of hours they watched TV.

One problem, however, that I have encountered in "giving voice" to students is that the voices that dominate are sometimes those of the more aggressive boys or those who are more academically skilled. I try to overcome this problem by using structures that encourage broader participation. During writing workshop, for example, I give timed "free writes" where children write about anything they want for a set period of time. Afterward they immediately share their writing with another student of their choice. Students then nominate classmates to share with the entire class, which often has the effect of positive peer pressure on those who don't normally participate in class. By hearing their own voice, by having other students listen to what they have to say, children become more self-confident in expressing their own ideas, and feel more a part of the classroom community.

Dialogue

The basic premise of traditional teaching is that children come to school as empty vessels needing to be filled with information. "Knowledge" is something produced elsewhere, whether by the teacher or the textbook company, and then transferred to the student.

This approach dominates most schools. "Reform" usually means finding more effective ways for children to remember more "stuff" or more efficient ways to measure what "stuff" the students have memorized.

I agree that children need to know bunches of "stuff." I cringe any time one of my fifth graders confuses a basic fact like the name of our city or country. But I also know that the vast bulk of "stuff" memorized by children in school is quickly forgotten, and that the "empty vessel" premise is largely responsible for the boring, lecture-based instruction that dominates too many classrooms.

The curricular "stuff" that I want the children to learn will be best remembered if it relates to what they already know, if they have some input into what "stuff" is actually studied, and if it is studied through activities rather than just listening. All three approaches depend on dialogue and on making students an integral part of their own learning.

To initiate dialogue I may use a song, poem, story, news article, photo, or cartoon. These dialogue "triggers" are useful for both classroom and small group discussion. I often use them as a starting point in a social studies, writing, or math lesson. I have a song, word, poster, and quotation of the week which, whenever possible, is related to our curriculum topics.

For example, during the study of the American underground railroad earlier this year, I used the song "New Underground Railroad," written by Gerry Tenney and sung by Holly Near and Ronnie Gilbert. The song compares the underground railroad of the mid–1800s in the United States to that of the movement to save Jews during World War II and to the sanctuary movement to help "illegal" Salvadoran refugees in the 1980s. My student from El Salvador connected immediately to the song. She explained to the class the problems of violence and poverty that her family had faced because of war in El Salvador. This one song raised many more questions. For example: Why did the Nazis kill people? What is anti-Semitism? Who runs El Salvador? Why does the United States send guns to El Salvador? Why are people from El Salvador forced to come to the U.S. secretly?

Another trigger that I use is overhead transparencies made from provocative newspaper or magazine photographs. For example, for a poetry lesson during writing workshop, I used a *New York Times* photograph taken during January's cold spell that showed piles of snow-covered blankets and cardboard on park benches near the White House. Many students initially thought the piles were trash. When I told them that they were homeless people who had been snowed upon while asleep, my students were angry. The discussion ranged from their own experiences seeing homeless people in the community to suggestions of what should be done by the President.

"That's not fair," one student responded.

"Clinton said he'd take care of the homeless people if he got elected and look what he's done," said a second student. "Nothing."

"I didn't vote for him," said a third. "Us kids never get to do anything, but I know that if we were in charge of the world we'd do a better job."

"Like what?" I asked.

"Well, on a day that cold he should have opened up the White House and let them in," responded one student. "If I were President, that's what I'd do."

One of my students, Jade Williams, later wrote a poem, "Homeless":

I walk to the park
I see homeless people laying
on a bench I feel sad
to see people sleeping outside
nowhere to go I felt
to help them let them stay
in a hotel
give them things
until they get
a job and
a house to stay
and let them
pay me back
with their love

A Questioning/Problem-posing Approach

Lucy Calkins, director of the Teachers College Writing Project at Columbia University, argues that teachers must allow student viewpoints to be part of the classroom curriculum. "We can't give children rich lives, but we can give them the lens to appreciate the richness that is already there in their lives," she writes in her book, *Living Between the Lines*.

But even that is not enough. We should also help students to probe the ways their lives are both connected to and limited by society. This is best done if students and teachers jointly pose substantive, challenging questions for the class to try to answer.

Any time a student poses a particularly thoughtful or curious question in my class we write it down in the spiral note-book labeled "Questions We Have" that hangs on the board in front of the room. It might be during a discussion, at the beginning of a day, or during a reflection on another students' writing. Not every question is investigated and thoroughly discussed, but even the posing of the question helps students to consider alternative ways of looking at an issue.

In a reading group discussion, for example, the question arose of how it must have felt for fugitive slaves and free African Americans to fear walking down the street in the North during the time of slavery. One student said, "I sort of know how they must have felt." Others immediately doubted her statement, but then she explained.

"The slaves, especially fugitive slaves, weren't free because they couldn't walk the streets without fear of the slave masters, but today are we free?" she asked. "Because we can't walk the streets without fear of gangs, violence, crazy people, drunks, and drive-bys."

In reading groups a common assignment is to pose questions from the literature that we read in common. For example, while reading *Sidewalk Story* by Sharon Bell Mathis, a children's novel in which the main protagonist, a young girl, struggles to keep her best friend from being evicted, my students posed questions about the ethics of eviction, failure to pay rent, homelessness, discrimination, and the value of material possessions over friendship. "Is it better to have friends or money?" a student asked, which formed the basis of a lengthy discussion in the reading circle.

Other questions that students have raised in our "Questions We Have" book include: Who tells the TV what to put on? Why do geese fly together in an angle? Did ministers or priests have slaves? How many presidents owned slaves? Why haven't we had a woman president? Why are the faces of the presidents on our money? How do horses sweat? If we are free, why do we have to come to school? When did photography start? Who invented slavery? Why are people homeless? What runs faster, a cheetah or an ostrich? Did any adults die in the 1913 massacre of 73 children in Calumet County, Michigan? (in reference to the Woody Guthrie song about a tragedy that grew out of a labour struggle).

Some questions are answered by students working together using reference materials in the classroom or school library. (Cheetahs can run up to 65 mph, while ostriches run only 40 mph). Other questions are subject of group discussion; still others we work on in small groups. For example, the question, "What is the difference between the master/slave relationship and parent/child relationship?" developed one afternoon when a child complained that his parent wouldn't allow him out in the evening for school story hour. A girl responded that we might as well all be slaves, and a third student posed the question. After a brief group discussion, I had children work in groups of 3 or 4 and they continued the debate. They made two lists, one of similarities and one of differences, between the master/slave relationship and the parent/child relationship. They discussed the question in the small groups, then a spokesperson from each group reported to the class.

The fascinating thing was not only the information that I found about their lives, but also how it forced children to reflect on what we had been studying in our unit on slavery and the underground railroad. When one student said, "Yeah, it's different because masters whipped slaves and my mom doesn't whip me," another student responded by saying, "All masters didn't whip their slaves."

When another student said that their mothers love them and masters didn't love their slaves, another girl gave the example of the slave character Izzie in the movie *Half Free, Half Slave* that we watched in which Izzie got special privileges because she was the master's girlfriend. Another girl responded that that wasn't an example of love; she was just being used.

In this discussion, students pooled their information and generated their own understanding of history, challenging crude generalizations typical of children this age. Students also started evaluating what was fair and just in their own lives. It was clear to all that the treatment of slaves was unjust. Not so clear was to what extent and how children should be disciplined by their parents. "That's abuse!" one student remarked after hearing about how one child was punished.

"No it's not. That's how my mom treats me whenever I do something bad," responded another.

While no "answers" were found, the posing of this question by a student, and my facilitating its discussion, added to both kids' understanding of history and to their sense of the complexity of evaluating what is fair and just in contemporary society.

Emphasis on Critiquing Bias

Raising questions about bias in ideas and materials — from children's books to school texts, fairy tales, news reports, song lyrics, and cartoons — is another key component of a social justice classroom. I tell my fifth graders it's important to examine "the messages that are trying to take over your brain" and that it's up to them to sort out which ones they should believe and which ones promote fairness and justice in our world.

To recognize that different perspectives exist in history and society is the first step toward critiquing materials and evaluating what perspectives they represent or leave out. Ultimately it helps children see that they, too, can have their own values and perspectives independent of what they last read or heard.

We start by examining perspective and voice. "Whose point of view are we hearing?" I ask.

One poem that is good to initiate such a discussion is Paul Fleischman's dialogue poem, "Honeybees," from *Joyful Noise, Poem for Two Voices*. The poem is read simultaneously by two people, one describing the life of a bee from the perspective of a worker, and one from the perspective of a queen. Children love to perform the poem and often want to write their own. They begin to understand how to look at things from different perspectives. They also start to identify with certain perspectives.

After hearing the song of the week, "My Country 'Tis of Thee My People Are Dying," by Buffie Saint Marie, one of my students wrote a dialogue poem between a Native American and a U.S. soldier about smallpox–infected blankets the U.S. government traded for land. In another instance, as part of a class activity when pairs of students were writing dialogue poems between a master and a slave, two girls wrote one between a field slave and a house slave, further deepening the class's understanding about the complexity of slavery. During writing workshop six weeks later, three boys decided to write a "Triple Dialogue Poem" that included the slave, a slave master, and an abolitionist.

Students also need to know that children's books and school textbooks contain biases and important omissions. I find the concept of "stereotypes" and "omission" important to enhance children's understanding of such biases.

For example, around Thanksgiving time I show my students an excellent filmstrip called "Unlearning Native American Stereotypes" produced by the Council on Interracial Books for Children. It's narrated by Native children who visit a public library and become outraged at the various stereotypes of Indians in the books. One year after I showed this, my kids seemed particularly angry at what they had learned. They came the next day talking about how their siblings in first grade had come home with construction paper headdresses with feathers. "That's a stereotype" my kids proudly pro–claimed. "What did you do about it?" I asked. "I ripped it up;" "I slugged him," came the chorus of responses.

After further discussion, they decided there were more pro–ductive things they could do than to hit their siblings. They scoured the school library for books with Indian stereotypes and found few. So they decided to investigate the first grade room. Two of the students wrote a letter to the teacher asking permission and then went in. They found a picture of an Indi–an next to letter I in the alphabet strip on the wall. They came back excited, declaring that they "had found a stereotype that everybody sees every day!" They decided they wanted to teach the first graders about stereotypes. I was skeptical, but agreed, and after much rehearsal they entered the first–grade classroom to give their lesson. Returning to my classroom, they expressed frustration that the first–graders didn't listen as well as they had hoped, but nonetheless thought it had gone well. Later the two students, Paco Resendez and Faviola Alvarez, wrote in our school newspaper:

> We have been studying stereotypes of Native Americans. What is a stereotype? It's when somebody says something that's not true about another group of people. For example, it is a stereotype if you think all Indians wear feathers or say "HOW!" Or if you think that all girls are delicate. Why? Because some girls are strong.

The emphasis on critique is an excellent way to integrate math into social studies. Students, for example, can tally numbers of instances certain people, viewpoints, or groups are presented in a text or in mass media. One year my students compared the times famous women and famous men were mentioned in the fifth grade history text. One reaction by a number of boys was that men were mentioned far more frequently because women must not have done much throughout history. To help facilitate the discussion, I provided background resources for the students, including biographies of famous women. This not only helped students better understand the nature of "omission," but also generated interest in reading biographies of women.

In another activity I had students tally the number of men and women by occupation as depicted in magazine and/or TV advertisements. By comparing their findings to the population as a whole, various forms of bias were uncovered, not only in how the media portrays the population, but in the structure of jobs that helps segregate women into occuptions such as office worker or waitress. Another interesting activity is having students tally the number of biographies in the school library and analyze them by race, gender, and occupation.

One of my favourite activities involves comparing books. I

stumbled on this activity one year when my class read a story about inventions in a reading textbook published by Scott Foresman Co. The story stated that the traffic light was invented by an anonymous policeman. Actually it was invented by the African–American scientist Garrett A. Morgan. I gave my students a short piece from an African–American history book and we compared it with the Scott Foresman book. We talked about which story we should believe and how one might verify which was accurate. After checking out another book about inventions, the students realized that the school text was wrong.

The Teaching of Activism for Social Justice

The underlying theme in my classroom is that the quest for social justice is a never–ending struggle in our nation and world; that the vast majority of people have benefited by this struggle; that we must understand this struggle; and that we must make decisions about whether to be involved in it.

I weave the various disciplines around this theme. When I read poetry and literature to the children, I often use books that raise issues about social justice and, when possible, in which the protagonists are young people working for social justice. In math, we will look at everything from the distribution of wealth in the world to the percentage of women in different occupations. The class songs and posters of the week also emphasize social struggles from around the world. I also have each student make what I call a "people's textbook" — a three–ring binder in which they put handouts and some of their own work, particularly interviews that they conducted. There are sections for geography, history, current events, songs, poetry, and mass media. I also have a gallery of freedom fighters on the wall — posters of people that we have studied in social studies and current events.

In addition to studying movements for social justice of the past, students discuss current problems and possible solutions. One way I do this is by having students role play examples of discrimination and how they might respond.

I start with kids dramatizing historical incidents such as Sojourner Truth's successful attempt to integrate Washington, D.C., street cars after the Civil War, and Rosa Parks' role in the Montgomery Bus Boycott. We brainstorm contemporary problems where people might face discrimination, drawing on our current events studies and interviews children have done with family members and friends about types of discrimination of which they are aware.

One day in the spring of 1993, my class was dramatizing contemporary examples. Working in small groups, the students were to choose a type of discrimination — such as not being allowed to rent a house because one receives welfare, or not getting a job because one is a woman — and develop a short dramatization. Afterward, the kids would lead a discussion about the type of discrimination they were acting out.

After a few dramatizations, it was Gilberto, Juan, and Carlos' turn. I had no clue as to what they were going to dramatize.

It was a housing discrimination example — but with a twist. Gilberto and Juan were acting the part of two gay men attempting to rent an apartment, and Carlos was the landlord who refused to rent to them. I was surprised, in part because in previous brainstorming sessions on discrimination none of my students had mentioned discrimination against gay people. Further, as is often unfortunately the case with fifth graders, in the past my students had shown they were prone to uncritically accept anti-gay slurs and stereotypes. But here, on their own initiative, were Gilberto, Juan, and Carlos transferring our class discussion of housing discrimination based on race to that of sexual orientation.

The dramatization caused an initial chorus of laughs and jeers. But, I noticed, the students also listened attentively. Afterwards, I asked the class what type of discrimination had been modeled.

"Gayism," one student, Elvis, yelled out.

It was a new word to me, but got the point across. The class then went on to discuss "gayism." Most of the kids who spoke agreed that it was a form of discrimination. During the discussion, one student mentioned a march on Washington a week earlier, demanding gay rights. (Interestingly, Gilberto, Juan and Carlos said they were unaware of the march.)

Elvis, who coined the term "gayism," then said: "Yeah, my cousin is one of those lesi... lesi..."

"Lesbians," I said, completing his sentence.

"Yeah, lesbian," he said. He then added enthusiastically: "And she went to Washington to march for her rights."

"That's just like when Dr. King made his dream speech at the march in Washington," another student added.

Before long the class moved on to a new role play. But the "gayism" dramatization lingered in my memory.

One reason is that I was proud that the class had been able to move beyond the typical discussions around gay issues — which had in the past seemed to center on my explaining why students shouldn't call each other 'faggot.' More fundamentally, however, the incident reminded me of the inherent link between the classroom and society, not only in terms of how society influences the children who are in our classrooms for six hours a day, but also in terms of how broader movements for social reform affect daily classroom life.

It's important not only to study these progressive social movements and to dramatize current social problems, but to encourage students to take thoughtful action. By doing this they see themselves as actors in the world, not just things to be acted upon.

One of the best ways to help students in this area is by example — to expose them to people in the community who are fighting for social justice. I regularly have social activists visit and talk with children in my classes. I also explain the activities that I'm personally involved in as an example of what might be done.

I tell students they can write letters, circulate petitions, and talk to other classes and children about their concerns. My students have gone with me to marches that demanded that King's birthday be made a national holiday and that there be

an end to the nuclear arms race. Another time, while studying the Sanctuary Movement and learning about the wars in
Central America, half of my class accompanied me to a
demonstration demanding an end to U.S. government support of the "Contras" fighting the Sandinista government in
Nicaragua. Two of my students testified before the City
Council, asking that a Jobs With Peace referendum be placed
on the ballot. Another time students at our school testified
with parents in front of the City Council that special monies
should be allocated to rebuild our school playground.

Such activities have gotten mixed reviews from my colleagues and supervisors. Is it proper for teachers to promote
student activism? Doesn't this run the danger of indoctrina-
tion?

Many teachers believe that teaching should be politically
neutral. That is impossible. Everyday decisions of what to
teach and not to teach are inherently political decisions. For
example, when a teacher chooses a read-aloud book or makes
a specific writing assignment, a certain perspective is being
promoted in the classroom. The presence of that perspective
and the absence of others is a political act. It might not be
conscious, but it is political nonetheless.

Likewise, if a teacher decides not to discuss past or current
social movements that address societal problems, it is a political decision, in this case of omission. The message, while
subtle, is clear: such social activism does not warrant the
attention of the class compared to the rest of the curriculum;
that social activism in the broader society is not of value and
should not be viewed in a positive light.

However, in a society based on democratic principles, a
key purpose of a public school system is to foster active participation in political and civic life. Some educators, and in
some cases entire districts like the Milwaukee Public Schools,
are advocating that students be encouraged to "demonstrate
more responsible citizenship" and "be involved with their
community." What better way than to encourage students to
act on their beliefs?

At the same time, certain safeguards must be taken. First, in discussing any issue, various points of view must be examined. At the elementary level this usually is the teacher's responsibility. At times, I take positions opposed to what I believe in order to challenge student thinking. For example, during a role play trial of a fugitive slave who faced return to his southern slave master, I was the attorney for the slave master, as many students had difficulty presenting a substantive case for the master.

Second, teachers shouldn't hide their personal opinions on controversial subjects, but they should be labeled as such, i.e., one person's opinion. It must also be clear that a student's grade does not depend on agreeing with the teacher.

For a teacher to pretend to have no opinion on controversial topics, however, is not only unbelievable, but sends a message to students that it's OK in a democracy to be opinionless and apathetic toward key social issues.

Such apathy is not OK. At a time when cynicism and hopelessness increasingly dominate our youth, helping students understand the world and their relationship to it by encouraging social action may be one of the few antidotes. Schools are a prime place where this can take place. Teachers are a key element in it happening. Teaching for social justice is a necessary priority as we approach the new century.

Chapter Five

GETTING OFF THE TRACK
Stories from an
Untracked Classroom
Bill Bigelow

In school, I hated social studies. My U.S. history class was, in the words of critical educator Ira Shor, a memory Olympics, with students competing to see how many dates, battles and presidents we could cram into our adolescent heads. My California history class was one long lecture, almost none of which I remember today, save for the names of a few famous men — mostly scoundrels. This marathon fact–packing was interrupted only once, as I recall, by a movie on raisins. Social studies — ostensibly a study of human beings — was nothing of the kind. "Poor History," writes Eduardo Galeano, "had stopped breathing: betrayed in academic texts, lied about in classrooms, drowned in dates, they had imprisoned her in museums and buried her, with floral wreaths, beneath statuary bronze and monumental marble."

Today, students who prove unresponsive to similar memory games are often labelled 'slow learners,' — or worse — and find themselves dumped in a low–track class, called 'basic' or 'skills,' understood by all as 'the dumb class.' This is victim–blaming, penalizing kids for their inability to turn human beings into abstractions, for their failure to recall disconnected factoids. And it's unnecessary. Tracking is usually advocated with good intentions; but its only educational justification derives from schools' persistence in teaching in ways that fail to reach so many children, thus necessitating some students' removal to less demanding academic pursuits.

Untracking a school requires untracking instruction. However, many of those who argue against tracking offer only the vaguest hints of what an effective untracked class could look like. Hence their critique that tracking delivers inferior instruction to many students, lowers self-esteem, reproduces social hierarchies, reinforces negative stereotypes, etc. may have ironic consequences. Compelled by these and other arguments, schools that untrack without a thoroughgoing pedagogical transformation can end up simply with a system of tracking internal to each classroom. I've seen this in more than one "untracked" school: students who come to class able to absorb lectures, write traditional research papers, memorize discrete facts — and stay awake — succeed; those who can't, sit in the back of class and sleep, doodle or disrupt — and fail. Those of us critical of tracking need to take responsibility for offering a concrete and viable vision of an untracked classroom. Otherwise, the results of untracking will replicate the results of tracking, and many educators will lean back in their chairs and say, "I told you so."

Components of an Untracked Classroom

As a classroom teacher, I've found that an anti-tracking pedagogy in social studies has several essential, and interlocking, components. And while the examples I'll use are drawn from my high school social studies classes, these components remain as valid in other content areas or can be adapted:

- Show, don't tell. Through role plays, improvisations, and simulations, students need to experience, not simply hear about, social dynamics.

- Assignments need to be flexible enough to adjust to students' interests or abilities. Teachers can assign projects, poetry, personal writing, critiques, etc., which allow students to enter and succeed at their own levels of competence and creativity. This is not a suggestion to give easy assignments, but to adopt a flexible academic rigour. And in no way should this detract from students developing traditional scholastic skills they will need to pursue higher education.

- The curriculum needs to constantly draw on students' lives as a way of delving into broader social themes. Knowledge needs to be both internal and external; history, government, sociology, literature is always simultaneously about "them" and us.

- The classroom environment needs to be encouraging, even loving. All students need to know that their potential is respected, that they are included in a community of learners. A rhetoric of caring is insufficient. Both the form and content of the class must underscore every child's worth.

- What we teach has to matter. Students should understand how the information and analytic tools they're developing make a difference in their lives, that the aim of learning is not just a grade, simple curiosity or "because you'll need to know it later."

- An anti-tracking pedagogy should explicitly critique the premises of tracking. Students need to examine the history and practice of tracking in order to become aware of and expel doubts about their capacity to think and achieve. We cannot merely untrack our classrooms; we have to engage students in a dialogue about why we untrack our classrooms. More than this, the curriculum needs to critique the deeper social inequities and hierarchies that were the original stimuli for tracking, and continue today to breed unjust educational practices.

- Finally, the method of evaluating students in an untracked class should embody the flexibility and caring described above. We can't advocate creating flexible assignments that adjust to students' interests and abilities and then hold youngsters accountable to rigid performance criteria. Evaluation needs to be guided by principles of equity rather than efficiency.

The power of an anti-tracking approach lies in the interrelationship of these components, not merely applying them checklist fashion. Lest my examples sound too self-congratulatory or facile, I should begin by confessing that all this is easier said than done, and my classroom is rarely as tidy as my written descriptions. My students, just like everyone else's, get off task, hold distracting side conversations and occasionally fail to complete their homework. The aim here is not to provide a cookbook of tried and true educational recipes but to contribute to a broader discussion about how we can teach for justice in an unjust society, and to explore how such a commitment can contribute to successful classroom practice.

Bringing the Curriculum to Life

Role plays, simulations and improvisations allow students to climb into history and social concepts and to explore them from the inside. It's a first-person approach to society that gives each student an equal shot at grasping concepts and gaining knowledge. Advanced students — advanced in traditional academic terms — are not held back with this more experiential approach, but nor are they privileged by their facility with, say, Standard English or their stamina in reading and memorizing textbookspeak. Indeed, all students learn better with a more experiential curriculum. Just about every unit I teach includes at least one role play, simulation or set of improvisations.

For example, in a unit on U.S. labour history, students role play the 1934 West Coast longshore strike [see *The Power in Our Hands*, pp. 74–77 and 148–163]. In five groups (longshoremen, waterfront employers, farmers, unemployed workers and representatives of the central labour council), each receiving detailed role sheets, students confront the choices that confronted the original strike participants. From each group's respective standpoint, students propose solutions to the strike and decide whether they want the governor to call in the national guard to protect strikebreakers and how they will respond if the guard is called upon. Not all groups have clear positions on the questions and so students have to use their creativity to design potential resolutions and their persuasive powers to build alliances with members of other groups.

The dynamics of the strike are lived in the classroom, experienced firsthand by students, not buried in the textbook. Longshoremen negotiate with farmers to support the strike, waterfront employers seek to entice the unemployed with offers of work, and more than one group threatens violence if the governor calls in the guard. Students must master lots of information in order to represent their positions effectively, but it's not just a memory Olympics — they have to use the information in the heat of deal making and debate.

Most students have a great time, running around the room negotiating and arguing with recalcitrant peers; often, students remain engaged after the bell rings. But the role play is not simply play. As Paulo Freire says, "Conflict is the midwife of consciousness," and the simulated conflict in role plays like this allows students to reflect on much larger issues: When are alliances between different social groups possible? What role does the government play, and should it play, in labour disputes? Is violence or the threat of violence justified in class conflict? Can people stand up for themselves, but also support each other? These are big and tough questions, but because they draw on an experience every student watched and helped create they are concrete rather than abstract. Regardless of past academic achievement, the activities and discussion challenge every student.

These and other questions can also lead us to explore the contemporary relevance of an almost 60-year-old strike. Often students-as-longshoremen cobble together an alliance including farmers, the unemployed and the central labour council. "What do you think happened in real life?" I ask.

"Sure we can get together," many a student has responded. "But we're just in a role play in a classroom. It's easy to get together in here. I don't think it could happen in real life." Most students are surprised to learn that it *did* happen in real life — working people in 1934 maintained a remarkable degree of solidarity. And from this knowledge we discuss situations in which people can and cannot get together. Students also reflect on their own cynicism about people's capacity to unite for worthy goals.

After the role play I sometimes ask students to relate our discussion to their lives, and to write about a time when they were able to stick together with a group for a common objective. In our class read–around the next day I encourage students to take notes on common themes they hear in each other's stories. Here, too, we can continue to pursue theoretical questions about unity, but it's a pursuit rooted in our experience, not one imposed as an abstract academic inquiry. It *is* serious academic work, democratized through students' in–class experience and its connection to their lives.

Improvization and Equal Access to the Curriculum

Improvization is another kind of "levelling" role play that seeks to give all students equal access to information and theoretical insight. In a unit on U.S. slavery and resistance to slavery, I provide students a set of first–person roles for different social groups in the South, which supplements information already gleaned from films, a slide–lecture, poetry, a simulation, readings and class discussions. They read these roles and in small groups select from a list of improvisation choices. They can also create their own improv topic or combine ones of mine to form something new.

The topics are bare–bones descriptions requiring lots of student initiative to plan and perform. For example:

- A plantation owner tells a mother and father, who are enslaved, that he's going to sell their children. He needs the money.

- An enslaved person encounters a poor white farmer on the road. The farmer accuses the slave of looking him directly in the eye, which is illegal.
- An enslaved person asks an owner if s/he can buy her or his freedom.

There's an obvious danger that students' performances of these and any role plays can drift toward caricature. Caricature may allow students to distance and insulate themselves from the enormity of the subject, but it can allow them, as well, to trivialize one of the most horrendous periods in human history. However, the alternative of students remaining outside, removed from a subject like the enslavement of African people, seems to me a greater danger. So we talk about how we can't possibly know what people experienced, but through our performance, imagination, writing, and discussion we're going to do the best we can. And students have responded with passionate skits that have moved many in the class to tears — that have, in Toni Morrison's words, given "voice to the 'unspeakable.'"

As students perform the improvs I ask them to take notes on powerful lines or situations, as they'll be writing from the perspective of one or more of the characters. After each skit we discuss the problem posed, and how students handled it. As we progress, I draw on their improvs to teach about laws, different forms of resistance, how certain practices varied from region to region or in different time periods. It's a series of mini lectures, but accessible to all students because linked to a shared experience.

Afterward I ask students to write an interior monologue — the inner thoughts — from the point of view of one of the characters in an improv. People have the freedom to write from the point of view of a character they represented or one they watched. I encourage students to "find your passion," as my teaching partner, Linda Christensen, likes to say — so they're free to rearrange and massage the assignment to fit their interest. Most students write the assigned interior monologue, but some prefer poems, dialogue poems or letters. This,

111

too, is a vital part of an anti–tracking pedagogy: students need sufficient freedom to enter an assignment at a point of their choosing; they must be able to reconstruct the task according to their interests and abilities.

For example, after one set of improvisations, "Diane," a young woman with a low track academic history, wrote a dialogue poem about childbirth. The paired perspectives are from the wife of a white plantation owner and an enslaved African American woman. It reads in part:

My man is not here to hold my hand.
My man is not here to hold my hand.

He's out in the field.
He's out in the field.

with a whip in his hand.
with a whip at his back.

I lay here on my feather bed.
I lay here on the blanketed floor.

The pain comes. I push.
The pain comes. I push.

Someone, please come and help.
Someone, please come and help.

The midwife comes, the doctor, too.
The midwife comes, no doctor.

Silk sheets in my mouth.
A wood stick in my mouth.

To halt the screams.
To halt the screams.

I push some more.
I push some more.

I sigh relief. The child is born.
I sigh relief. The child is born.

Strong lungs scream.
Silence.

It squirms there, full of life.
It lies there, cold and blue.

It is a boy.
It was a boy.

Another born to be big and strong.
Another one born to be laid in the ground.

A babe suckling at my breast.
This babe lying in my arms.

Tomorrow I will plan a party.
Tomorrow I will go to the field....

None of the improvs had been about childbirth, but this was where Diane found her passion.

There are virtually no wrong answers here. Almost every interior monologue, every poem, is plausible, even if students approach the same character's thoughts in very different ways. Chaunetta writes from the point of view of a woman whose children are sold off, Eric from a man contemplating escape, Monica from a plantation owner reflecting on his dissatisfaction with his overseers. Some of the pieces, like Diane's, are publishable, some not even close. But each student gains an insight with validity, and together their portraits form an emotional and empathetic patchwork quilt. And again, the assignment challenges all students, regardless of supposed skill levels.

Untracking the Big Questions

Before students begin the read-around I ask them to take notes on three questions: 1) In what ways were people hurt by slavery? 2) How did people resist slavery? and 3) Explain why you think slavery could or could not have ended without a violent struggle. We circle-up for the read-around. I encourage, but don't require, everyone in class to share his or her writing. As students read their pieces they compliment each other, offer "aha's" and take notes on the questions. This is not an editing session, so critical remarks aren't allowed — thus students know they'll only hear positive comments if they choose to share. The read–around, or sharing circle, builds community as youngsters applaud each other's efforts and insights. The medium is the message: we all count here.

Afterward, people look over their notes and write on the questions. Unlike textbook questions, these encourage students to make meaning themselves, not to parrot back the meaning decided by some publishing company. The third question is a difficult one, calling for students to reflect on the obstacles to social change. It's a question that ordinarily might be set aside for the "advanced" class, but because of an anti–tracking pedagogy it can be approached by everyone: they all watched the improvs, they all participated, they heard my mini–lectures, they discussed their questions and insights, they entered someone's head to write from his or her point of view and they listened to the 'collective text' created by the entire class. Wrestling with a question like this is simply the next step. Everyone can succeed, and everyone is intellectually challenged. And because theory is grounded in students' in–class experience, the assignment doesn't privilege those students who may be more practiced at abstract thinking.

If we want our classes to be accessible to students regardless of academic background and confidence we have to discover ways of bringing concepts alive. Simulations are another show–don't–tell strategy. For example, in exploring the history of work in the U.S., particularly "scientific management" or "Taylorization" — owners studying and then chopping up the labour process into component parts and assigning workers one repetitive task — a simple lecture would reach some students. But using paper airplanes and students as skilled workers to simulate changes in the production process provides all students access to a vital piece of history that can help them reflect on their own work lives.

We can tape off the floor and offer pieces of chocolate to simulate land and wealth distribution in different societies; unsharpened and sharpened pencils can represent raw materials and manufactured products to help us show the dynamics of colonialism; and with balls of cotton, shirts, wheat, "guns," and bank notes, we can walk students through pre–Civil War sectional conflicts. An untracked classroom can be both more playful and more rigorous than a traditional read-this/listen-to-this/write-this approach.

We can also allow kids to get out of the classroom and into the community, both as social investigators and change-makers. Students can visit a senior citizens' centre to interview people about a particular time period, they might tour a factory to learn about working conditions, or travel to a Native American community to meet and talk with activists. Often, I conclude a major unit or a semester by encouraging students to become 'truth-tellers' — to take their knowledge about an issue beyond the classroom walls. One year, a student of Linda's and mine choreographed and performed for a number of classes a dance on the life of Ben Linder, the Portlander murdered by the Contras in Nicaragua; numbers of students re-write children's books from a multicultural standpoint and use them to lead discussions at elementary schools; one group produced a videotape, cablecast city-wide, about the erosion of Native American fishing rights on the Columbia River. Several years ago, a student in a global studies class wrote and recorded "The South Africa Rap," questioning why corporations leave communities in the U.S. and invest in Apartheid; it was subsequently played by several community radio stations around the country. A real-world curriculum aims to give students an equal opportunity to understand society — and to change it.

A New Teacher-Student Covenant

An anti-tracking pedagogy needs to offer alternatives to traditional teaching methods and critique these methods as well. The traditional teacher–student covenant proposes to rehearse students for alienation: I give you an assignment over which you have no or little control. It's not about you, it's about subject X. I think it up — or more often a textbook company thinks it up — I design it, you perform it and I evaluate it. In exchange for successfully carrying out your part of the bargain I give you a reward: your grade. Neither the work nor the grade has any intrinsic value, but the grade has exchange value that can be banked and spent later for desired ends. Conception and execution are separate, and this dichotomy prepares young people for a life of essential powerlessness over the conditions of their labour and the purposes towards which that labour is used. An anti-tracking pedagogy needs to offer a new covenant, one that promises students an education rooted in their lives, with much greater initiative and participation.

In Linda Christensen's and my Literature and History course we constantly draw on students' lives as a way of illuminating both history and literature and, in turn, draw on the history and literature as a way of illuminating students' lives. In the slavery and slave resistance unit, mentioned above, we read an excerpt from Frederick Douglass' autobiography in which a teenage Douglass defies and physically confronts his overseer [*Narrative of the Life of Frederick Douglass*, pp. 68–75]. We discuss the conditions in Douglass' life that propelled him into this confrontation, and from the discussion ask students to describe a time in their lives when they stood up for what was right. The assignment gives a framework for students' writing but offers them lots of room to move, and as with the other assignments described, this one adjusts to a student's skill level. Some students may be able to write a personally probing, metaphorical piece while others may struggle to write a couple paragraphs — but the assignment offers all students a point of entry.

The read-around celebrates the diversity of students' experience, and in some cases their bravery or self-sacrifice: Nate writes about confronting a racist and abusive police officer, Stephanie about attending an anti-nuclear power demonstration, Josh about challenging a teacher's unfairness, Zeneda about interrupting an incident of sexual harassment. But the stories also give us the raw material to reflect on when and why people resist, and the relative effectiveness of some forms of resistance over others. And we can test our findings against Frederick Douglass' experiences.

In a unit on the history and sociology of schooling, students write about an encounter with inequality in education, and at a different point, about a positive learning experience. In a lesson on the Cherokee Indian Removal they write about a time their rights were violated. After reading a Studs Terkel interview with C.P. Ellis [*The Power in Our Hands*, pp. 145–147], who quit his leadership position in the Klan and became a civil rights advocate and union organizer, students write about a significant change they made in their lives.

The personal writing and sharing undercuts a curriculum designed to inure students to alienated work, as the assignment also equalizes students' opportunity for academic success and theoretical insight. Moreover, it is a key part of creating a classroom discourse that in both form and content tells each student: you matter; your life and learning are important here. That's another aim of breaking away from a curriculum that is traditionally male dominated, and extols the lives of elites over working people and people of colour. Unless we reorient the content of the curriculum to more accurately reflect the lives of all our students, we implicitly tell young people, "Some of you are better than others, some of you are destined for bigger things."

An Explicit Critique of Tracking

Ultimately, an anti-tracking pedagogy needs to engage students in an explicit critique of tracking. As Jeannie Oakes and others have shown, one of the by-products of tracking, even one of its objectives, is that low-tracked students blame themselves for their subordinate position in the scholastic hierarchy; students come to believe that they are defective and the system is okay. Consequently, the unequal system of education, of which tracking is an important part, needs a critical classroom interrogation so that students can expose and expel the voices of self-blame, and can overcome whatever doubts they have about their capacity for academic achievement.

In our unit on the history and sociology of schooling, students look critically at their own educations. We start with today and work backwards in time to understand the origins of the structures that now seem as natural as the seasons. From David Storey's novel, *Radcliffe*, we read a short excerpt that poignantly describes the unequal treatment received by students of different class backgrounds and, as mentioned earlier, ask students to recall an episode of unequal schooling from their own lives. We use the novel excerpt and students' stories to talk about the hidden curricula embedded in school practices — the subterranean lessons students absorb about democracy, hierarchy, power, solidarity, race, social class and resistance. Students make observations on their own educational experiences, both past and present, and informally inventory the building's resources: who gets what kinds of equipment, facilities, class sizes and why? Our students' research is subversive in the best sense of the term as they engage in a critical inquiry that subverts the apparent legitimacy of a system of privilege that benefits some at the expense of others.

We read excerpts of Jean Anyon's 1980 *Journal of Education* article, "Social Class and the Hidden Curriculum of Work," which attempts to demonstrate that schools' expectations of students vary depending on the social position of students' parents. For example, through her research Anyon found that schools in working class communities value rote behavior and following directions; "affluent professional schools" value creativity and student initiative. The article, written for an academic journal, is a real stretch for a lot of students and might stay beyond their reach if we confined our conceptual exploration to reading and discussion. Instead, we test Anyon's theory by travelling to a wealthier, suburban school to make observations on classroom and school dynamics. We return to compare these to their observations of our own Jefferson High, a school in the centre of a predominantly African American, working–class community. Their first–hand experience makes theory student–friendly, and allows every-one to participate in the discussion as we evaluate Anyon's argument.

To provide at least a partial historical context for their find-ings, students participate in a mock 1915 school board delib-eration. Students represent different social groups as a way of examining who promoted and benefited from the introduc-tion of intelligence testing and differentiated curricula. We read excerpts from the second chapter of Jeannie Oakes' *Keep-ing Track* on the history of tracking, and a chapter on the his-tory of the SAT test, "The Cult of Mental Measurement," from David Owens' *None of the Above*. From Paul Chapman's *Schools as Sorters*, we review a 1920 survey (p. 126) conducted by Stanford University that found high school students had aspirations that were too high for the jobs available — over 60 per cent of them wanted professional careers, whereas fewer than 5 per cent of jobs were in the professions. Concluded Stanford psychologist William V. Proctor: "For [students'] own best good and the best good of the nation a great many of them should be directed toward the agricultural, mechanical, and industrial fields." Could the 'problem' of students' high expec-tations help explain certain social groups' commitment to intelligence testing and tracking? My students react with some anger at this conscious attempt to deflate children's dreams.

Providing new information and ways to question the charac-ter of schooling is a vital component of untracking any school or classroom. As suggested, tracking is not just a bad idea, but is a practice linked to the legitimation and maintenance of deep social inequality. Undercutting the legitimacy of unfair privilege is thus another needed piece in an anti–tracking strategy. As indicated in the classroom examples provided, the curriculum can offer students permission and encouragement to critique social inequities and to think about alternatives. Further, introducing into the classroom a legacy of resistance to injustice helps nurture an ethos of hope and possibility. Learning from individuals and movements working for democratic social change, both past and present, provides inspiration that not only can societies change for the better, but so can we. Because tracking rests on a premise that people's intellectual capabilities and potential for achievement are fixed, an anti-tracking curriculum needs to demonstrate a more hopeful — and realistic — view of human possibility.

Grades and Equity

At the end of the first quarter Linda and I taught together, Alphonso came to complain about his grade. "I don't think I deserve a C," he argued. "Maybe I can't write as well as Katy. But she came in writing like that, and I've worked really hard. Compare what I'm doing now to what I wrote when the year began. I think I deserve at least a B." Alphonso's complaint illustrates a dilemma of evaluating, or more precisely grading, students in an untracked class. Alphonso was right: Katy knew more history, wrote with more detail and clarity, and had a firmer grasp of course concepts. But Alphonso had worked hard, made important strides in his writing and comprehension, and regularly shared his insights with the class. Still, were we to grade on a curve or based on some fixed standard of achievement, a C would have been fair, even generous. However, we had told the class we wouldn't grade this way, but on effort, openness, growth, consistency of written and oral participation, respect for one another, as well as clarity of analysis. Thus we gladly changed Alphonso's grade and confessed our mistake.

"Fair grading" is an oxymoron and I'd prefer not to give letter grades at all. I attended an ungraded college, Antioch, where professors wrote students end of the term letters indicating academic strengths and areas needing work. Students responded with self-evaluations that commented on teachers' assessments. It all seemed to make more sense. Of course Antioch professors didn't see 150 students a day. Nor were they ordered by school or state authorities to sum up a student's performance with a single letter grade.

An anti-tracking pedagogy needs a system of student evaluation that does not reward students based primarily on the skills and aptitudes with which they begin a class. A system of fixed criteria from the outset benefits some and penalizes others largely on the basis of class, race, gender or nationality. An untracked class needs an egalitarian evaluation system that lets all students know they can succeed based on what they do in class, not on what they have or have not accomplished in the past.

Linda and I do not assign letter grades on individual assignments during the term. Instead, we write comments on students' papers indicating our evaluation and keep track of in-class participation and completion of written work. Students maintain folders of their work and at the end of each term write extensive self-evaluations analyzing all aspects of their achievement in class, and present a case for a particular letter grade. Linda and I read their evaluations, review their folders, discuss their overall progress and conference with students. Only then do we assign letter grades.

As in Alphonso's case, sometimes we blow it. But students are always free to challenge us, call our criteria into question and draw our attention to factors we may have overlooked. Every year we tell students about Alphonso to underscore our fallibility and to encourage their vigilance.

Ours is obviously not the only way to grade. But whatever system teachers adopt should derive from a broader anti-tracking philosophy and strategy. In evaluation, as with everything else, we must be bound by considerations of equity, not tradition or efficiency.

An anti-tracking pedagogy is more than just a collection of good teaching ideas strung together in a classroom with kids of different social backgrounds and educational histories.

That may be a step in the right direction but we still need to ask: Towards what? Is it enough to offer quality education in a heterogeneous setting, as some untracking proponents suggest? I don't think so. Once out of school, our students will still be 'tracked' by jobs that require little decision making and initiative, by high unemployment, by racism and sexism. We can't truly untrack schools without untracking society. Thus an anti-tracking pedagogy should equip educators and students to recognize and combat all inequity. Its organizing principle should be justice — in the classroom, in school and in society at large.

Chapter Six

*Streaming beyond
highschool
= streams (- college
university*

TEACHING STREAMED
STUDENTS

Bob Davis

I

Responding To A Class Reality

The streaming system in our schools is not something that is easily abolished. Some of its most obvious structures can be removed — like the different programs labelled General and Academic — and that would be a good thing. But much of the old sifting and sorting that might have taken place within these programs would still continue — in how marks are awarded, in the divisions within specific classes (Crows and Bluebirds) and in who is actually qualified to sign up for certain post-secondary programs.

The core of our streaming problem — and the reason for its tenacity — can be understood more clearly if we first grasp how teachers respond to it: how they understand the framework of social class in which their students live and are educated and how they cope with this understanding. It's not easy analytic territory, and I thought the best way of getting to it was to share some of my experiences with teachers while I was myself a teacher of General Level students.

A number of years back, when General Level programs were much more in fashion — and we may well see a new emphasis on these programs with the recent Harris reforms for Ontario secondary schools — my old sidekick and friend Jim McQueen and I used to do the conference circuit as G–level schtick men. While we gave our spiel about teaching history, next door another G–level expert gave his about positive peer culture, and down the hall another gave hers on co–operative education. We vied for the cutest title to our talks. One seminar leader called his "How I learned to love the sweat hogs."

We undoubtedly had some good effects on some people. Alongside inspirational roadshow types like Zachary Clement, we probably got a few teachers to begin thinking about the curious beast called the G–level kid. But we also served a very negative purpose in deepening teachers' cynicism, which, I might add, has grown apace since those days. Like others before and after us, we added weight to this society's twisted notion that learning about such a problem is just a matter of lining up a whole bunch of people who can sell their success at this or that little piece of the action.

The Cynical Teacher often senses the weakness in approaches like this. I think he or she understands that just because you line up 57 varieties of narrow, specific G–level successes you have not necessarily helped analyze the problem as a whole. Of course, you may not want to understand the problem as a whole. That's fair enough. Many teachers feel that all they can hope for from a big conference or a P.D. day are a few clues for handling some things better in their own subject in their own classroom: "Leave the administrators to think about the problem as a whole; isn't that what they're paid for?"

There are profound pressures on all of us who work for giant agencies like schools and businesses to leave the thinking about "problems as a whole" to the chiefs. It's a dangerous practice, but a very difficult one to avoid.

What the "Cynical Teacher" Knows

Despite these pressures, my Cynical Teacher doesn't really give up on "general systems thinking." He or she understands on an intuitive level that a problem like THE GENERAL LEVEL STUDENT is connected to deep basic matters that cannot be significantly changed without spending millions of dollars and making very far-reaching changes in the school system. I am not thinking of "radical" teachers here. I'm thinking of the kind of quiet conservative cynic who believes that if a lot of his G–level students don't want to be in school — yet are compelled to stay there — you have a deep and serious problem. He or she is rightfully skeptical of one of the Heinz 57 seminar leaders who implies that big changes will result if teachers develop a "more positive attitude" to their students, or stop using a red pencil — the main suggestion of another seminar leader I heard. Our Cynical Teacher knows that virtually every G–level class contains three or four students who raise such hell that he or she must be a tough disciplinarian merely to keep order and a modicum of sanity. The wonderful curriculum that I am about to claim might change his or her classroom will sound like a naive dream. A Cynical Teacher with this kind of experience is not far off deciding that the essence of the G–level problem is that "you can't make a silk purse out of a sow's ear." Such a teacher is indeed thinking about the G–level problem as a whole — and in the only way that makes sense to him or her. And unfortunately, all our P.D. days and conferences are ill-designed to assist such a teacher (the majority?) to deepen his or her thinking.

You might consider this section a small contribution to thinking "as a whole" about G–level students. I'll talk in some detail about my own teaching, but these details aren't so important; it's the analysis behind them that really counts.

"Basic" and "General" — The Same Problem

One of my first general thoughts about General level is that the problem of the "General level student" is part of the same problem as that of the "Basic level student."

When the Ontario Secondary School Teachers' Federation (OSSTF) first began offering their big conferences on General level students in the early 80s, their conference formula had three ingredients: one element was the 57 varieties of detailed seminars, which I've commented on already; second, was the big inspirational launching or closing plenary speech from some American preacher–cum–standup comic like Zachary Clements or Barbara Colorossa (more about them later); and third, there was the handy wisdom of a keynote speech, ostensibly derived from the research of Dr. Alan King which OSSTF had paid for and were justifiably proud of. The message in some of these keynote speeches was clearly proven by King's studies. Others were not, but were presented with the same certainty. One of the unproven ones was that somehow we in Ontario high schools were doing a great job with Advanced (Academic) and Basic (Lowest) level students but that we were failing with the in-betweens, the General–level students. The conference spiel and overheads implied that all Basic level students were learning a useful skill and getting jobs in their "field" and that all Academic level students were heading to college, university or desirable employment.

To frame the problem for General level teachers in this way makes it virtually impossible for them to look at their stu–dents as part of the total streaming system. And that's my first point: General–level students are part of the school streaming system as a whole, and that system has serious problems. Until we realize this and begin to attack it we will not get far with the G–level problem.

The Streaming Picture at Stephen Leacock

Back in 1977 some English teachers at Stephen Leacock Collegiate in Scarborough approached my colleague, Jim McQueen, about getting some help in teaching General level students. Jim and I piloted the setting up of a 15–person committee, the main accomplishment of which was to do an "every student (anonymous) survey" of our 1300 students. The survey gave us the opportunity to make some links between the stream (Advanced or General; there was no Basic stream at our school) the student was in and various other items like participation in intramurals, participation in extra-curricular activities, average marks given by teachers, absenteeism, attendance, AND — here was the unusual feature — the ethnic and socio-economic background of the student. (Only aggregate totals were sought since the survey was anonymous.) The principal had approved one period for the survey school-wide, and all items were covered either by student memory or by having a recent report card in their hands. They filled in a computer card and wrote the occupations of their parents or guardians on the back. The Blishen Scale was used to allocate a number to the parents' jobs, thus putting jobs on a scale by income, education, and social status.

The socio-economic spread of our school, I should mention, reaches all the way from a major upper middle class area north of the school through small upper working class homes south of the school to a public housing project next to the school's football field.

Streamed on all Fronts

The results of the survey showed that a large percentage of the higher socio-economic level of students were in the academic stream and a high percentage of the lower socio-economic kids were in the general level stream. Ethnically results were not significant; in 1976 Stephen Leacock was what McQueen called a mayonnaise and white bread school. (By the mid-1980s there was a new middle class Chinese group largely in the Academic stream and a new, predominantly working class, black group largely in the G-level stream.) The survey also showed that participation by General level students in intramural and extra-curricular activities was markedly lower than by students in the academic program. The survey indicated as well a much higher General level rate of absenteeism and lateness. *can't interest, them they just won't attend.*

In addition, the survey showed that teachers were giving lower marks to the General level kids even though they were already in a lower stream. In 1976 I took this phenomenon to be teacher prejudice, which we hoped such survey results would help to eradicate. I now believe it implies that teachers have an unconscious or common sense notion of what constitutes basic literacy and, because of this, they refuse to give high marks to students who don't have these fundamentals. In fact, many teachers, if they were allowed to, would be failing a lot more students than they do. Teachers generally do not buy the hand-holding, warm-body approach to G–level and Basic level which is currently forced on them. These survey results at Stephen Leacock Collegiate in Scarborough show basically the same results as the mammoth *Every Student Survey* conducted throughout the Toronto Board in 1970, 1975 and 1980.

Responding To A Class Reality

When I reported on this survey to teachers in the 1970s there were many skeptics who said, "That's not true in my school." Nowadays, I find the studies only confirm what most teachers observe on their own. The issue has now shifted from whether there is a class–streamed school system to why there is and what can be done about it. Today when I say to G–level teachers that they are dealing with working class students for whom school is yet another example of a hostile class system and who develop an elaborate resistance to it, I get a number of different responses:

(1) *You're stereotyping these kids, Bob. By talking about economic class you're almost "creating" class divisions, which wouldn't be significant if you treated them all as equals.*

This view, common among liberal administrators, reminds me of Malcolm X's rejoinder to liberals who accused him of "creating" racism by calling it racism. Malcolm said that white capitalism, slave ship owners, plantation owners, and the Jim Crow laws caused it; he was, he said, merely calling racism by its right name so it could be understood by his own people and fought against.

One principal said I should not have allowed a Grade 9 G–level class to name a magazine of their writing, photographs and drawings *The Dead Beat Bugle*. This same group for whom I was supposedly "perpetuating a low self–image" proceeded to sell the magazine throughout the school for twenty–five cents a copy. They sold out their 500 copies in two days, and the majority of copies were bought and enjoyed by academic level kids. My class had a better sense of irony than their principal: they knew and everybody else knew they were called dead beats. In this case, they also knew that dead beats had produced a very "undeadbeatish" magazine, something they were proud of.

This liberal fear of stereotyping is important up to a point, but it is a reactionary notion if it is used to pretend there are no different interests, different cultures, different classes in society. At its worst this approach makes it harder to get a grip on the problem, and with some liberals that is exactly what the line is meant to do.

[margin annotation: Stereotyping]

One of its variations is the insistence from Ministry, Boards and teacher federations that we avoid the expression General level "student." We must only talk, they say, about General level "courses" or "programs"; these students are "stereo-typed" otherwise. The liberalism involved here is seriously misguided. With 62 percent of these students dropping out of this program and with the vast majority taking only General-level courses, these are clearly an identifiable group of people. They aren't just kids who happen to be taking General level courses among a range of the courses they attend. They are being streamed into one set of courses, which are largely a failure for them. This has to be evident in the language we use to describe their school identity.

(2) Sometimes I hear this:

> *Sure Bob, the working class are in the lower streams. But you have to face it, they don't have the brains to get ahead. Smarts are inherited, and there's nothing you can do about that.*

Every school staff has its natural superiority people. Most

often they have this view particularly about black inferiority, but many blur racial and class ideas into their personal version of good old-fashioned genetic natural selection. I haven't the time to deal with this view here, but I mention it to remind my liberal readers that this view, which liberals consider a Neanderthal throwback, is alive and kicking in many modern Canadian teaching staffs.

(3) A third response reflects what some teachers think is a hard-nosed approach to the realities of social class and working class kids' hatred of school. It goes as follows:

> Bob, of course I know it's students from the lower socio-economic strata who fill up my G-level classes. But that's not the problem. The problem is that they don't want to be there, and they're forced to be there because we've raised the school-leaving age. However admirable it may be to try to teach everyone up to high school graduation, which we've been doing since World War II, the effort has been a failure. Nobody who hates school as much as most G-level students do will learn very much. I'm trying to teach them only because I'm forced to, but if was running the school system people would get their walking papers way before sixteen if they were doing very badly and especially if they were goofing off and not showing up half the time.

[handwritten margin note: some believed G. level students don't like school + that's the prob not vise versa]

I don't usually find I can change a person's mind with this point of view. I wish more of the public knew what a strain it is for teachers dealing day by day with so many hostile students (most of whom are in General or Basic level). So I sympathize with the strain of the job. That's what I always mainly notice about this kind of person. When it comes to saying something to them, however, I usually simply state that modern governments love having us teachers stuck with the problem of handling masses of unemployed teenagers, and such governments are not about to turn them loose onto the streets, although that may be starting to change now. So since we're mostly stuck with late-leaving compulsory schooling, wouldn't it be great if we could find a different answer to lower the strain rather than daydreaming about lowering the school leaving age?

(4) But the most common response from teachers is this:

Yes, we have a class-streamed school system, but it's not our fault. It's the parents; it's the peers; it's the street; its the culture.

This theory is the official sociological answer: the cultural deprivation theory. No books in the home, no talking in the family about the news, no proper breakfast, no proper study space, no good work habits encouraged, no encouragement from friends to do well in school, no role models of success-ful parents.

where does school fit in

All these things have their truth when the results of short-age of money are separated from the patronizing attitude toward working class life that the middle class usually indulges in. But without implying that a sentence or two is sufficient answer to a theory that is deeply held conventional wisdom in this society, let me pose one question: whatever the truths in this view, are the people who spout it, often with such touching pathos in their voices, implying that school has absolutely nothing to do with the problem? Can a place where kids spend six and often seven hours a day for thirteen to fourteen years of their lives have no effect on them whatsoever? Must we go from the naive view of some of our ancestors that schooling was the key to the total trans-formation of society to a view that school is nothing but a eunuch? Some of us might be forgiven for thinking that this is such a preposterous view that the institutional sponsorship of the cultural deprivation theory is there to take the spot-light off what the school does or does wrong, and make this school experience look like a minor blip in the lives of youth. A mighty expensive blip!

No, the school is not a eunuch. It is not all powerful, but it's not a eunuch.

Yet even teachers who blame all the problems of G–level students on their parents and peers have to teach these kids. A few avoid it by landing jobs in upper middle class schools or by being in a position to give themselves academic classes only. One of the things our G–level committee at Stephen Leacock Collegiate checked out was how different departments chose to assign G–level classes to their teachers. In our history department, McQueen and I specialized in the field. In some departments the task rotated based on the department's sense that G–levels were a strain and should be shared. In some departments new teachers were given these classes, and in some schools we even heard of systems where G–level assignments were given as punishment.

How Teachers Cope *What Approach do Teachers Take?*

So some General level classes are being handled by choice and some are not. But teach them we must, and when you try to assess what different approaches are being taken by teachers you get answers like these:

(1) *One teacher told me: I just talk to them about their girlfriends and boyfriends. They can't learn much, and their basic skills are nil, so we just have a good gab every day.*

This teacher was cynical, but he was also aware that he had fairly official (if somewhat blurred) blessing for giving up on teaching his students anything and settling instead for being a friend.

G–level conference speakers often lend a lot of support to this approach, although this support has been diminishing these last few years of neo–conservative "reforms." For those who still hang in with this point of view, their speeches have two ingredients: one is the standup comic re–creation of every real scene in a teacher's life in brilliant dramatic form, which gives you the kind of affirmation that TV cops must give real cops. (Because we teachers are not heroes on TV much, these popular speakers must do for us what TV does for police, doctors, journalists, and parents — i.e. to accept that although the way things work is the way they'll go on working, there's nonetheless a kind of rough dignity to being a teacher.)

The second thing these speakers pass on is a gentle religious message that we should love the unfortunate G–level students — they're real people, too; they have a lot to teach us, etc. It doesn't matter what Mike Harris and Company think. And many teachers are responsive to this warm–hearted message, even though it completely avoids the issue of what they should be teaching. After all, teaching these kids is a bitch, isn't it? We're not sure they can learn anything at all, are we? So why not stick to love, relationships, self–image? As if our relationships with others and a good self–image have nothing to do with knowing something!

This first teaching approach is still common. In its extreme form it is the teacher talking about their (students) girlfriends and boyfriends. In its more prevalent form, it is the warm friendly classroom — lots of right brain intuitive stuff ... therapy rather than learning ... "going nowhere at your own speed."

(2) The second approach I call the Dittoes and Discipline approach.

This approach often has some learning theory behind it that says "these" kids need to have learning broken down into small discrete steps and to stay away from grand theorizing. Teachers with this perspective give out a new xeroxed sheets every period and run a tight ship. The extreme and pathetic example to me is the teacher who asks a G–level kid to describe in minute steps how to get to the corner of Yonge and Bloor, then ties the kid up in knots about how imprecise his directions are, and then uses the example to illustrate how concrete and simple his teaching of "these people" has to be. This is the "Neanderthalizing" of G–level students.

(3) The third solution for a few teachers is to adopt one of the current fads ranging from co-operative education, to mastery learning, to 4-Mat, to learning styles theory to life-skills.

As I suggested earlier, not many teachers get swept away by fads — and I don't deny that many fads have their good points — so it's best to think of this solution as a side show. Administrators, consultants, teacher union professional development specialists, college conference circuit people, and Ministry advisors may talk as if some of these fads are sweeping the nation or should sweep the nation or would sweep the nation if teachers were more venturesome, but it's a kind of fanfare that affects very few and hides a void in the school system as a whole.

(4) *A fourth solution proposed a number of years back as something of a panacea for the ills of working class students is an unconnected dismantling of the present structures for streaming in our schools.*

The class nature of our streaming system started to embarrass some governments as parent groups continued to raise the issue. In Ontario, George Radwanski's Report, commissioned by the Perterson government's Ministry of Education, suggested that streaming may be nothing more than an embarrassing mechanism and should therefore be abolished. Add a new non–embarrassing mechanism like periodic province–wide testing, and maybe skills will shoot upward and equality will flourish. Because these suggestions were usually made with no comment whatsoever on the changes in curriculum content or teaching methods which would be necessary if these external streaming arrangements were abolished, the proposals show either an unbelievable naivete about how class discrimination actually works or, which is more likely, these authorities were quite prepared to dump on local school boards and teachers the problem of recreating streaming within each class–room — along the lines of the old Crows and Bluebirds reading groups in the elementary schools. Of course, we have to get rid of these larger structures, but we have to know what we're putting in their place. Otherwise the new system will also fail working class kids, and the cynicism among teachers will grow.

(5) *A much harder-edged streaming system now seems to be in the works with neo-conservative secondary school "reforms." In Ontario, these reforms, following on the logic of the NDP's Royal Commis-*

sion on Learning, are a year or two away from implementation . Since they haven't reached the classroom, and most teachers aren't consciousness of what they might mean in practice, I'm going to put them aside for another time.

(6) At present most teachers are just plain confused.

They know the strain. They try many different things. They even talk about the students' girlfriends and boyfriends occasionally. They may even give out a few dittoes, but they are still frustrated with the whole enterprise. They want to be teachers not social workers. And what they are doing right now they call "babysitting".

(7) My own answer is more prosaic. It's about curriculum.

It is to ask what we're trying to teach G-level students. We're teachers, aren't we? Is it too old-fashioned or maybe new-fashioned to ask what we're trying to teach? You see, most of the Heinz 57 wares being marketed at conferences on lower-stream students imply that these students are too stupid or too neurotic (or even psychotic) to learn much of anything. Underneath both the girlfriend/boyfriend classroom and the dittoes and discipline classroom is the same patronizing attitude. Too dumb or too disorderly. Of course, good teaching techniques are important, and of course a sympathetic personality is very important. But why this near conspiracy to suggest that what is learned is not important?

I start with the premise that despite the obstacles many working class kids face that come from lack of money, they can learn just as well as middle and upper class kids and deserve to have a curriculum and learning standards as serious and as challenging. When we examine the General level curriculum, however, and we keep in mind what economic class its students largely come from, we soon notice some big problems with the curriculum. (Problems which are even bigger at the Basic level.) I am mostly a history teacher so the

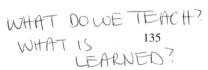

WHAT DO WE TEACH?
WHAT IS LEARNED?

135

missing ingredients are more obvious to me in the history curriculum. I therefore start with history, which is what I want to talk about in the next section of this chapter.

[handwritten: What's missing in /wrong with the curriculum that leads to G-Level failure?]

II

History and Work: Rewriting The Curriculum

The following is a poem on my classroom wall that is a motto for what I think is missing in traditional school history:

So Many Questions

Who built the seven gates of Thebes?
The books are filled with the names of kings.
Was it kings who hauled the craggy blocks of stone?
And Babylon so many times destroyed,
Who built the city up each time? In which of Lima's houses,
That city glittering with gold, lived those who built it?
In the evening when the Chinese Wall was finished
Where did the masons go? Imperial Rome
Is full of arcs of triumph. Who reared them up? Over whom
Did the Caesars triumph? Byzantium lives in song.
Were all her dwellings palaces? And even in Atlantis of the legend,
The night sea rushed in,
The drowning men still bellowed for their slaves.

Young Alexander conquered India.
He alone?
Caesar beat the Gauls.
Was there not even a cook in his army?
Philip of Spain wept as his fleet
Was sunk and destroyed. Were there no other tears?
Frederick the Great triumphed in the Seven Years' War.
Who triumphed with him?

Each page a victory—
At whose expense the victory bell?
Every ten years a great man.
Who paid the piper?

So many particulars.
So many questions.

[handwritten note: where are these students represented in our curriculum, our texts, our teaching?]

Bertolt Brecht

Does it not seem likely that children of footsoldiers, stonemasons, cooks, factory workers, and clerks identify poorly with a history which fails to mention footsoldiers, stonemasons, cooks, factory workers and clerks?

All our children should be learning about the trials, struggles, frustrations and accomplishments of these missing heroes, but the children of the working class especially suffer from their absence from our history books.

This is not the place the explain why these "peoples'" stories are absent in these books, but it is the place to point out that the teacher, who understands what socio–economic class his lower stream kids come from and who wants to affirm the dignity of their background, will understand that all courses must be revamped to correct this monumental silence. Once again, let me emphasize two things: (1) Everybody, including upper and middle–income kids, needs to hear the history of all classes. (2) Working-class kids by the same token do not just need a package of "working–class" curriculum, especially an ersatz version — a bunch of S.E. Hinton novels (like *The Outsiders*), for instance, combined with some hip social history focussed on flappers and model T's. To add challenging curriculum to lower stream history courses is not a matter of adding "social colour" (like costuming in early Ontario), but rather of incorporating the roles "ordinary people" have played in the central activities of the society — in politics, family, work, etc.

[handwritten note: Not just a "packaged" curriculum for them, but incorporate representation into a well rounded curriculum.]

The Scope of the Task

If the revision I have in mind were to be done right, it would be a very extensive job. It means, at its most extreme, the rewriting of all courses to include the dimension of ordinary people's history. It does not mean tacking on a "social history" chapter at the end of each unit, which happened in one of Ricker and Saywell's famous old texts, *The Modern Era*. That approach gives students the impression that ordinary peoples' history is a kind of relief from the mainstream history of politics and economics — a pause that refreshes; more flappers and model T's. Neither is it satisfactory to do "easier" G-level versions of the prescribed courses. They may ease some teacher/student anxiety by simplifying the reading material, but they do not solve the problem of what's missing in the course content itself.

But if the full task of this curriculum reform is daunting, it is not so difficult to make a start with a specific new unit, which I want to talk about shortly. First though, I'd like to lay out what seem to me some basic principles for the rewriting of classroom history.

As a preface, let me say that when such a central element of our history is so absent from most of our courses, proper change cannot happen merely by the introduction of a nibble here and a dabble there. Some changes must happen slowly, but many very small changes are so unnoticeable that we are not necessarily better off with them than we were without them. In *The Modern Era*, for example, you are left with the impression that the only time "workers" get on to history's stage is when they're living it up or causing trouble (Model T's, flappers and strikes). Current texts are no better. Other books push this line even further: workers are pictured as boozing pleasure-seekers, who periodically turn into a violent mob. It is essential to introduce experimental units and courses which correct this neglect and distortion.

I should add here that if extensive changes were to take place in the regular courses, these experimental units might cease to be needed. They should not be thought of as models

can usually read complter texts if interest is there.

for a whole program; they are meant to highlight elements missing in the regular program. They are not concerned, for example, with the central process of political development and change, which must, of course, be part of a total history program

First Principles for a History Rewrite

1. The Dignity of Ordinary Lives and Work

If you spend most of your historical study learning about famous missionaries, explorers, kings and queens, politicians, financiers, writers and inventors, you pick up the message that the life of the average peon is unimportant. If, in addition, you are from a humble background yourself, you pick up the additional message that you and your own folks are not that memorable either. So my first principle is that a corrected version of history would stress the lives and histories of ordinary people; this is primarily to offer them proper recognition and dignity. Fortunately, there has been a burgeoning of social history in the last fifteen years in Canada, England and the United States, so that the number of available sources for improving our high school history texts have increased significantly.

2. The History of Conflict is Central

Battles over hunger, wages, work conditions, housing, children, schooling, politics, transportation, possession of property, etc., have always been a central part of the history of ordinary people. Conflict has always had a primary place in history teaching, but some kinds of conflict have generally been more acceptable to record than others: conflicts between religious sects, barons and kings, colonies and mother countries, dictatorship and democracies. These are the central conflicts we find in our history books.

The conflicts that are underplayed or are virtually absent

include conflicts between slaves and owners, peasants and lords, soldiers and officers, workers and management, tenants and landlords, rich and poor. These are conflicts which suggest serious division within our own societies and, worse still — imagine it — some of these conflicts continue today. When these conflicts are present in our history books, they are there so infrequently and in so chaotic a form that the message students get is that there is little historical rhyme or reason to them; they appear as mindless mob violence. A point appreciated by those who have power in our own society.

3. Exploitation is an Ongoing Fact of History

History books that set out basically to defend the status quo do not present exploitation as an ongoing fact of history. Yet once you begin to present the history of ordinary people in any systematic way, you find it difficult to avoid putting exploitation centre stage.

You do not have to be a socialist to come to this conclusion. With enough distance between present and past, exploitation is usually accepted as a root interpretation by historians of all political affiliations. Most historians agree, for example, that peasants were exploited in the middle ages or that the main motivation for the monstrous crime of black slavery was economic. But just try to persuade an utra-rightist that today's small farmers or blacks are exploited for profit.

4. Ordinary People Fight Back

If you take ordinary peoples' battles out of the mob violence category and put them into the category of a natural response to being exploited, you inevitably get into a coherent history of the riots, strikes and organizations ordinary people have formed to gain new rights or hold on to old ones.

5. The Union Movement is a Central Part of the Story

The best known working class organization is the union. The union movement is central to the struggle by working people for a decent life. Certainly, this movement has many problems and weaknesses, which ought to be dealt with plainly in school, but to have its history popping in and out of our curriculum the way it does, suggests it is largely insignificant. This is a serious distortion.

6. Political Parties are also Key to the History of Ordinary People

When ordinary workers and farmers have been very angry about conditions — and have not obtained sufficient satisfaction through their unions — they have sometimes formed new political parties to look after their interests. Our history text writers acknowledge this to some extent. The strength of farmer–worker parties after World War I is often mentioned as is the rise of radical farmer parties in the West during the 1930s. What's usually missing — a depolitizing absence — are two major elements of our political party system: (1) the extent to which ordinary people's demands, mostly moving in a left–wing direction, are reflected in all political parties, and (2) the extent to which popular support has arisen, at the same time, for parties at both ends of the political spectrum (communist and fascist parties in the 1930s, for example).

An Experimental Unit on "Work" for Grade Nine General Level History

I now present a ninth grade General Level history unit on "Work," which I designed for my Scarborough, Ontario high school. Its students were streamed by local elementary schools into what amounts to a "self–contained" General Level program. The class invariably reflects the predominantly working–class makeup of this program, which was identified in our school's Every Student Survey. Let me once again remind you (too often?) that I believe students of all social classes and academic levels would benefit from this unit, but working class students benefit especially from it.

1. Sparking Interest

I get students started by asking them to write down what they consider the five most dangerous jobs, the five most boring jobs, the five most unhealthy jobs, the five most physically exhausting jobs, and the five jobs which most produce nervous stress.

I learn a lot about them from this, and we have a good discussion. I bring in some information I have from surveys of dangerous jobs by organizations like the Ontario Federation of Labour or the National Farmers' Union. What do I learn? Such things as this: none of my city kids has ever listed farmer as a dangerous job, yet it rates in the top three jobs in Canada for deaths and bad accidents. I have also realized that students are heavily influenced by TV so that a common dangerous job they listed was "stunt man," a job not known to employ many full-time people but big in TV hype.

Jobs which students list as producing stress are also commonly affected by TV, so that doctor and nurse crop up a lot, but key-puncher does not appear and neither do factory jobs.

At the same time many students have stories from home about jobs that are unhealthy and unsafe. We discuss whether the government ads suggesting that unsafe or unhealthy conditions are the fault of workers for not taking care or for not wearing safety boots, a mask or a helmet.

2. Work Terms

I then ask my students to explain each of the following terms from the world of work.

1. Blue collar job
2. White collar job
3. A strike
4. Equal pay for equal work
5. Equal pay for work of equal value
6. Fringe benefits
7. Collective bargaining
8. Overtime pay
9. Getting fired
10. Layoff
11. Pregnancy leave
12. Assembly line job
13. Piece work
14. Management
15. Shop steward
16. Minimum wage law
17. Seniority
18. Workmen's compensation
19. U.I.C. (unemployment insurance)

Students are expected to learn the meaning of these work terms, if they don't know them already. We discuss them in class. Then they do a test on them. There is a common assumption by conservative critics of liberal school reform that "new curriculum" is just gazing at your navel and telling each other how it feels. In fact, the topic of "work" has lots of precise knowledge connected with it, as much as any "science."

3. Your Rights Under Ontario's Labour Code

I then turn to look at the rights of Ontario Workers under the law, going through following the work sheet:

THE RIGHTS OF ALL WORKERS IN ONTARIO BY LAW
(ON PAPER ANYWAY)
WHAT ARE THEY?

Minimum wage required to be paid:
adult _____.
student _____.
waiter _____.
Minimum number of hours of work per week before over-time pay must be paid _____.
Amount of overtime pay must be at least _____.
Pregnancy leave rule for management _____.
Is it paid leave?_____.
Vacation — number of weeks after how long _____.
Vacation pay _____.
What is "pay equity"?_____.
Is it guaranteed by law in Ontario? _____.
Are any seniority rights guaranteed for all workers? _____.
How about paid sick leave?_____.
When is a person entitled to UIC (unemployment insurance)?
_____.
How much do you get for how long?_____.
The regulation about when and how long a compulsory break must be given _____. Is this more favourable to management or the workers? Give reason. _____
_____.
What are the statutory paid holidays that all workers must be given?_____.

WHAT KIND OF BENEFITS AND RIGHTS CAN A GOOD UNION GET FOR WORKERS THAT THEY DON'T HAVE FROM THE ONTARIO LABOUR CODE?

In working out this sheet students are to ask for information from their parents. Later they learn where this information can be obtained from government information services, usually a single phone number. Precise information here is combined with a knowledge of personal rights. This opens up a very solid discussion, and the writing tasks focus on how these rights came about and whether they are adequate.

4. Organizing a Union: The Film "Maria"

The next unit starts with a film called *Maria* written for TV by Rick Salutin and directed by Alan King. An Italian textile worker in her mid–20s, after 10 years in a Toronto plant where her sister and mother also work, decides to try to start a union. The story shows the tough organizing battle, which unfolds at the plant, as well as the opposition Maria encounters first from her father and then, especially, from her boyfriend, when she takes on this "man's job." Maria is just one hour long. It is a totally absorbing personal story and very informative about union organizing, the law which frames it, and the attitudes and responses of companies, unions, and male workers to new organizing among low paid immigrant women. It is also a film that gives a very clear view of the difference between labour code rights and the protection that only a union can obtain.

Apart from the new topic here, I also judge that students are ready to deal with a more substantial writing project after two sheets of factual terms and labour law.

Here is a summary of the movie written by a grade nine general level student:

MOVIE: MARIA *by Seth Sibanda*

This movie was about a bunch of foreign workers who were from overseas. They included such countries as Greek, Italian, West Indies and Portuguese. The youngest of all the workers was an Italian girl called Maria. Maria unlike the older women had soft feelings, in other words it didn't take much to get her mad. She didn't like the way the fashion company was being run and she wanted to get a few people together to do something about it.

You see the fashion company payed the workers less than they should get pay. They provided awful, steamy, hot smelly work conditions and the man and the lady who watch the workers were too cruel and harsh to the men and many ladies who worked there. These and many other reasons were the reason for Maria and the others trying to form a union.

They started by getting addresses of all the ladies who were interested in helping them to form a union. But the bosses did not take to kindly to this action and therefore several girls were laid off for several months. But then the bosses were starting to get nice. They fixed the washrooms and sinks and other little appliances. But that was the only thing that they did. They refused to do more because they thought it was unnecessary.

Then one day the workers and the bosses had to present there arguements to a group in a giant assembly hall. A black worker had been fired to scare the other workers. But the men in charge decided to pursue the case only two more months later. This made the bosses very happy and the workers still had to work under there orders and awful conditions. My question about this stage of the movie was why didn't the workers go on strike? Because I feel that they had the bosses scared and that they could get what they want by going on strike.

Well the time came for the workers and there bosses to cast there votes for labour union or not. The day before the votes were casted and counted, the man-forman of the workers threatened that he would cut this workers heart out if he told anybody about the threat.

The day of the voting came, but before the workers and bosses casted there votes, the head boss and owner had a few words to say to his workers. What the boss said pleased some people and disappointed and upset others. Well it was time for the voting. I like the way the camera moved in to give the movie a different atmosphere. And to also show the pressure on the employees faces. Now all they had to do was wait and count. Maria and the boss counted.

Outside the warehouse company the other workers stood around trying to stay warm and wait for Maria. Each person wondering what the results would be. Well in a short time Maria was out. The look on her face said enough. But the workers still thought they won. The results a tie 76 to 76. In other words they loss. Tie goes to the company.

Everyone congratulated and thanked Maria for her efforts. They didn't win but they sure scared the hell out of their bosses. In six months later they planned to try again, and I'm sure with more planning and organization they will come out on top and get what they want !

I felt that there was a lot to be learned in this movie. I also know a bit more about a union than I ever did before. This movie in its own way that if you want freedom and good enjoyable work conditions you have to fight for your rights. And don't be afraid to express yourself.

This girl Maria is really a inspiration to shy people who always get shoved around. She took her time, gave up her boyfriend, and helped others to get what they need to enjoy working.

My concluding assignment on this movie is twenty–nine key quotations for which students must answer who said it, to whom, in what situation, with what significance, and whether they have any personal reaction to the quote. They work in groups on this, helping each other. Naturally this quotations assignment also forms the basis of class discussion and debate.

5. Work Songs

I now introduce the following work songs*:

Bud the Spud, Stompin' Tom Connor
Pickin' for a Dollar, David Campbell
Dark as a Dungeon, Dolly Parton
9 to 5, Dolly Parton
The Maintenance Engineer, Sandra Kerr
The Farmer's Song, Murray MacLachlan
Black Fly Song, Wade Hemsworth

These songs are taken from various records and converted to a single cassete tape. I give students copies of the lyrics. I always add current songs and work songs they bring to class. I focus on difficult words, and students are tested on their knowledge of the lyrics. Labour curriculum must be integrated with art as any other successful piece of curriculum must be. Songs also open up the chance to discuss why songs about work are so rare in the mainstream radio, record and video businesses. It also opens up the possibility for students to write a work song of their own.

---

* Readers should remember that I'm talking about songs from the late 1970s and early 1980s.

6. Interviews of Two People Who Work Full-Time

It has struck me for some time that schools usually fail to make good use of the human resources available to students. Libraries and vertical files are not students' only source of information. Indeed, they are often out of date and extraordinarily boring. In my experience, reliance on libraries and vertical files has produced two miserable travesties of education: the "Research Essay" and the "Term Project." The Research Essay, much beloved by many teachers as a training for university, usually turns out to be a mostly undigested, pretentiously-worded pastiche of slightly re-worked quotes from fat textbooks. Of course, that's what many university essays are as well, and that's what many professors actually like. So I guess I shouldn't be so hard on teachers who hold up the same ideal to their high school students. The Term Project is often worse than the Research Essay. The essay at least insists on words and sentences. The Term Project, however, is often nothing more than a glossy duotang collection with cover photograph, coloured headlines, and lots of vertical file quotes, which are entirely undigested by the student. These essays and projects pass as our high school contribution to the "information society."

I'm not opposed to formal research, provided it's serious, but in the context of a normal school schedule good human resources will often get students much better information much faster. Students are an obvious source of information for each other, though they are rarely tapped as such. The surrounding community is equally, if not more, fertile ground, though with limited class time it's hard to get out collectively to this community. Classroom guests from the community are essential, and they should be paid. And, obviously, students should be encouraged to do it on their own, particularly with their parents. This is what I do in my next unit.

In this unit I assign students the task of interviewing two people — parents or guardians, relatives or friends — about their work. I've prepared a sheet of 29 questions for students to use (which readers can have by writing to me c/o *OS/OS*). At the head of this questionnaire is a note to those being interviewed. It goes as follows:

This class is now taking a unit on WORK. They are discussing what different kinds of work there are — also the pay and the working conditions. They have been discussing the different interests of workers and management. They have been learning about some of the problems of health and safety in jobs. They are also considering whether men and women are treated differently in jobs in ways that are unjust.

They will write about these things to develop their writing ability.

They are also reading books about the topic to improve their reading ability.

These interviews are part of this work. They have two purposes:

(1) To help the students to realize that they can learn a lot from people around them like relatives and friends.

(2) To develop their abilities in interviewing and in getting on paper the main things that you say. (A few kids will be using a tape recorder.)

Note: *No names are needed in these interviews and the information is confidential. Each student is to interview any two adults. Women who work in the home can answer the special question page.*

7. *Working* by Studs Terkel

After the interviews I move on to a book called *Working* by Studs Terkel. Terkel interviewed hundreds of "ordinary Americans" about their jobs and their off–hours, and the book is a compendium of these lively and honest statements. Terkel knows how to get people talking, and his characters include everyone from prostitutes to steelworkers. I don't use much of this fat book for my Grade 9 class. I require them to pick out any five selections, however short. Almost all of them pick the prostitute, and some of them pick the next four shortest selections, which is fine with me. With 30 students doing the choosing, they end up covering a lot of the material, which helps extend their general knowledge when we come to discuss the reading with the whole class. Individually, I require each student to write a paragraph on each person they have chosen mentioning "the main things that stand out about them." I also require them to write another paragraph telling who their favourite character was (or "least hated" — picking favourites is often a lie for many students, who might not like anything about what they've experienced or read).

8. Your Own Story

I now give an assignment that requires delicate preparation and encouragement. I tell them that they should imagine that they are older and already have full-time jobs and that Studs Terkel is going to interview them for his book. Their task is to write out a selection about themselves as it might have appeared in Terkel's book. They must decide whether they are married or living with someone, whether they have children, whether they are single. How do they spend their spare time? What are their bosses like? How about their fellow workers? What, in detail, do they do in their job? Is there a union at work? Are they workers or management? What happens in breaks? Do they like their jobs? What were some funny or miserable incidents at work? There are a lot of questions that can be asked.

For those students who say, "I can never do those imagination assignments", I suggest they get a detailed rundown of the job of a parent, guardian, brother or sister or friend, pretend they have that job themselves, and add their own feelings.

What usually comes out of the assignment is a revealing spread of TV dream world jobs (beauty salon operators, professional hockey players, stunt men, night-club dancers) through pretty bizarre stuff (one South American kid was a big time gun runner on the Amazon River with a harem of women) to the most painful and dull jobs. The writing is

(handwritten margin note: Forces them to think of what's available to them. Realistically)

150

sometimes remarkably strong and almost always leads to deeper thinking on the subject of work and the students' future. ✷ Isn't that our purpose as a teacher?!

Here are a couple of recent and representative examples of student work on this topic:

LAWYER *by Gino Damiano*

I am an ordinary man who works minding my own business. I am twenty-nine years of age and married to a beautiful woman. I have two children who are as beautiful as my wife.

Now, continuing on with my job, I like my job some of the time when the other workers aren't bothering me. I get a good salary because I receive a lot of clients. People like me because they think I work so well. I work five days a week and nine hours a day. I take the weekend off and enjoy it with my family.

I work in a full-sized office with a few secretaries and bosses. Our building is pretty big, filled with criminal lawyers such as myself and business lawyers (corporation) and family lawyers. Even though there are a lot of people working in this building, we are not a union. We work with our own clients and make money off them. I like this job very much because I get to associate with different people.

On special occasions at work I like to take some of my friends out to lunch. We celebrate during lunch somewhere fancy. I sometimes take my wife along with me so she can associate with my secretaries and bosses too.

One time, if I can remember long enough, there was an incident that took place at the Supreme Court of Law. I was hired to help this innocent person accused of murder and theft. I gave it all I had. But even though he was innocent, he was sentenced to jail for two years or five thousand dollars bail.

This job took me five years through university and four years through law school. I never really had time for other jobs, because I was too busy studying every night. But I did have jobs when I was younger and, believe me, those jobs don't come anywhere near the job I have now.

I feel like a new man now that I've passed through school and, though it was years of hard work and studying, I pulled through.

When I have my holidays I take about two weeks off. My family and

I run away somewhere far like the Bahamas or Italy, Greece or Africa and have fun in the sun.

Though I'm not really a lawyer I sure wouldn't mind being one.

I'M A CAB DRIVER *by Susan La Monthe*

I'm a cab driver, and I don't really like it. Life is hard and it's rather difficult to raise enough money to support 4 children. All I get a week is 150 dollars. I get $2.50 an hour. My husband left me when I was having my last child, Tommy, who is now 3 years old.

My life feels wasted. It's just the same thing every day. I get up miserable and tired as usual, get ready for work, make the kids' lunches, leave a note for the milkman saying if I need anything today, take a bus to the subway station, which is so dirty, crowded and swishy. Get to work almost always late. Get a yelling from my goddamn boss, who has the largest mouth you ever saw. Get in my cab and start driving.

Being a cab driver is a very dangerous job. I have had knives pointed at me, threats, my money stolen, and lots of other things, but I can't seem to leave my job. It's part of me.

Well, anyway, after the day is over I hit the subway again, cook supper for the kids, and go to bed. The next day it starts all over again.

I consider myself rather young to be putting up with all this shit. I'm only 30 years of age, and I don't deserve it. This is the only job that I've ever had, and that's why I'm scared of trying anything else. There's nothing amusing about my job. It's the same every single day of my sickening life. The people I work with aren't that interesting because I hardly ever talk to anyone. I'm just too busy all the time. I'm telling ya, if you ever think of becoming a cab driver, don't. IT'S HELL.

9. Field Trip

Next we visit some instructive place like the GM Van Plant, which was near our school in Scarborough. Here we are shown around by company personnel, but we also get together with a union representative after the visit to the plant. One inevitable feature of a visit to an auto factory is the shouting, cat calls and hyena screams the workers make to the group from a distance and through the protection of various production lines. A union person explained this phenomenon to my students: (1) the job is boring (2) from a distance workers are safe from management reprimands (3) our visits make them feel like zoo animals so they act the part for a lark. Without this analysis, students often mistook these actions as simply whistling at girls.

On field trips to factories and other workplaces a teacher must always try to go beyond the glossy management view of the operation or the natural attraction to students of a free coke or a free chocolate bar.

10. Two historical novels & projects emerging from them

I end this unit with two historical novels for young people by Bill Freeman, *Shantymen of Cache Lake* and *Last Voyage of the Scotian*. What we did with these remarkable little books you can read about in the next section on "Bean Bakes, Models and Murals."

III

Bean Bakes, Models and Murals

This section describes two different "giant-project" conclusions to the work unit I have described in the proceeding section.

Imagine this recipe: 200 lbs. of white beans, 50 lbs. of salt pork, twelve two-kilo bags of brown sugar, twenty cups of molasses, twelve cups of dry hot mustard, twelve bags of onions.

And instead of a gas stove, imagine that you're going to cook these pork and beans in three giant iron pots (used formerly for dunking pigs!) over a large, outdoor wood fire which will burn two cords of wood for eighteen hours.

Imagine as well that on the previous weekend you have baked — this time inside, with proper ovens — 1500 rolls of bread, and imagine, finally, that your guests for this strange meal are 1500 high school and elementary students from Stephen Leacock–John Buchan schools in Scarborough, Ontario.

This is exactly what 40 Grade Nine general level students and four of their teachers have laid on for four years in a row. The students and staff who handle this giant feed start the fire and "pour" in the food about 6 pm on a Thursday in cold mid–December. They then take shifts right around the clock watching the fire, and they serve the beans and the bread to 1500 students the next day at noon. After the meal the students forget rock and roll for one hour and have an old–time hoedown to the music of a top fiddle band.

Learning about Lumberjacks

The whole thing began with a book. I was desperate for some reading material about work that my grade nine general students would find interesting. I ran across a kids' book, part mystery story, part historical novel, called *Shantymen of Cache Lake* by Bill Freeman. It caught my eye because my grandfather was a lumberjack in the Ottawa Valley. I've also canoed on Cache Lake, which is in Algonquin Park. I was aware that for most teenagers, especially those who've had trouble reading, historical novels are about as exciting as keypunching bank cheques. This book turned out to be different. I won't exaggerate to you. I don't mean there were stampedes to get at it or pleas for extra reading homework. But when five or six students out of twenty–five mention on their own that they like this book, or that "this book is starting to get good," or that "this book is better than the usual stuff we have to read," you know you have a find.

In the course of reading this book I discovered — since the historical setting was Algonquin logging in the 1870s — that the night and day diet of the shantymen was pork and beans. It occurred to me that most students, if they had eaten pork and beans at all, had probably got them out of cans. I therefore went to the principal and asked if two general level classes could get permission to cook pork and beans old–

style on an open fire for their own nourishment and enlight-
enment. He was not your average principal, I should tell you.
With an eye to a weird kind of morale–booster day, he suggested we cook beans for the entire school.

"It's A Gas"

After I got over the complete madness of the idea, I consulted
some teachers and students and we decided to try it.

The biggest scare every year is that the beans will either be
too hard or burned. The taste we can adjust during the last
few hours by adding ingredients. But if the fire is not hot
enough, the beans will be hard; and if the fire's flames lick
up around those pots for too long, the beans will burn. Our
guests will let us know if they don't like the meal and 1500
complaining teenagers equals a failed project. This adds an
air of deadly seriousness to an event full of raucous fun and
wild fatigue.

People who like this event have different reasons for
remembering it. My own reason is the reaction of the students who put it on. Virtually all student–run, morale–boost-
ing events at our school are run by senior, academic–level
students. The Bean Bakers, on the other hand, are first year,
ninth grade students. They are also "general level" — a group
which make up over 40% of our school population. As I've
said earlier: from a careful survey of the entire school population, we discovered that that these general level students
come predominantly from the working–class section of our
school district. We also discovered that they have much less
participation in the school's intramural and extracurricular
programs than the students heading for Grade thirteen.

Yet the Bean Bake — which is voluntary of course —
attracts almost all the students from my two general level
grade 9 classes. I judge that they like doing something that is
overnight, that is a bit wild and that has a real and satisfying
ending — that 1500 people eat a good meal and marvel a bit
at the stamina of the cooks. "It's a gas," as the Bean Bake
posters say.

A Special Ghost

But at this point I should tell you something quite personal. For me a special ghost attends the Bean Bake each year. It's my old lumberjack grandfather, who used to take me on his knee when I was a kid, and tell me stories of wrestling the bears and fighting the French. To an Orangeman like him, the French were more devilish than the bears. I think of him when I read *Shantymen of Cache Lake*, and I resent how few books there are for young people about his life — a life which so many Canadian men experienced, struggled with and some of them died of.

So I'm grateful to Bill Freeman and his publisher Jim Lorimer for bringing out this series. I use Freeman's other two novels as well: *The Last Voyage of the Scotian* (the life of Canadian sailors in the 1870's) and *First Spring on the Grand Banks* (Newfoundland fishermen in the 1870's). My grandfather's generation of farmers and fishermen and lumberjacks don't deserve the silence they've met in our schools. In class we find a few words to break this silence, and the Bean Bake lets us take this new knowledge out to the school as a whole. And for a little while, the food and the fiddle music remind us all of another time and another place … but something still our own.

Murals and Models

But I must take you back to my Nine G's.

Since we work on a semester system at Stephen Leacock, teachers have to start over with a fresh batch of students in early February, often teaching the same courses we taught from September to January. In the past, when my second semester G–level class asked why they had no special event like the Bean Bake, I had to tell them flatly that once a year was plenty for me, thanks.

But last spring, partly by accident, I finally stumbled on another event which took up the slack for these students. It had occurred to me the previous year that the lives of lumberjacks and sailors suggested lots of ideas for building models — making ships, shanties, rafts, log chutes, houses of rich owners and poor workers. Among the educational establishment, model building — the whole schtick of papier mâché and murals, bits of wood and bits of paper — has been considered an elementary school activity, suitable for young children but not for your sophisticated high school type. And among high school teachers themselves model building appears a bit demeaning, what with our specialized university degrees and all. Also, it's so messy. My department head, nevertheless gave me permission to use our daily class for the entire month of May for this project and I plunged in.

Since I have no special talent in this line, I decided to have the large mural done by two senior art students. (All the rest of the project was done by Grade Nine). The mural contained three panels of 8' x 4' plywood: the left-hand one was Cache Lake, the scene of the lumber camp, the centre one was Ottawa, and the third, Quebec City. These three scenes we chose because the logs flowed through the Madawaska from Cache Lake into the Ottawa River and in turn into the St. Lawrence and down to Quebec City.

The mural sat on three tables, each the same length as a plywood slab. These tables then became the surface on which to put a papier mâché continuation of the murals. All models made eventually sat in place on the paper maché base in front of an appropriate picture — a model shanty, sleighs and a log chute in front of Cache Lake; houses big and small in Ottawa; and three model ships anchored in front of Quebec. Each model was made by a group of two to four students. Since the class contained thirty people, everyone couldn't work on a model. So some students collected pictures and made slides of lumberjacking and sailing, some made the papier mâché, and one group even wired up the whole set-up so that all shanties, houses and ships lit up in the dark.

After about ten days' work, I realized that students were liking this activity and that there was a fine sense of calm starting to develop. I then got the idea that this would be an excellent project to invite their parents to see.

Meeting The Parents

We sent home an invitation to an inside sit-down party with bean supper (cooked inside this time!), a bit of music by students and myself (with the principal on hand to sing "My Daddy Was a Logger"), the presentation of the murals and model project (which we carried with great hazard and great commotion to the staff lounge the night before the party), and finally the showing of the Alan Ladd movie — *Two Years Before The Mast*. (This film was part of my actual curriculum since it gives an excellent picture of 19th century conditions for seamen and also a good depiction of the sailors fighting back to improve their conditions. The students, of course, also know this is Cheryl Ladd's father playing the hero!)

Would parents show up? Very few parents of G level students come to the regular parents' nights. "Would you come if you had bad memories of school and you were going to be told your kid had 'to apply herself, etc?" was the way one friend put it to me.

With each invitation we sent out new copies of *Working* by Studs Terkel and of our two historical novels along with a letter. The letter read: "Some parents say they don't know what their kids are studying. Have a look at these. Your kids are taking them in a history class and we'd love to get your reactions." With two weeks to go, we had only received back five confirmation forms from parents.

I then made the decision that tipped the balance. I decided to visit each of the thirty homes personally. I did it over two evenings, usually staying only a couple of minutes at each home. One parent and I had a great debate about the language in the Terkel book. Another was sitting at the back door when I was let in by her daughter. "I just wanted to invite you to a free party and movie when you can see Karen's work," I said. "I didn't read the books!" the mother shot back from her perch. She was obviously thinking: "Not only are they giving students homework; now they're giving it to parents." "That doesn't matter," I said. She showed up bringing her younger child as well.

On June 7th at 6:30 pm, 78 people arrived, counting the class of thirty, parents and brothers and sisters. The event went very well indeed and was sealed as a success for me by the way the students presented the project to their parents and colleagues. Three days before the Big Night I decided to ask each student group to appoint one person to explain to the assembled people what they had done and why. We got a microphone hooked up on a long cord so people could move around to the different models, maps, cartoons and drawings.

I swear to you that the people who described the life of shantymen and sailors, as shown in the slides they had made, were so good, so natural, that most teachers could have learned from them. I had taken the risk of asking the students to talk, knowing that they might get stage fright or might say things that were dull and maybe embarrassing. I took the risk because I didn't want that kind of parents' night where all you see are pretty pieces of work with slides clicking away by themselves. That kind of show is a lot like most books which purport to teach about work processes. They talk about coal mining, steel–making or clothes–making as if no people are involved. "First the coal is taken" etc. By whom? To whom? With what human energy? At what cost to human health and emotion and life?

I wanted real students to be seen and heard that night, and they were. These are students who are often called *dumb*, a word which in English means both "stupid" and "can't speak."

If I may be allowed a Biblical comment: on this grade nine parents' night, it seemed to me, that "the dumb" were speak-ing. They had something to say about what they had learned, and they were saying it loudly and clearly to their parents and their peers.

IV

Propaganda and point of view: Can a teacher speak her mind?

When I present units like the one found in the previous two chapters, a question is often lurking in people's minds which now deserves an answer: Bob, aren't you merely replacing right wing or liberal propaganda with left wing propaganda?

My main answer to this question goes like this: We are not dealing here with "my bias" versus the objectivity of school texts and official courses. I have made this point at length in Part I. No presentation of curriculum in any subject, even science and mathematics, exists without a point of view. The material does not make sense without this point of view. In English and history the standpoints and messages are strong even if hidden.

In English, for example, while there is an official stress on techniques and forms (thus giving it that peculiar bloodless and numbing quality for many students and teachers), there is nonetheless a fairly clear point of view, lifestyle and ideology that comes through when you look at the sum total of the officially approved books. Let me offer a small illustration. In most English programs anti–utopias are favoured over utopias: *Animal Farm, Brave New World, 1984, Lord of the Flies, The Chrysalids, Fahrenheit 451*. All these are valid school books and pass the "good literature" test, but put them all together and we are passing on a canon of cynical, sad, and by now even a bit smug Western musings from post World War II — very time–bound, very place–bound. The smugness of Western thought about utopian ideas is bound to increase with the current breakup of the Russian empire. Students are taught, of course, that no such Western sermon is being preached; they are really just learning the characteristics of a novel or how to write an essay comparing two novels! As I indicated earlier, this kind of mind–twist is at the core of our official English curriculum. And a very similar version of it is at the core of our official history curriculum.

History courses — what few are left — still reflect a pro-Western civilization, free-enterprise capitalist framework. They also increasingly reflect the skills-training framework, i.e. that history is merely the point of view of this or that historian and must be learned as an investigative craft. Given who runs our society these frameworks could not be otherwise.

What I mind being told is that this official line is objective truth while mine is propaganda. I also object, given my stress on open debate and reason, to being lumped with bigots. My point of view is the only one which makes sense of the information for me.

If I properly represent the official point of view (and hopefully I may be allowed to defog it since it is often so fogged), if I also encourage the widest possible debate, if I respect all student points of view, and if I do not favour people who agree with me with better marks, then I believe I should have the liberty to throw my own point of view into this mix as well. In a context like this I do not call my view propaganda any more than I call the official view propaganda.

I believe the authorities should be able to tolerate my view (within the context laid out above) the same way as many American schools tolerated Carl Becker's point of view when they used his great high school textbook in the 1950s. Note the vitality of a clear, unblurred framework contained in these chapter headings from Becker's Modern History:

Chapter 6: *The French People in the Eighteenth Century: How the Few Lived Well Without Working, and How the Many Worked Without Living Well.*

Chapter 10: *How the Great Powers Tried to Safeguard Europe against Revolutions, and How the People Kept on Making Revolutions in Spite of Them 1815–1905.*

Chapter 19: *How the Industrial Revolution Led to a Scramble for "Backward Countries" 1875–1905.*

Chapter 20: *Alliances and Armaments: How the Great Powers Prepared for War in Time of Peace, and How the War Came because the Great Powers were so Well Prepared for it.*

In fact it is often a disservice to students, especially to those who see less value in studying, to hide the framework within which a multiplicity of information makes sense to a particular person. The assumption that such clarity and upfrontness always lead to intolerant propaganda or to higher marks if you agree with the teacher is based on a misunderstanding of how knowledge is passed on. Knowledge does not pass on well if the teacher's or the textbook's point of view are buried under a foggy PR which pretends that objectivity itself is now talking. Students do not grasp specifics which have no credible framework.

I should also stress that to me history investigation is a search for "The Truth." I see no problem in working with this premise while still encouraging debate and a clash of ideas. If instead we discuss frameworks only as equal choices or biases, the consequences in real life of holding different philosophies, as I have already said, is turned into a game of Trivial Pursuit. Theories become pieces of trivia equal to useless facts. Any connection between such theories and building or even preserving a certain world flies out the window.

Making Ideas Come Alive

In opposition to this approach, I want to argue that it is possible to debate theories and evidence openly, to be exposed to official theories and unofficial theories — including the teacher's own theories — and still find students surviving with their own minds and souls intact. This approach also assumes that it is good for education to have teachers who are allowed to be excited and serious about their beliefs. This is not a matter of wanting teachers who jump up and down, who whoop and yell. It's rather that when a teacher's passions hang out (the non-sexual ones, that is), this communicates something very important to students — especially those turned off school: Ideas can excite people.

And they are exciting because they touch what students already have in their minds.

Students already carry around a whole set of theoretical

assumptions and frameworks about race, class, history, capitalism, communism, etc. however dimly articulated or inaccurate these may be. I remember discussing the movie *El Norte* with a class a few years ago. The plot of the movie is as follows: Two Guatemalan Indian young people, whose father has been involved then killed in the revolutionary resistance, flee through Mexico to THE NORTH (el Norte), to the dream world of the United States where everyone is supposed to have a car and a TV and be happy. Of course the United States does not come through as promised. Quite by accident I found out one day that virtually everyone in the class assumed that the brother and sister's father had been fighting against a communist Guatemalan regime. The media and the schools had done their job well since a few short scenes involving soldiers, raids and foreigners spelled communism to them. Ideas like this sit in a student's mind in the form of stories (e.g. how communists take over countries and how they run them). Often it takes only a few code words like "terror" or code scenes like "army going in to citizens' homes" to suggest the whole story to a student. Most adult historical and current affairs judgements also work this way. To correct or expand the ideas that sit in a student's mind, the main responsibility for a teacher is to present more true stories from reality, not (if I can make this point again) by first giving techniques in detecting bias.

Another common technique of history teachers is open to the same problem.

Huge charts are widely used to teach the difference between Facism, Communism and Liberal Capitalism. Apart from their overemphasis on political structures instead of economic systems, these charts also discourage students from learning true stories about who did what, to whom, when and why, how it turned out.

Both the big charts and the lessons on detecting bias become a quick way to spot nasty communism and nasty facism. Facism, however, will disappear from most students' minds since it has few specific stories now to keep alive its separate reality. Many students and much of the public think Hitler was a communist.

Most students don't know enough history (stories) to use these bias-detecting techniques properly. Pressing these techniques more and more on students, therefore, undercuts the true meaning of historical study which is to learn the true stories. (Not one truth to be imposed, but a search for the truth of what really happened.) When this function of truth-telling is undercut, what history becomes is more and more skills applied to less and less substance. Of course, history courses must keep a critical eye on their stories, but let this enhance the main function, not crowd it out.

The One and the Many

The pre-Socratic philosophers of ancient Greece used to say that our experience of the world was a mixture of encountering the One and the Many, large basic truths and the concrete details of life; theories, principles, anchors on the one side and the multifarious texture of life on the other.

This is not the so-called fact/value distinction of our history skills people. The fact/value distinction was invented by modern science and capitalism to get religion, philosophy, and the poor off its back. Rulers and scientists could co-operate better when morality became primarily a matter of individual feeling, not one of social responsibility. They argued that facts were firm and impersonal while values were floating and personal and couldn't be depended upon for making important decisions.

The real world, in my understanding, doesn't have this kind of separation, but rather has always has a deep interconnection of "facts" and "points of view": How we are and how we ought to be (and how the world is and ought to be) are dependent on each other, and because they are, they intertwine and cannot be separated by saying that one is firm and the other is floating. A history teacher's principles are not anything so floating as biases. They are rooted in getting hold of the truth. Taking in the multifarious, detailed texture of life that we must share with our students is light years away from learning hard and boring facts, and offers us much more real knowledge. The Mickey Spilanes of this world are never going to find out what really happened.

Canadian philosopher, George Grant, recalling Nietzsche, used to tell us at university that one could understand the change from his grandfather's time to the present by noticing that his grandfather's generation started the day off at breakfast by looking up to God in prayer. His own generation started the day with the morning newspaper looking across horizontally at the hurly burly of present events. I have a similar choice in driving half an hour every day from downtown to my suburban teaching job. At times I listen to the CBC's *Metro Morning* program, to interviews and news. At other times I prefer to put on my own music tapes for a more timeless experience.

Teachers need to help their students do both. Teachers need techniques that will regularly bring out both these aspects of experience: the One and the Many, the anchors of life and the passing waves. So much of teaching, especially for lower stream students, gets stuck between these two poles having neither the firmness and reassurance of discovering a real truth nor the light-touch pleasure of sampling life's multifarious detail. What kids mostly get is the numbing and dumbing experience of the grey middle ground.

Waves and Anchors

The Waves, the multifarious detail:

My regular focus for this side of things is a daily set of thirty-five newspapers (*Toronto Star*, half-price, paid out of our department budget). Every period begins with five to ten minutes of reading of each student's own choice of articles. I can then assign certain readings, writings and discussions on certain days. The old current events period played a similar purpose for some teachers. Both these techniques focus on the present. The detailed texture of the past or of life in other countries is harder to pass on and like many teachers I rely mostly on movies, even bad ones, to do this.

The Anchors, the principles, the theories:

Finding regular ways of developing the deeper insights is very difficult in a modern history program since the official system is so frightened by ideas, points of view, passing on beliefs, etc. I suggest only one technique here. If I decide a movie or a novel or some other work contains some gold that can profitably be mined — in other words it's worth spending some real time on it — I often extract a large number of quotations from it and do what some would recognize as a modern variation of the old "exegesis of a text." There are dangers here, of course. The text can be destroyed by picking and hacking away at it. Usually I have found it is wise to let students experience such works fresh the first time. The exegesis is usually meant as deeper reflection on what has taken place more naturally first time round.

I'd also recommend that when you find a work that invites deeper attention, use the whole work: whole books, whole speeches, whole movies. Not chopped up little snippets. All students, not just academic level ones, need solid curriculum. A diet of chopped up extracts produces chopped up minds. Don't sell your students short by giving in to this publishers' scrapbook game. Curriculum snippets, by the way, are sold as part of the process of making education entertaining. But underneath this is the view that substantial curriculum is not so important if it is mainly a skill you are teaching. Who needs to know the story of the Russian Revolution if you can learn from a chart "the nature of communism"?

The approach I am recommending here is a bit like the approach of believers to sacred texts like *The Bible*, *Das Kapital* or the works of Freud. Most people are aware that there have been abusive, chapter-and-verse approaches to sacred texts. Yet these abuses do not mean that no texts can be treated as sacred. I also find sacred works in unlikely places as you have already seen in my description of how I taught the film *Maria*. And I have found such texts in pieces of epic Hollywood schlock like *Dr. Zhivago*, or in old white-knight war movies like *Paths of Glory*, which starred Kirk Douglas.

It is not by accident that I used a metaphor like "sacred text" about history books or films. From my college days in the 1950s I have always thought of philosophy and history as my "pulse subjects," as the places where the big questions of life could be studied and debated. Such also was the philosophy behind the official high school history program when I started teaching in Ontario in the early 1960s.

That conception of history as a "pulse subject" is all but gone now as the number taking history steadily decline, as the skills emphasis crowds out content, and as the notion of offering a large number of students a comprehensive look at our "origins in Western civilization" is largely abandoned.

In the light of these changes, this debate over whether a teacher with strong views is a propagandist is a bit unreal. Over the last thirty years people like myself found it invigorating to debate what was missing in the traditional "Western civilization" curriculum. And plenty *was* missing. But then, right before our eyes, we found we were debating a curriculum, which was itself vanishing. It was as if we thought we were debating changing the rules of hockey only to find we were playing Pac Man.

This does not mean that all teachers and students have ceased to debate the big questions. The debates are happening in new places: in Canadian family courses in Family Studies, in various sociology and world religions courses in History departments, in Law classes, in classes on the environment in Biology and Geography, in world issues classes in Geography, in classes on the Canadian novel and women's literature in English. This rise in enrollment in relatively new courses suggests some out-of-control computer mouse hopping around searching on behalf of grassroots teachers and students for places where serious contemporary issues can be discussed with passion and intelligence.

I am encouraged by this development, though I miss the historical dimension in these courses. Of course, the propaganda issue is still very much alive in these new places. Teachers eager to expose students to debate on modern issues like abortion, ecology, feminism, new family patterns and the fight against racism are again being called propagandists.

Conclusion

As you can see, I personally reserve the word propaganda for ideas that are rammed down my throat or are slipped by me in a commercial that seems to be about something else. The kind of buried pitch for free enterprise capitalism which the total school program gives our students qualifies far more as propaganda than my openly debated teaching. If I have the right to call this official slant what it is, I have no trouble fulfilling my obligation to teach the official view. And once that is defogged I no longer call it propaganda. It is a point of view, an ideology. Finally, to repeat my earlier position, if I am fair to my students and if I also debate and tolerate all ideas, I should also be permitted to express my own views, which make sense of the course material for me.

Subscribe & Save
YES! Start my subscription to OUR SCHOOLS/OUR SELVES Magazine today

INDIVIDUAL
- ❏ $38 Regular
- ❏ $32 Student
- ❏ $50 Cdn Outside Canada

ORGANIZATION
- ❏ $50 In Canada
- ❏ $60 Cdn Outside Canada

SUSTAINING
- ❏ $100 ❏ $200 Other $_____

TOLL FREE ORDER NUMBER 1-800-565-1975

Name _____

Address _____

City _____ Province_____ Code _____

Occupation _____

❏ Cheque enclosed   ❏ VISA/Mastercard

Card No. _____ Expiry date _____

Signature _____

Pass to a friend

Please enter my subscription for 6 issues of OUR SCHOOLS/OUR SELVES starting with issue number _____

Please check one:

INDIVIDUAL
- ❏ $38 Regular
- ❏ $32 Student
- ❏ $50 Cdn Outside Canada

ORGANIZATION
- ❏ $50 In Canada
- ❏ $60 Cdn Outside Canada

SUSTAINING
- ❏ $100 ❏ $200 Other $_____

TOLL FREE ORDER NUMBER 1-800-565-1975

Name _____

Address _____

City _____ Province_____ Code _____

Occupation _____

❏ Cheque enclosed   ❏ VISA/Mastercard

Card No. _____ Expiry date _____

Signature _____

MAIL ⟹ POSTE

Canada Post Corporation / Société canadienne des postes

Postage paid	Port payé
if mailed in Canada	si posté au Canada
Business Reply	**Réponse d'affaires**

0110253299   **01**

0110253299-B3H1G4-BR01

OUR SCHOOLS/OUR SELVES

5502 ATLANTIC STREET
HALIFAX NS   B3H 9Z9

MAIL ⟹ POSTE

Canada Post Corporation / Société canadienne des postes

Postage paid	Port payé
if mailed in Canada	si posté au Canada
Business Reply	**Réponse d'affaires**

0110253299   **01**

0110253299-B3H1G4-BR01

OUR SCHOOLS/OUR SELVES

5502 ATLANTIC STREET
HALIFAX NS   B3H 9Z9

Chapter Seven

THE GULF BETWEEN
A School and a War

Chris Searle

I want to concentrate upon the impact of the Gulf War of 1991 on the lives of our students, and on our school itself as a living institution — but in doing this, I am all the time conscious of a certain irony in using the word "gulf."

For, in the curriculum terms and within the scope of what we teach and learn, throughout this war there was another "gulf" — if not an abyss. The war not only presented to us issues about internal school relationships, the pressure upon unity and the school's attitude to the communities it serves. Over and above these crucial aspects was the war's function as a formulator and conductor of knowledge itself, and the gulf over which it stood between two versions of knowledge, two registers of assumed fact, that were in currency all around and through the school, its neighbourhood and communities.

On the other hand, there was a state–licenced, state–approved stratum of knowledge. This was one–track in its perspective, national–chauvinist in its orientation, anti–Arab, anti–internationalist, and largely prevalent in the public consciousness outside the school. It was formed through televison, tabloid newspapers, the positions (and consensus) of govern-

ment and mainline "opposition" — and squared with the ideology set down in the "National Curriculum" currently being
imposed on all British schools. On the other hand, there was a
view that was organic and critical, arising from the real lives of
the students at the school — in particular Arab students, for
many of whom internationalism was a necessary aspect of
their lives, having either been brought up in the Middle East,
in countries like Yemen, Syria or Jordan, or having been for
long family sojourns there. This view was grounded in a community's real knowledge of life and its struggles, in a living
understanding of the importance of the oil economy and the
effects of imperialism.

There is no doubt that in many British schools the Gulf War
had a damaging and divisive impact. Schools with all-white
student populations often found themselves, almost automati-
cally, because of force of culture, nationalism and the imperial
legacy, taking active sides with British and U.S. political and
military objectives and strategies. These schools became the
domestic cheerleaders for the allied war efforts, giving jingoistic support to "our boys," the new crusaders of the Gulf, with
mass letter-writing to the troops, parcel sending, fund-raising
and other such publicity exercises.

For other schools, composed of black and white British
cohorts, a potentially more volatile situation emerged, with
Pakistani and Bangladeshi students often supporting Saddam
Hussein (whom many even saw as an authentic Islamic hero)
while the white students retained an uncritical loyalty to the
British military intervention. Sometimes inter-communal bit-
terness and violence broke out, both in and out of school.

While some of these schools futilely tried to press down
the lid on their students' responses — others took what they
saw as a neutral and objective line, while still defending the
allied position. The largest and most progressive British
teachers union, the National Union of Teachers, took a cau-
tious approach in its "advice" leaflet, "Gulf War: the impact
on schools." This argued that "it may be helpful to hold discussions about conflict resolutions whilst in no way seeking

to influence beliefs of individuals about the rightness or justice of the war. This would have been in keeping with the
Union's long held belief in education for peace."

A few schools set out to create a spirit of genuine openness and discourse, while unashamedly standing up for
peace and for a solution to be found by the Arab people
themselves. The account that follows sets down the processes
of response to the war in one such comprehensive school in
Sheffield.

I write as the school's headteacher, but also as an active
English teacher. The students all live in the neighbourhood of
the school, a working-class district close to the industrial end
of the city, where its once-great steel industry was located.
With just under half the students from local white families,
the others come from Pakistan, Yemen, Somali and Caribbean
communities. One of the school's teachers is an exiled Iraqi.

During the days before the war, and as the two huge armies
face each other across the desert with the UN deadline
approaching hour by hour, there is fear and uncertainty
among the students. Many of them can sense the scale and
conflict of the events as they unfold. Many of them write
down their reflections and read them out to each other in
their English class. Some of these are marked not only by
their honesty, but by a sense of being overpowered by huge,
uncontrollable issues which they cannot fully understand.
One 12-year-old boy, Lee, writes:

> I do not think that Britain and the UN should go to war
> against Iraq because it would mean a lot of peole would
> die, including people who are not soldiers. Iraq says that
> they are taking back land which already belongs to them
> and which the British took away from them...
>
> Some people say that America only want to protect
> Kuwait because of the oil in the area, which is bought by
> other western countries.

The environmental impact of a war in the Gulf would last for many, many years, causing further destruction of the ozone layer which would have a disasterous effect on everyone all over the world.

There are many issues involved when discussing the Gulf crisis and some of them I don't understand. This makes the question "Should Britain go to war with Iraq?" difficult to answer. But I would like to see a peaceful solution to the matter.

Jackleen, a 15–year–old Yemeni girl who has only been in Britain for five months, is also tentative, but from a completely different perspective and exploring the contradictions she sees all around her:

I don't know what I can say about this problem. Really it is a big problem because we do not know what will happen.

I really don't like the war and every one I know doesn't like the war. Why the war, why? I get in my head more questions about this problem, I know I don't agree with anyone … but this doesn't mean I don't like the leader.

Why when Israel went to Palestine did no one do anything, it's just all countries said, "It's not my problem, it is a Palestine problem." Why does no country care about the Palestine problem? And the same things in Afganistan, why and why and why?? In this letter I want to ask America, England and all countries why, in an Arab area, have these countries come to help Kuwait?

I know some peole from America and England don't like the war and don't want to go to Kuwait to fight because it is not their country … but the heads of state want to help Kuwait, not only because they love Kuwait, not all this, it's because they want oil. I am sorry if I said this … but this is all in my head.

I don't like the war so please leave the Arab countries to solve this problem among themselves. I really want to see all Arab countries working together, not like as they do now.

And contradictions there are, rising around our students. In the recently united Yemen, many of their families are suffering the direct consequences of their government's neutrality and its refusal to support US/British/Saudi military alliance against Iraq. The Saudi government has expelled nearly a million Yemeni migrant workers, and their remittances are no longer there to boost the national economy and provide a financial base for thousands of dependent Yemeni families. On the other side of the frontier, one of our fourth-year students, Abdullah, on an extended visit to his family in Jeddah, has been conscripted into the Saudi army. Abdullah is a tall, burly youth who looks much older than his fifteen years, and his uncle came to the school, seeking help to get him back to Britain. We wrote to the Saudi authorities asking them to secure his release from military service and allow him to continue his education with us. He came back just before the war began, beaming all over his face as he walked back into school. Now he laughs and fools around with his Yemeni classmates, who are obviously glad to see him. "In Saudi when we dig in the sand, we find oil," he jokes, "Not like you Yemenis. When you dig, all you find is dirty water!" The Yemenis, taking all this in good humour, seem to have a final laugh. "He is a Yemeni like us, we know his family. His father lives in Saudi so he thinks he's Saudi too."

For some of the other students there is also closeness to the war. A Pakistani girl, Majida, writes: "I don't want the war to go on because my friend's dad has been to the war and this time he will have to go again. If he doesn't, he will be under arrest." Brian, in his second-year class, also seems affected by the call-up of British military reservists, in the heart of his family. He sets down:

> Another reason why I don't want the war to start is because my Dad and my brothers will have to go back in the army, and they might get hurt and maybe get killed.

You would think that such opposing loyalties would polarize these young people. Everything around them is persuading them to take sides simplistically and emotionally: religion,

national chauvinism, family connections, plus the media bombardment in the tabloid press, particularly the Murdoch press
and the *Sun*. Morning after morning come the banner headlines pouring hatred and scorn on the Iraqi people. "We'll
bomb them till they drop" screams the *Sun* on 31 January. In
the local daily, the *Sheffield Star*, there are photograph of school-
girls up against the Union Jack, raising money to send gifts to
British troops in the Gulf, and a story about another girl writing to the soldiers who have "gone to the Gulf for the Queen
and our country."[1] Whose country? The *Guardian* publishes an
article about an 11-year-old schoolgirl at Falla Park Primary
School near Gateshead. She wrote a poem about Saddam Hussein that was published in the local newspaper, the *Gateshead
Post*, after a local group of the Territorial Army sent it in to
them. It goes like this:

> Saddam Hussein is the man we hate
> We'll get him just you wait!
> He's trying to take over, get him out,
> "He doesn't belong there,' we'll all shout.
> We'll take his head and mash it up,
> Until it fits an egg cup
> Take off his arms, take off his legs
> Bend them back until he begs.
> Take his head, take his heart
> Rip the stupid man apart
> Poke out his eyes, chew off his nose
> Kick him in the head, pull off his toes.[2]

Reading these published words, this sadism from one so
young, I suddenly understand again something so horrific,
residual, still there throbbing in the British and European
mind towards the Arab peoples, welling out of their imperial
past. I am reminded of the "Crusades," the siege of Ma'arra in
1098, and how European historians themselves wrote how
"in Ma'arra our troops boiled pagan adults in cooking pots;
they impaled children on spits and devoured them grilled."[3]
Or, closer to our own time in Yemen in 1967, of the Argyll
soldiers and their inter-platoon rivalry in Aden, and how

Robertson Jam golliwog stickers were awarded to any officer whose soldiers succeeded in killing an Arab. One officer had admitted:

> At one stage my platoon had notched up 13 kills and another platoon were one kill behind. The corporal even told the private he was to use his bayonet, for it was to be that kind of killing.
>
> They went into an alley and killed a young Arab who was out after curfew.[4]

Yet in the midst of this historical and present hatred, our young people could keep their minds level, remember their schoolmates and friendships and still resist division. One 14–year–old Pakistani girl, Shazia, wrote:

> Soldiers are fighting for oil. People are dying because of this war. Innocent lives are involved in this crisis. people in Iraq and Saudi Arabia are all scared because of this war, President Bush and Saddam Hussein do not think about people, soldiers and their families, They just want oil. When people ask me, "which side are you on?," I say I did not want this war to happen in the first place. But it has. But I am on no one's side. I want it to end. I do not want it to become a world war just because of oil.

During the first week of the war, while British, American and Saudi aircraft are bombing Iraq and the sorties go into their thousands, we hold year assemblies on the subject of the war. The objective is to formalize the dialogue going on between the students at the playground and classroom level, to hold their views together, and create more mutual under–standing within the framework of peace. Of course there are differences which come across strongly in these assemblies. Corin, a 14–year–old white boy, makes these points out loud:

> Even though war is a horrible occurance, sometimes it can't be helped. People being killed isn't a pleasant thing, but when someone just walks into a country and tries to

take it over, something has to be done about it. Different people have different views, like some say England and America should mind their own business. I think this is true, but Kuwait asked the help of England and America, so I think they should stay where they are.

Other views are that England are only in Kuwait because it's full with oil. This may be true, but why is Saddam Hussein in there? It can't be just that Kuwait was part of Iraq, because what's the point in fighting for a bit of land unless you get something out of it at the end?

Nadia, his Yemeni classmate, gives her reply with all her year listening:

I don't think Britain should go to war with Iraq because it would be very dangerous and it would affect the whole world. It was very dangerous for the Americans and British to get involved in the Gulf crisis! The Arabs should talk about it and sort everything out between themselves.

Very innocent people will get killed around the world, especially in the Arab countries. The Americans and British are only in Saudi Arabia because they know that Fahad would give them something e.g., oil, land.

Why didn't the Americans and the British go to help Palestine? In my opinion, I think the Americans and British didn't help Palestine because it is a poor country.

The Americans and British would not like the Arabs to interfere with them!

The question of Palestine was at the centre of the students' argument. This year group had recently been studying the *intifada* and the lives of Palestinians on the West Bank, and several of the students have written letters to young Palestinians in a school in Ramallah, with the intention of setting up a permanent link between our two schools. "Why don't [the British and Americans] stop Israelis taking over Palestine?" protests one Pakistani boy in his essay on the war, while another Yemeni boy answers the question: "The Palestinians are not rich and they have no oil." In a similar vein, James, a classmate of Corin and Nadia, adds: "But why should we have to fight? Why should we be greedy, and have all the oil. The consequences will be dreadful." And, with strong insights on the same question and her mind on the Al–Sabah ruling dynasty of Kuwait, 13–year–old Haifa from Yemen writes:

> No, I think that Britain should not go to war against Iraq because it is an Arab people's matter and the matter should be solved between Arab countries…. The British people should take care of their own people not send them to battlefields as mercenaries, fighting to bring back one family rule to a country because that family is under the influence of the British government.

At a second–year assembly, spontaneous applause by almost all those present breaks out when Nicola, a 13–year–old white girl, reads her thoughts to all her year mates. Muslim and Christian backgrounds, national origins, race and culture all seem in agreement and to be at one when she reaches her final suggestion.

> No!
> Just simply no!
> Britain should not go to war against Iraq. It's all Mr Bush's fault. If they hadn't roped Mr Major into sending forces, it would be all right.
> On TV last week, two wards at a hospital had to be closed down because two paramedics had to go on stand-by in the Gulf. Just think about all those peole missing medical treatment.
> Saddam Hussein and Mr Bush should talk about what they're going to do about this war and leave everybody else out of it. Bring everyone home from the Gulf and re-unite them with their families! And if Mr Bush and Saddam Hussein can't make up their minds, we should let them fight it out among themselves.

As the aerial bombardment of Iraq continues during the first three weeks of the war, the students continue to discuss and write about its meanings and implications. For teachers, these raids have a special resonance. Our Arabic teacher, a much-liked colleague, is an Iraqi. His parents live in the neighbour-hood of the bunker in Bagdad that is destroyed with a terrible loss of life. The war comes to the staff room too. Daily news bulletins are shown in the lunch hours in the Resource Area of the school, where national and local newspapers, from the Conservative *Daily Telegraph* to the Communist *Morning Star*, are also on display. Yemeni students also bring in Arab newspapers, and often lunch hour sessions are full with watchers, readers and talkers, all concerned with the latest situation in the Gulf. We find some enthusiastic graffiti about Saddam on the wall in the languages room, and there are a couple of pro-Saddam slo-gans in the boys' main toilets. But while there is frequent dis-course and open discussion about the war, there are no fights or violent arguments, and no evidence of jingoism, warlike talk and antipathy towards either Islamic or British students.

The war, ironically, has become a stimulus for those stu-dents struggling to learn English as a second language. This is particularly true for the Arab language students, for they feel a deep urgency and real motivation to express their views to their English peers across the school. Safa has been in Britain only five months before the start of the war. Yet the passion and poetry of her beginner's English produces its own form of eloquence.

> No one can go to an Arab country to protect it unless they want something from this country. But it's always Sad-dam's fault because he can't take Kuwait from its people and get them out of their country. And I think they have to look for a good idea for them all. I think that the good idea is that Saddam has to get out of Kuwait. I think this is the best idea for them all because we don't want war and we don't need it, because war is the worst thing in the world. Because it burns everything, it will make the world very bad and thousands and thousands of people will be killed, and the animals and everything. It will kill the smile on the lips and make everything look bad.

For Samich, another newly-arrived Yemeni, there are so

many questions about his Arab people and those who are interfering with their lives. It is the forming of such questions and the finding of anwers to them that will bring him the language he is learning so quickly — as well as the truth for which he craves.

As I hear in ITN news that President Saddam Hussein has attacked Kuwait because he thinks that Kuwait is his country. I have seen, too, many people on television shouting "we do not want war," and I have also heared children saying "why do we the children, always have to bear the costs?" Why don't Mr Bush and Mr Major, the prime minister of the United Kingdom, why don't they bear the costs why, why why?....

And I also hear an old man saying why don't Mr Saddam Hussein and Mr Bush and Mr Major the prime minister of the United Kingdom solve this out with peace and without any war? Why does Mr Bush want to help Kuwait for the oil, and this oil will destroy our and their armies and their nation and our friends, and they have got nothing to do with these problems? Why don't they solve the problems in the Middle East, since 1967? I will answer this question, because in the Middle East, which includes Palestine, the Palestinians are not rich and they have no oil.

I am saying this especially to Mr Bush and Mr Major to do nothing about themselves. Nothing will happen to them because they are in England and the USA. Think about the Arab countries and about what will happen in Yemen or in Iraq or in Kuwait or in Saudi Arabia. I like to say these words, and I am saying this especially to Mr Bush and Mr Major, who do not think about them since nothing will happen to them.... Think about what will happen in Yemen or in Iraq or in Kuwait or in Saudi Arabia. I like to say these words....

And I am saying to Mr Saddam Hussein, please do think about what will happen to him and his army.

If there will be a very long war I am ready to give my life and my blood to protect my Arab countries and my Arab families. I am ready to give my life and my body to save the truth.

God will be with the truth.

✦ ✦ ✦

As students like Samieh work out their thoughts, and go to the computers to project them on screens and bring them out, the questions they raise are about subjection, imperialism, national liberation and economic independence. In their own words, they are dealing with complex issues, and their English-born peers are listening to them and learning from them. The same questions are being put in the form of poems, and answers, too, emerge that are being shared by everyone. Mohammed Kassim asks:

Why is the world at war?
Why do the rich hate the poor?
Why can't the whiteman love the blackman?
Why can't they be friends, what don't they like?

But there were powers behind these questions.

But no
They want to rule what is not theirs
They make excuses and support millionaires.
If only they could stop and think of their demands
Maybe war would stop and they could shake hands.
Peace could stop killing in the sand.
Peace could remove the gun from the hand.
Solidarity is the way we should live today
And together we should stand up for our say.

There could hardly be poetic thoughts so different from those of the girl in Gateshead. We manage to persuade a Sheffield local paper to publish Mohammed Kassim's poem too. The truth is that the presence of such a highly-motivated and clear-thinking cohort of students in our school as those from the Yemeni community has a genuine impact on the thinking of many other students. The Yemeni community has its own school; it organizes its classes three evenings a week in our school buildings, regularly attracting over a hundred students to each session. It is voluntary, being completely organized by and through the community's contacts and infrastructures. It teaches Arabic, Yemeni, history and culture, Islamic studies, and "manners" — or how to treat other people. All this has a dynamic effect on the mainstream daily classes in our school.

Then, in the middle of the war period, some stone-throwing racist whites attack the Yemeni Community Association minibus as it brings a group of children to the evening classes. The community has already felt the lash of other racist acts — abusive telephone calls, insults in the street and graffiti scrawled over their community centre — but the attack on the minibus is particularly dangerous, it could have caused serious injury, or worse, to the children. When the community asks whether the classes can be switched to weekend daylight hours to make attacks less likely, the school immediately agrees, and also asks whether some Yemeni speakers could conduct an in-service for our entire teaching staff on the history of the community in Sheffield, its links to the homeland and its responses to the Gulf.

This is a very productive session, and it is pivotal in helping to raise the understanding of all our teachers. The film, *Thank you, that's all I know,*[5] by Christine Bellamy, which describes the history and struggles of Sheffield's Yemenis, is shown. It includes some grim footage of British colonial brutality in Aden, and the rounding up and mistreatment of Yemenis on the streets of the city — which is a revelation to some of the teachers. There is also an explanation of the literacy campaign being run from within the Yemeni community, delivered by one of its young women teaching assistants. Mohammed Kassim, himself a fifth-year student at our school, addresses his teachers and describes the curriculum and organization of the community language school. What also comes out of the session is the realization that one of our black colleagues, Owen (a Barbadian) had served as ground crew in the Royal Air Force for two years in Aden, in the early 1960s. In an interview, recorded later, with two Yemeni fifth-years, he tells them of his experiences as a part of the British occupying force during the years of the Aden insurrection. He recalls how the

British officers prevented the black servicemen from mixing with the Aden population in case they showed sympathy for them, of the friendliness found during the times they did mix, and of the racist barriers in the British armed forces that stopped him, or any other black recruit he knows, from achieving promotion.

"Think of the people that are going to be killed. Don't just think about yourself, think about other people in the world, they may be in the war while we are in England." This message, written at the beginning of the conflict by Azra, a second-year Pakistani girl, becomes even more truth-laden by its end. International Women's Day falls during the week following the cease-fire, and among the visitors and speakers who come to the school to commemorate it is Jenny Hales, an elderly peace campaigner who lives in the neighbourhood of the school. Speaking on the theme of "Women and Peace," she tells how she had been a member of the international peace mission that camped on the Kuwaiti/Saudi border, between the opposing armies, at the onset of the long stand-to before the war. She speaks of the Iraqi soldiers who were guarding the camp, and how they and the campaigners opened up their lives to each other during the cool desert evenings. She tells of the horror and betrayal that she felt when the allied bombers first flew overhead to bomb Bagdad, and describes how, when the campaigners were evacuated to Bagdad, the Iraqis there — even though her countrymen were flying the planes that were causing such death and destruction — approached them with warmth and friendship.

Jenny Hales' talk has a strong effect on many of her listeners, and as she speaks, she shows them the awesome photograph of an incinerated Iraqi soldier that has been published in the *Observer* the previous Sunday, above the headline "The real face of war."[6] This one, terrible image of the carnage which followed the massacre of the retreating Iraqis on the

Basra road during the last hours of the "ground war," shocks and stays with many of the students. This is the "enemy" that the triumphing allied commanders and their men have so roundly vanquished. During their English lesson the next day I suggest they write down the last thoughts of the Iraqi soldier.

Nadia begins in this way with the soldier looking for a "sense of peace":

> My wife I'll be back.
> Please don't grieve, I'll be back.
> Son, I'll be back,
> No, don't cry—
>
> I'm on my way home.
> Mother and father
> Do not weep.
> Soon I will be home, to keep you strong.
> I'll bring money, food and clothes,
> We shall build a house,
> or even own a car.
>
> Do not worry,
> The war is nearly settled,
> So do not weep!

Marie, a white classmate, seems to find a kind of freedom in his mind:

> Free at last,
> Free from the danger
> Of shooting guns,
> Free from the danger
> Of whistling missiles,
> Free from the guilt
> Of what has been forced upon me.
>
> I'll see my family soon,
> Not to mention my friends,
> I hope they don't ask questions,
> I don't want to live through pain again,
> Tomorrow cannot come too soon.

While a Pakistani student, Izat, creates three lines that hold a whole war within them:

> I can hear a voice of oil burning
> Back in Iraq there are people crying for food
>   and yearning
> I want this war to end.

But perhaps the most moving response is from Safa again — now a few war weeks further in her learning of English. For her soldier it is only the family that matters, and in particular his brother whom he protects and loves as a parent.

My last thoughts

My little brother Saleh I am coming back to you as soon as this war has finished. I want to stay beside you, feeding you and giving you everything you want. I'll give you your books, pens to learn how to write and read. I will give you clothes for school, and new clothes for Eid.

Don't worry brother, I'm your father and mother and everything. I will stay near you and keep looking after you to protect you.

I will do all these things when I come back.

I want you to grow up to be a doctor or a soldier and anything good that you want to be. But I want you to remember your country and how to build it to be a prosperous country. I wish I could do all these things if I came back to you, if not, God will be with you.

Perhaps some people are happy and their families are around them, but I know for others they are not.

I don't want you to cry. I want you to be a man, a strong man to feed yourself and look after yourself if I don't come back. I want you to be the best, not for me but for yourself first, and for your country second.

I want you to know that I don't want to kill anybody, for we are not animals, we are people.

I don't want you to forget this. I want you to remember it all your life. I am dreaming, and I wish to do all these things when I come back.

Afterword

Just as the war ended, another, different one began for the school. The local education department, as a part of its effort to cut back its general school budget, announced that either our school, or a neighbouring comprehensive school on an almost all-white working class estate, would have be closed. This appalling decision virtually pitched the two schools against each other in a battle for survival: one would be the winner, the other the loser. Both schools resisted this pressure to fight it out, and embarked on a unified campaign for joint survival, but the danger for both communities, in the potential loss of their main local education resource, was real.* For what kind of system was it that could spend 4 million pounds daily on sustaining an interventionist war on another continent, and close its schools at home?

For us, the unity, made stronger by the weeks of the war, remained precious as we went into our campaign to save the school. As Shameem, a third-year Pakistani girl, wrote in her campaign poem which we published in our parents' newsletter (in an obvious rhyme that no one had discovered before):

Asians, Somalis, Saudis, Syrians, English and Yemenis —
We all come to this school and we're not enemies.

And her classmate Elizabeth reinforced this same message in another unifying image:

I don't want this school to close. Here I feel I've known everyone since I was small. We are all a family, teachers and children, black and white.

It doesn't matter who you are. If you are in our school you are part off this family. There may be war in the world, but at our school we are at peace with each other.

As these campaigns begin, two fifth-year girls come to my office with a idea which has gripped them. One was Sawsan,

* After an intensive community campaign, both schools were saved from closure in May 1991.

a Jordanian, the other her white English friend Kay. They spoke of some Iraqi families that Sawsan had got to know. Unsupported by their own government, and not qualifying for any assistance from the British social services, they had no money at all. The next day, the girls brought in an Iraqi mother and, while her child played among the books in my office, she explained how her husband — a medical student — was now without his scholarship, and how the family had been financially stranded. The girls decided to organize a series of fund-raising events for these families, and began with a sponsored lunch for the teachers.

This lunch had some publicity in the local paper, and the same evening Sawsan received a threatening, anonymous phone call, promising "acid in your face" if she continued to raise money for Iraqis, plus a battery of racist insults. Frightened, but undaunted, the girls carried on.

Two weeks later, after the first payment had been made to the families from the money the girls had raised, Sawsan brought in a beautiful hand-sewn tapestry, made by the Iraqi mother who had visited us. It was a gift for the school. Across the black fabric and written in Arabic in golden sequins, was a verse from *The Koran*, praising human unity and the God of the daybreak.

FOOTNOTES:
1 The *Star*, Sheffield (12 February 1991).
2 Andrew Moncur's Diary, *Guardian* (7 February 1991).
3 Amid Maalouf, *The Crusades through Arab Eyes* (London, 1984).
4 "the Aden File," *Sunday Mail* (17 May 1981).
5 *Thank you, thats all I know*, a film by Christine Bellamy (Sheffield Film Co-op, 1990).
6 *Observer* (3 March 1991).

Part III

Issues of Equity: Gender, Race and Culture

TACKLING SEXISM in a gutsy and meaningful way with adolescents is a daunting task. The Equity Studies Centre at the Toronto Board of Education embarked in the early 1990s on a new and exciting program of gender–issue retreats for high school students. Novogrodsky, Wells, Kaufman and Holland — teachers and counselors who organized this effort and who are also the authors of this piece — describe their 1991 pioneering four–day retreat involving forty young men and forty young women from grades eleven and twelve. The event gave them an opportunity to meet for the first three days with their own sex and get together for the fourth day to learn from each other. The topics included sexism, sexuality, violence, male-female relationships, homophobia and changing expectations about what it means to be women and men. Students partici-pating in these retreats were chosen to reflect the racial, ethno-cultural and social class diversity of Toronto. They were chosen as well for their emotional maturity and leadership potential which would be necessary to bring the retreat's message back to their schools.

Using many approaches to stimulate discussion and debate, including family–type groupings, skits and psychodrama, stu-dents found an extraordinary level of common ground first within groups of their own sex and during the final day in mixed groups as they tackled many thorny and sensitive issues. When they met two months later at a follow–up retreat, the positive bonds forged were still felt. The participants were also able to report on many activities they had initiated in their schools on gender issues. The authors stress the many valuable lessons learned in such retreats. Perhaps the most notable of these is the importance of sex–segregated activities as well as group work with both sexes present. They write: "Although our goal is to break down gender divisions, and power–relations between sexes, the reality is that separate male and female groupings can provide a type of safety and security that isn't always available from the start in mixed groups."

Equity in schools means both equal opportunity and respect for differences. For Canada's indigenous people it has meant — and continues to mean — a long and arduous struggle in both areas. Marie Battiste, a Mi'kmaq educator in Nova Scotia, speaks to George Martell in 1992 about the challenges of creating a curriculum where Mi'kmaq is a living language. She describes her own work as the curriculum co–ordinator for the band–operated school at the Eskasoni Reserve. She was instrumental in developing a programme which utilizes the prescribed content established by the province while at the same time enriching the students with local community–based knowledge and information. She also tells about the successes they've had in reclaiming Mi'kmaq language and culture, stressing that there is a strong interconnectedness between language, culture, traditional forms of government, the church, and the role of women.

Battiste speaks of the growing pride local Mi'kmaq's now have in passing on their cultural ways and traditions to the children at the school, and the communal support the school enjoys. However, she admits that some parents still have questions about the use of Mi'kmaq as the language for instruction. "People don't see that my fancy English education has been at the cost to my identity, to my language, my culture, my connectedness," she says. Her hope is that those students who go on to university under the Mi'kmaq Studies at the College of Cape Breton will solidify a commitment to their language and culture while struggling for political and social power. Hopefully, they will bring that message home to their own communities with the education of their own kids.

While some Canadian First Nations people like the Mi'kmaq in Nova Scotia are beginning to take over the education of their children, children from many "visible minorities," like African Canadians, have to contend with much less knowledge about their own experience, writes the Antigua–born educator and author Althea Prince, who lives in Toronto. She describes her own experience during Ontario's Black History Month — "the shortest and coldest month of the year" — breathlessly crisscrossing the province to read from her Antigua–based children's book, sometimes with nervous librarians hovering around, patronizing her by worrying about whether her story will be "suitable" to children who are not Black.

In the wake of examining the tokenism implied in compressing the African Canadian experience into one month, Prince also critiques the shallowness of much of official multiculturalism and calls for a more inclusive curriculum with a "world historic perspective." Within such a perspective the experience of African Canadians has much to offer not only to children of African ancestry but to all children, who need to know the truth about colonialism and imperialism, the reasons Europe carved up Africa. To those pro–establishment educators who want to "protect" children from such harsh truths, she insists that children will be able to genuinely understand this terrible story and the long shadow it still casts in present day Canada, if it is taught with an enlightened, humanist commitment to historical truth. In the end it is more cruel to remain silent of this past.

Keren Brathwaite, an African Canadian educator and parent activist, echoes many of Prince's concerns in "Keeping Watch Over Our Children." She speaks of the frustrations of the African Canadian community in dealing with the Canadian public school system. Despite the fact that Black Canadian parents have been engaged in a struggle for educational change since the 19th century and even earlier, the results continue to disappoint them. African Canadian students are not achieving at the level of their potential and they remain over–represented both among school dropouts and in dead–end programs.

Brathwaite, who has been a parent–organizer for over 20 years in the Greater Toronto area, puts the blame squarely on the school system which she still sees afflicted by systemic problems of racism, particularly labeling and stereotyping. Like Prince, she points to the lack of an inclusive curriculum where children of African Canadian parentage can see their collective experience reflected. This, she argues, is a major source of alienation and frustration among Black students.

There are two roads to improvement that she can foresee. The first one consists of even greater militancy on the part of African Canadian parents. They will have to insist on playing a more active part on their children's education team, being ready to intervene and advocate for them when necessary. At the same time, she is also favourably disposed to exploring some alternative models for education, including African–centered schools in the community. She argues these may provide a source of inspiration and expanded learning–opportunities for some African Canadian students. They may also, she hopes, offer an opportunity to demonstrate what Black students can achieve in an educational environment which does not look askance at them.

Chapter Eight

RETREAT FOR THE FUTURE
An Anti-Sexist Workshop for High Schoolers

Myra Novogrodsky,
Michael Kaufman, Dick Holland
and Margaret Wells

Sometimes, it seems, school deals with everything except what is most relevant to young people. This is nowhere more apparent than with issues of gender identity, relations between young men and women, and learning to understand the dramatic challenges to our male–dominated world. Every adolescent female experiences sexism in various forms in her daily life at school, home, and on dates. Every adolescent male is caught in a complex web of perpetuating sexism while being negatively affected by the demands of becoming A Man.

And yet, our schools rarely touch these issues. Many things keep all this out of sight: There are the traditional biases of educators and, in some cases, a lack of consciousness and discomfort with the material. For those staff who would like to deal with gender issues, the many demands on their teaching time, the tightly defined curriculum, and the lack of training in this area all get in the way.

In the Spring of 1991 we set out to break that mold and led a four-day retreat for forty young men and forty young women from Toronto high schools. Actually, it was two retreats. Males and females met separately for the first three days, leading up to a final day together. We covered topics such as sexism, sexuality, violence, male–female relations, homophobia, and changing our expectations of what it means to be women and men.

The previous year the Toronto Board of Education had sponsored a retreat on sexism and sex equity for young women. The forty female student participants were enthusiastic about the opportunity to have in–depth discussions and activities which focused on their experiences of gender. The students came from a broad spectrum of socio–economic and ethno–cultural backgrounds, but it wasn't surprising that all of them said they were afraid of the increase in violence against women. Many admitted they had practiced unsafe sex and were terrified of contracting the HIV virus. Most were aware of the increased opportunities for women in the workplace, but few had enough of a historical perspective to understand the role of the women's movement in spearheading these changes.

Most of all, participants told us they were very interested in their relationships with young men. When we talked about issues and the possibilty of change, they asked us, "What about the boys?" After all, not only do we have to address men if we want change to occur but, as some of the women noted, even though the retreat was a wonderful experience, in isolation it created distance between them and the boys and men in their lives whom they care about. The Board decided it was time to begin to answer that question. The idea of parallel retreats was born.

We set out to design a retreat for students in grade eleven and twelve (generally, sixteen and seventeen–year–olds). They would still have a year or two left at school so they could take their learning back to their home schools and put it into prac-

tice. Individual self awareness and empowerment were important goals, but real change in the schools that would reach
more than the eighty participants would be a core objective.
To contribute to the diffusion of ideas from the retreats, we
knew that the selection of participants was a major factor. We
wanted to involve students who reflected the racial, ethno-
cultural, and social class diversity of the student population.
These young people would also have to be sufficiently mature
to deal with the issues and have the leadership potential necessary to bring the messages of the retreat back to their
schools. We advised teachers selecting the students to think
carefully about what leadership meant in their own schools
and not to be restricted by the sometimes narrow definition of
that term. These selection criteria would help make the retreat
an important learning experience for the larger school community.

Our retreat set out to provide an opportunity both for students and for teachers to focus on these matters for a short,
but intense time.

The Philosophy Behind the Retreats

The parallel retreats for young women and young men represented an extension and departure from much educational
work on gender equity. Most gender equity work within
school boards has tended to focus on providing equal opportunities for girls and women. Compensatory programmes,
especially in such subject areas as math, science and technology, attempt to develop a more inclusive curriculum. Such
curriculum attempts to reflect the experiences of women as
well as men, adapt to their learning styles and personal goals,
and eliminate stereotypes of girls and women from teachers'
practice. This approach is understandable when one considers
how the sexism of society privileges male students and their
experiences. In this context educators attempt to provide
"catch-up" for female students so that all can compete on that
famous level playing field of life. Given the fact that female
students must learn and live in the world as it is, it is worth-

while for school boards to devote energy to these equal opportunity efforts.

However, if our work on gender is to produce significant and long lasting results, we must go further than efforts to create equity between female and male students within the existing social structure. We must consider how we can help students and teachers examine the very construction of gender roles and the societal power relationships which shape their construction. In planning the parallel retreats we wanted participants to begin to understand some difficult concepts: One is that sexism is a form of systemic discrimination which ensures the power of one group in society over another group. Sexism isn't just what individuals say or do, it relates to the entire way we've set up a male–dominated society. The second is the perplexing idea that patriarchy is a system not only of oppression of women, but one that has a contradictory impact on men as well: men's privileges and power are linked to the pain and alienation suffered by men themselves.

Sexism is a difficult form of systemic discrimination to examine critically, since it dictates notions of masculinity and femininity which are integral to our self-definitions and which come to be seen as natural. This difficulty is compounded for adolescents, since they are at an age when they are being subjected to so many complex and competing feelings and demands in terms of their own identity and desires. While we acknowledge that a four day retreat cannot, on its own, counteract the sexist messages and the gender constructions surrounding young men and women, we felt able to develop a program which would begin the process of deconstructing gender and allow participants to begin to imagine a different way of being.

What this meant for the young men was that while we encouraged them to understand their privilege as males within a sexist society, we did not want them to become caught in a position of guilt, unable to recognize their ability to work towards becoming anti-sexist men involved not just in supporting women's struggles for equality, but in challenging the very construction of a sexist society. The bridge for them was what one of us has termed "men's contradictory experiences of power": the way men have defined power within patriarchal society is a source of real distress for men.

At the same time we encouraged the young women to recognize the many and diverse ways in which their lives had been circumscribed by sexism. Judging from the previous year's experience, we expected some would realize for the first time how bad things really were. They would be able to re-examine and recognize sexism within things they took for granted. Indeed, as one young woman said, "All this stuff has happened to me and I didn't know it was sexism." Her insight was more than analytical; she realized she no longer had to put up with certain things. Our plan was to encourage the young women to see their individual and collective strength to challenge sexism and to explore how they could do this in concert with anti-sexist men. However constrained women might be, they have the power to fight and to change things. In the women's movement, women have a tremendous resource at their disposal – a collective vision of change, the wisdom of women of different ages and cultures, and a collective ability to challenge isolation and individual pain.

As part of this focus on gender issues we attempted to remain conscious that gender isn't isolated from other class, race and ethno-cultural relations in society as a whole and in the lives of individuals. The challenge was to design a programme which did not make universal assumptions about gender, but which allowed each participant to explore the complex ways that gender privilege or oppression operates in her or his own life. Our ideas of masculinity and femininity vary from culture to culture and era to era. Our experiences as women and men vary greatly under the impact of other forces that define our lives, things such as our sexual orientation, race or class background.

The Retreat Format

The plan for the retreat not only had to grapple with the issue of content, but with how to devise a format in which students would be able to confront productively a number of challenging issues.

We realized we needed to provide a different environment and a different context. The difficulty of education around sexism and patriarchy goes far beyond problems created by the traditional curriculum and its biases. The problem of schools and patriarchy has been the lack of a safe context for adolescents to deal with issues such as violence, sexuality, body image, household roles, assertiveness. In fact, most young people don't have any context in which to deal with these issues. What's more, the hierarchy of schools itself reproduces patriarchal relationships. Authority – of men at the top or of women who have managed to make it to a top in a system designed by men in the image of men's power – is something imposed over students.

The need for a different context and approach was partially to allow young people to get away from their normal routines of school, families, friends, and part-time jobs. The drudgery of daily life for adolescents and for participating staff would be interrupted by having the retreat outside the city in a fresh physical environment. The schedule would not be dictated by bells and disembodied voices over the P.A. system. The atmosphere would be informal; the one-sided exchanges still so common in many schools would be replaced by dialogue and mutual listening.

The learning process would be based on a variety of experiences: Each student was assigned to a small "family group," a support group that would function at the centre of the process of learning and self-exploration. Something between one-half and two-thirds of actual meeting time would take place in these groups of about ten students with two or three adult resource people. Our hope was that this would allow the development of safety, intimacy, and trust – encouraged in part by an agreement that all discussions would be confidential – and the chance for equal participation of all students. The family groups were not to be a location for mini-lectures by the teachers, but for group discussions, personal exercises (some using art or drama), and personal exploration.

The second component was activities with the whole group. These would range from sessions on sexuality (jointly facilitated by a man and a woman), to violence and sexual harassment. Speakers, films, drama and group discussions were to be used.

At each retreat, there would be a daily meeting of students from each school as a means to deal with common problems and to begin to relate the themes of the day to problems in their schools.

As noted, drama was to be used both in the large group and in the small groups as a method for exploring several issues. Drama techniques would give many students more scope to express their feelings and thoughts and to demonstrate what they were learning.

There was structured time in the small groups for students to write a journal, sometimes sharing their entries with their group if they chose.

Teachers as Participants and Facilitators

The parallel retreats offered not only a unique opportunity for students, but also offered staff an opportunity to hone their skills both in gender issues and in effective facilitation.

Locating staff was our first challenge. Through a network of Women's Studies representatives the project was announced to the school system. Each of eight participating schools was to select a male and a female staff member, and five male and five female students. While female teachers readily volunteered, enthusiastic male teachers were slightly more difficult to locate. In the end, with support from senior school administrators and the Status of Women Committee and with the promise of staff development to support the teachers, sixteen teachers volunteered.

The teachers were all people who were risk-takers and capable of bonding with students, even if much of the material was new and experimental. They met for three training sessions before the retreat. The first session shared the vision of the planning team and introduced teachers to one another. The goal was to make them part of the process of designing a retreat appropriate for students from diverse backgrounds.

From the start, the most contentious issue was how to get students to share their intimate thoughts and experiences about issues of sexism and violence, about growing up male and female in our society. Should we begin the retreat with a personal experiences, or should we open with an exercise which would give students some emotional distance but at the same time introduce the issues? The concern was voiced most strongly about the young men. "There's no way a six-teen-year-old boy is going to start talking about his insecurities or his real views about men or women," was a typical comment.

At issue here was more than an assessment of the capabilities of these young men in terms of emotional expression and self-awareness. We realized that the structure of the educational system and the usual position of the teachers as resident experts with power over the students had been one which normally creates a barrier between students and teachers. This barrier prevents the type of openness we were striving for in the parallel retreats. The education system sets up teachers as arbitrators and judges, as distant adult figures. The problem of openness worked in both directions: After all, if you were to ask most students if they expected their teachers to open up emotionally in a discussion, they too would say no. The system just isn't set up that way.

If the retreats were to be a success, if they were to be more than just an extended class-room situation, then we had to dramatically shift the relationship between student and teacher. The teachers had to become co-participants and facilitators. Most of the teachers had experienced the more relaxed and informal relationship between teachers and students which occurs on extended field trips. But we were asking them to go beyond that and to model redefined power relations with students. We challenged teachers to talk about the things they wanted students to talk about. We encouraged use of first names. We assigned two or three teachers to each small group discussion, so they could take turns acting as facilitators and as participants. We urged teachers to make a leap of faith. Going somewhat out on a limb, we suggested that if the teachers met the students as equals in a process of learning, the rewards would be rich.

The concern and doubt among the teachers, which was quite legitimate in the context of their teaching experiences, didn't go away until we were into the retreat.

The second training session, led by a professional staff development trainer, focused on the development of facilitation skills, team building, the stages of group development, and how to work productively with dissent in a group. Teachers had an opportunity to discuss their nervousness and their excitement about the coming event. They were able to see how much they already knew that would be useful at the retreats.

A week before the retreat all of the eighty students came together with the teachers for an introductory session. Students met in the small groups in which they would be working for much of the retreat. The room hummed with excited voices. The students wanted to have this experience and felt privileged to have been selected. Many groups quickly became involved in discussion; students began to talk about their feelings and thoughts around gender issues. Their enthusiasm was infectious and carried along the most hesitant teachers. At the final training session, which occurred immediately after the student session, teachers were presented with the completed retreat design package. Every activity was included in the binder along with supplementary reading material on group process, warm-up activities, and aspects of content about which teachers had expressed concerns, such as the particular challenges of discussing men's violence.

Teachers and students were ready. A week later the two buses pulled out of a parking lot taking the participants to separate conference centres north of Toronto.

The Men's Retreat: Sailing Through Uncharted Waters

As far as we knew, nothing of this kind had ever been done before with young people. There were simply no models for this work. We did know that our society and the schools within it desperately need chances for men to talk with other men about issues around sexism, but we kept thinking it just might not work.

But, by the end of three days together, even those teachers who were skeptical were surprised at our success. The young men had risen to the occasion: Instead of the machismo and sexist behavior that we thought might break out in a group of forty adolescent males, we found genuine displays of sensitivity, awareness and a growing desire to play their part in ending sexism. Theoretically, after fifteen or sixteen years, traditional socialization has had quite a chance to shape human behavior, but its veneer is thinner than many of us might think. This isn't to say changing patriarchy is a simple task. Rather, as the retreat showed, we can provide opportunities to men to express elements of masculinity that are normally suppressed and, while doing so, examine their own place within a system of male domination.

Our success with the men was based on maintaining a balance between helping them understand how they are part of a system of oppression and how they too are victims of that system. We looked at how sexism is not just an individual problem of harassment or assaults, but is promoted by the institutions of our society. The risk of these messages is that the male students will feel disempowered or resentful. For this reason activities were designed to show how men can make a difference; how men can individually and in groups begin to disassemble the sexist behaviors and structures in their own lives and work against sexism.

The students seemed to absorb and understand both these messages. In small groups they talked about feelings of shame about the activities of their fellow males, but they also expressed the desire to change things. Our capacity to maintain the balance between critique and personal growth was affirmed by the comments of some of the students. One said, in his confidential evaluation of the retreat, "Thanks for helping me become a better person," and another boy said, "I could see other people feeling better about themselves." For them, anti-sexism was becoming an essential part of being better human beings.

The decision to focus on the small "family" groups was critical in this process. The knowledge of confidentiality, the role of the teachers as co-participants, and the informality of the groups allowed a tremendous amount of creative thinking and growth. It was indicative of the success of the small groups that the only displays of sexist behavior (usually in the form of humour or taunting) was in the larger group, and even that was minimal.

In all this, the changed role of teachers was critical; they modelled the openness and risk-taking they expected from the young men. By being fellow men, and not merely adult authority figures, the teachers created a situation where the young men found themselves listening to and respecting the adults in a way that is seldom found in our society.

Drama provided some of the most surprising instances of the type of rupture of which the young men were capable. On various occasions they worked out skits about situations ranging from date rape, to locker room banter, to wife assault, to being caught by your parents while you were masturbating, to telling your parents you were gay. Over and over again we were surprised that the men created roles that included gay men and women that were not based on crude stereotypes but which attempted to portray real people. The lack of anti-gay portrayals (at least in formal sessions) was especially encouraging because of the extreme insecurities of teenage men in our culture and because of the complex ties between anti-gay attitudes and the misogyny of our culture.

The Women's Retreat: Difficult Passages

Three miles away the women were meeting. Unlike the boys' camp, the atmosphere was charged with a newfound defiance and strength. Nothing made this clearer than the workshop on WenDo — women's self-defense. The instructor modelled the self-assurance and strength which WenDo encourages women to develop. Through discussions and through practising basic WenDo exercises (designed to escape from and respond to attacks) the young women developed a sense of strength which was palpable. The first tentative attempts at the WenDo soon developed into strong assertive physical movements; the group shout of the WenDo yell grew in volume and confidence. For one woman in a wheelchair, the instructor made sure that she understood how to adapt WenDo strategy to her physical abilities and ensured that the young woman was aware of a special course for differently-abled women, which she later enrolled in. What happened in WenDo was indicative of the larger impact of the retreat. At its end, one girl wrote, "I enjoyed seeing women feeling so powerful and saying good things about themselves."

In spite of the sense of strength, or possibly because of the strength, some young women began worrying whether male-bashing was creeping into the program. This concern, which first came up in a drama session on men's violence, continued to be expressed throughout the three days. At the same time, some of the young women and some of the adult women felt that this concern was unduly influencing the young women's engagement with the program. The most dramatic example occurred on the last evening of the retreat when small groups were preparing their skits to present to the young men on the last day. One group which had decided to dramatize the effects of rape on a young woman started to discuss the possibility of making the rapist a lesbian woman instead of a man so that their male peers would not feel under attack. Through discussions with the facilitators the young women decided to stick to their original script; however this incident illustrated to the planners the extent to which young women are concerned about being labelled as anti-male when they express concerns about sexism and men's violence.

One of the challenges in this type of program is to respond to the diverse experiences of young women. Some of them experience positive family life in which there is an attempt to work towards sexual equality, while many face obvious gender discrimination within their families, such as preferential treatment of their brothers. Some have experienced abuse within their families or in other relationships. Indeed, during the retreat there were disclosures by several participants of past sexual abuse. Some of this took place as a part of the small group sessions and some during the day on violence. On that day we had a staff person on hand who had expertise in counselling young women who were victims of violence.

As at the young men's retreat, the half-day workshop on healthy (and fun) sexuality was a positive feature of the three days. The male and female co-presenters set the tone for the session with a humour and openness. Their use of props — such as "Woody," a wooden penis — and of role playing some of the more difficult and potentially embarrassing moments in dating engaged both the young women and the adults and created an atmosphere in which all questions were acceptable. Questions were flying about body image and body parts, safe sex and STDs, "what's normal" and what's fun, and the difficulties and pleasures involved in intimate relationships.

In the group sessions, the young women and adults created a supportive and open atmosphere. This mood continued after the sessions as informal groups sat around in pyjamas and nightgowns to continue intense discussions late into the night. The adults found themselves sharing stories of their frustrations, successes, fears and hopes with each other and with the young women who were no longer just students but younger partners in the challenge of achieving a non-sexist and equitable society.

Two Retreats Become One

There was excitement in the air as the bus from the young men's retreat pulled into the young women's camp. The young women were nervous, worried they'd be too harsh on the young men and felt protective about their feelings. But their nervousness and protectiveness were muted by a sense of strength, self-confidence, and, in some cases, anger, generated by their three days together. The young men, for their part, seemed anxious, even terrified. For the previous two days they'd been asking, "What's happening with the girls?" and now they were about to find out. They were nervous about being attacked but, perhaps most strongly, they were nervous that the young women would not recognize and accept the hard work and the self-searching they themselves had done. They, too, they knew, could be anti-sexist and they wanted to hear some acknowledgement that they were trying.

The day started with skits from the two groups that the students had worked out on their own. They looked at date rape, violence, sexual harassment, and sexist attitudes in the classroom and on the streets. The most remarkable thing about the skits were how similar the two sets were: the themes and approaches were the same. The men took responsibility around sexism. One difference did emerge. For the men there was a sense of outrage, anger and opposition to sexism, inequality, and violence. But there wasn't necessarily a lot of strength or a positive sense of pride. This isn't surprising for in many cases when males deal with their own sexism for the first time, guilt and self-blame are often up front. It takes some time to learn to sort through the complex feelings associated with being an anti-sexist man in a male-dominant culture. The women, too, showed outrage and anger, but also tremendous strength and defiance. This was clear at the end of a skit on sexual violence where the women actors gave a WenDo yell and punch. The room exploded with the cheers and yells of all the women in the room and brought them all to their feet. It was one of two moments of the day when the young men were genuinely stunned by the change their friends and classmates had gone through.

A second moment that exemplified this new-found strength, anger and assertiveness, came after one skit when one woman stepped forward in front of the group. She said she had been told that as the men's bus pulled up to the women's retreat, one young man yelled out, "You can smell the poontang." She said, "For those who don't know, poontang is a sexist word for vagina." She said she didn't want to spoil the day, but she felt she should put some realism into the air. She wondered what all the celebration was about if people still had this attitude.

Boys reacted defensively. A male student from her school, who was an amateur boxer and, in the past, not particularly known for non-sexist attitudes, said that the guys have to take responsibility and that many of them felt ashamed at what the other boy had said. The young woman said, "I'm not trying to say you all did this, but it makes me angry because someone did it."

It was an important moment. It made it clear that sexism doesn't vanish after a three-day retreat. It showed the un-evenness in impact from one man to the next. It also showed how, in the larger group of young men, many reverted to tried-and-true sexism. A sexist joke to cut through the ner-vousness about meeting with the women, showed the tremen-dous insecurity and the drive for control that is the substance of so much garden-variety sexism. On the positive side, the situation as a whole — the young woman confronting the men and the response she got — shows that men can and will listen to women and take seriously their concerns when they are shown the importance of doing so and are made aware of the consequences to women and men of the current gender system.

One final event during the skits bore witness to the risks that the participants were willing to make and the safety they felt in the group. One boy did a solo sketch, a soliloquy about being a male, ending with him talking about being sexually abused by his father. Whether it was autobiographical or a character portrayal wasn't clear, but this scarcely mattered. The room was spellbound, several people started crying and we were left, not with a sense of voyeurism, but of the recovery and strength that is possible in a collective and supportive process.

Well, this was all in the first ninety minutes of the day. We spent the rest of the day in school meetings, where the men and women from each school got together for the first time to make plans for their return. Students met twice with their teachers who acted only as resource people or, in some cases, were simply asked to leave. In the end each school brought back a short report — usually delivered by a boy and a girl, sometimes just by a girl, in one case by a teacher — in which they detailed some rather ambitious plans. Some decided to set up equity clubs or hold assemblies, others wanted to make presentations to staff meetings and encourage fellow students to speak out against sexism.

Summing up the day, one female teacher said: "I must admit I was skeptical about bringing both groups together... but I do think it worked. I am concerned though that the young women and some of the facilitators were so concerned about the men [being freaked out by the response of the women] that I feel in some ways it interfered with the process over the week. In sharing their experiences and acquiring information about violence there was a sense that we were male bashing. This is a common accusation, and I know how difficult it is to get around it, but I feel perhaps it's important to stress that if we are going to educate men, we have to identify the problem and have faith that the young men who come and the men who run the retreat are supportive."

The Work Goes On

The positive bonds that we felt were still apparent two months later when we gathered for a reunion. One by one, schools reported on their activities. At one school, students who had participated in the retreat developed a play on date rape which was presented to the student body. In several schools students addressed staff meetings and found they were opening a Pandora's box. They talked about addressing teachers on issues of sexism and sexual harassment in schools. During and after those meetings some teachers talked openly for the first time about how they had learned to live with sexual harassment. The students were challenging them to rethink this acceptance. The students had become facilitators.

Girls experienced the difficulty of being feminists in a milieu that misunderstands and often denigrates feminism. On the positive side, one young woman said, "Before the retreat I thought feminism meant that women thought they were superior to men. Now I know it means that women want equality, it makes me feel better about using the word." Nonetheless, many young women found themselves a bit isolated or having to endure the baiting of male friends who knew they had gone to the retreat.

One young woman said several months later that the retreat helped her "realize that I was in an abusive relationship with my boyfriend. I had just moved, was lonely, and was at a low point in my life. The retreat made me realize that I had the right to put boundaries on relationships. I broke off that bad relationship. It changed my perception of who I was."

In several schools male and female students who had attended the retreat set up an equity group. In the fall of the next school year they were still meeting. In one school, the group so impressed the administration that the principal underwent a sea-change in his attitudes and became the most enthusiastic booster of the club. In these schools, the young women, while experiencing some isolation, felt stronger and more confident than ever about the direction they were taking and were becoming role models for some of their peers. One young man, the school's star football player, reported how he had told his friends that he didn't want to hear any more sexist joking. Another male talked of the relief at finding older men who understood the difficulties of being men and who provided alternate role models: "You make it all better," he said. "You make it all easier." The students held an assembly for the student body and, encouraged by one of their teachers who went to the retreat and with the assistance of the retreat organizers, did a presentation and theatre piece that brought the students to their feet.

This same group presented their piece to a gender equity conference for grade seven and eight students at which several boys from the retreat gave a presentation to their younger peers talking about their own experiences. They were realistic about the difficulties in challenging sexism among high school males, but they expressed their belief that the efforts were more than worthwhile.

In a couple of the schools, students organized the White Ribbon Campaign, the December 1991 campaign on men's violence against women. One boy said the retreat had given him "a chance to stop and think; it took away the pressure and intolerance." One result for him was participation in the White Ribbon Campaign which made him proud to use the word feminist.

And in yet another school, staff decided to embark on an intensive training program for male teachers on gender issues.

Extending the Model

Through our months of preparation and the four days themselves, we learned some valuable lessons:

- We have a better chance than many of us would have thought in promoting equity, new gender definitions, and anti-sexist attitudes among both young women and young men.

- With a supportive atmosphere, male students are able to open up, talk about their experiences, and be vulnerable. Some young men, who appeared to be the last ones who would champion equality, surprised us again and again.

- Young women need opportunities that help them recognize for the first time how sexism has affected their lives and, just as importantly, the potential for collective empowerment.

- Key to our success was an atmosphere based on respect for the students in which their experiences were valued. Teachers were facilitators, resource people, and fellow human beings in struggle and change, and only authority figures and experts in the last resort. Teachers set an example by speaking in a personal and open way and by showing their respect for the students through their actions and attention. In turn, students clearly valued the experiences of the teachers.

- As participants in this process, teachers were able to learn more about their own experiences in a patriarchal society. At the retreats, teachers sat around talking candidly about their own experiences. After returning home, one man cried for the first time in decades and mentioned this without embarrassment in his report to his fellow staff members. One woman who had felt unable to do work on sexism in her school returned feeling clearer on the issues and empowered to do something.

- We were reminded of the importance of sex-segregated groups. Although our goal is to break down gender divisions and power relations between the sexes, the reality is that separate male and female groups can provide a type of safety and security that isn't always available from the start in mixed groups. Our format allowed us to take advantage of the benefits of separate and of mixed meetings. Participants come into the mixed group on the basis of mutual clarity and strength.

- Many of us discovered the value of role playing and drama as a means to communicate ideas and for students to work through issues and to adopt various solutions and problems as their own. The drama situation provided the bit of distance from a problem or a character type that made identification and openness possible.

- The enthusiasm with which the retreat was carried back into the schools indicated that such retreats can have an impact well beyond the small numbers directly involved. At the same time, the frustration expressed afterwards by some students suggests the importance of developing programs that can directly reach large numbers of students.

There are many ways our retreat model might be extended, including the establishment of similar retreats by other school boards and experiments with mini-retreats or in-the-community retreats in order to reach more young people.

Most importantly, though, is the integration of some of the retreat experiences into our daily educational environment. Many of the lessons of the retreats are nothing new to education reformers: we know that learning works best in a situation of mutual respect, where those learning have a sense of their own strength and power, where the learning environment is not dominated by a set of authority relationships, where learning is fun, and where teachers act as resource people and facilitators of learning (who themselves are learning too), where teachers are, in a sense, merely people who are older who have had many of the same concerns, problems, joys, and insecurities as the students we teach. In a sense, this whole experiment was not simply one in gender relations, but served as a pedagogical case study as well.

As valuable as these qualities are for education as a whole, when it comes to the area of gender relations and sexuality education, it appears these elements are indispensable. After all, gender relations are power relations. Untangling and dismantling current gender relations is only effectively done in an environment that is free of relations of hierarchy and domination.

We are convinced that many of the elements of the parallel retreats can be integrated into our daily curriculum and school environment. However, this requires teacher training and the view that men and women can be allies in the process of change. It requires development of new teaching resources. And, finally, it requires developing learning approaches – such as the use of drama and role playing, small group discussions, separate male and female support groups, a willingness to reassess the role of teachers — so that we can treat these topics in a fluid, critical but supportive and down–to–earth way.

Chapter Nine

TEACHING MI'KMAQ
Living a Language in School

*Marie Battiste interviewed
by George Martell*

In *April, 1992, while George Martell was in Cape Breton, he stopped at the Eskasoni Reserve to interview Marie Battiste, who was then a Mi'kmaq Cultural Curriculum Coordinator for the local band-operated school. After completing her Ed.D.in Curriculum and Teacher Training at Stanford University, where she did an historical analysis of Mi'kmaq literacy, Marie returned to Cape Breton in 1984 to serve as principal and education director at the band-operated Mi'kmawey School on the Chapel Island Reserve. At that time, the school had a student population of under 40, and offered multigraded classes for children in pre-school and in primary to grade six. In 1989, Marie moved to the band-operated Eskasoni Elementary and Junior High School in Eskasoni, with a school population of over 700.*

In the discussion, Marie refers frequently to these two Cape Breton schools. The Eskasoni School, she says, "provides a curriculum based on the provincial system for kindergarten through grade nine. The school has enriched its curriculum with Mi'kmaq language from kindergarten through to grade six. The language of the community is Mi'kmaq, and students usually enter kindergarten speaking only Mi'kmaq. In the past decade, the number of students entering kindergarten with English is growing. Approximately 20 per cent of the total school population now considers their first language English." The Mi'kmawey School at Chapel Island "utilizes the same curriculum as is prescribed by the province, and enriches their students with local community-based knowledge and information. Almost all of the students are English speakers, although the elder and most adult population still continues to speak Mi'kmaq as the lingua franca."

Marie talked to George about developing a curriculum and a way of "being" in Mi'kmaq schools which reclaims Mi'kmaq language and culture. In their conversation, they made connections to broader concerns of language, culture, traditional forms of governance, the church and the role of women.

Anne Manicom, Halifax, N.S.

Using the Language

GM What led you to your current focus on teaching the Mi'kmaq language?

MB My doctoral dissertation was a starting point. Initially, my specialty was bilingual–bicultural education, and I was looking for a thesis topic. I had exhausted the literature on every social, psychological, linguistic aspect of language and had been looking for "the problem." I decided one night just to not think about my research while I was with my advisor, and I said, "Let's make it a social evening, don't talk about research, let's not talk about my writing." So we talked about my family and home and all those sorts of things, and at one point she asked me whether we had bilingual education, and I said that we didn't, partly because there are several writing systems for Mi'kmaq, but no-one can agree upon which writing system is the best one to have. At that point in the discussion my advisor said, "Why don't you write your dissertation on that?" I was taken aback — I knew so much about it — I knew the systems, I knew the issues. I said, "It's as easy as that??!! Just to take something you like to do and know a lot about — you can do that?" It seemed it was, and I began writing my proposal to do an historical investigation of the writing systems.

GM What writing systems are there?

MB First of all, there's the system, still in use, that was developed by Father Pacifique, a missionary priest in the latter part of the nineteenth century who produced a 13-letter Roman script system. Then there was the Silas Rand system, but no-one used it because he was a Baptist missionary. Mi'kmaqs have been Catholics since 1610, and they were advised by their priests not to listen to Rand. Then came Bernie Francis and Doug Smith, who worked in the 1970s with the Mi'kmaq Association of Cultural Studies. Francis and Smith came up with a writing system by 1974 which was more linguistically appropriate than the systems developed by either Pacifique or Rand, reflecting the fact that we are now using English as a second language in most of our communities — in some places it is the first language. But that still hasn't solved our problem. While the Francis–Smith system is the most linguistically sound, and therefore the easiest to teach, a lot of people are uneasy about it. It seems to undercut the power of the old language for many. The whole issue has stirred up a great deal of discussion.

GM So, how do you think this issue should be moved forward? Should Mi'kmaq educators be actively encouraging the new system throughout their communities?

MB That's a hard question. When I was doing my thesis I had the chance to think about the functions and usages of our writing systems and how they were connected to different people, and from that I hoped to come to some conclusion as to what should be done with the current writing systems. But what I ended up with wasn't very hard and fast. Looking at the history of how the Mi'kmaq actually used these systems, and how the language itself was moving (with lots of erosion in the function and usage), I decided that it would be best to support whatever system people felt most comfortable with in their community, and to try to use it to promote their language. It wasn't the writing system that in the end was going to be the important aspect, it was whether they *used* the language at all.

GM Writing it too?

MB Yes. But the strength of the spoken language community will determine whether people have any strength in writing it. If they didn't talk the language, they'd have no use for writing it; there'd be no call for it. In the last century people knew how to read and write in Mi'kmaq, and they spoke it fluently as their main language. In my childhood my mother taught me how to write in Mi'kmaq and how to read the Pacifique system. Mostly, though, we read the prayer books. Beyond our prayers, the Pacifique approach was very difficult to work with, especially because of its vowel system, which was very much like French. By this time, of course, English had been our community's second language for a long time — and sometimes its first language. That's why a lot of people have found the Francis–Smith system to be more amenable to reading if they were also reading in English because there are a lot of similarities, especially in the way the vowels are used.

Teaching at the Chapel Island Reserve

GM In 1984 you went to Chapel Island Reserve in Cape Breton. Can you tell me about your time in that school? Were the kids learning Mi'kmaq when you arrived or did you start it up?

MB The Chapel Island Reserve wanted me to develop the educational program at the Mi'kmawey School. I asked them if we might be more experimental. I didn't want to run a system where everybody had to fill out the proper forms and do things in the standard way. At that time, all of their teachers were English except for the Mi'kmaq teachers in the Headstart kindergarten program. Basically they didn't have Mi'kmaq in the school. So I asked if it was possible for us to bring in all Mi'kmaq teachers and a Mi'kmaq curriculum. I wanted to develop a model as we went along. The Band Council approved and so we began by hiring our Mi'kmaq language teachers.

GM How did you develop your overall approach to curriculum?

MB Well, it was a matter of taking everything we knew and trying to lay it out into some themes, utilizing the Whole Language approach. Most of the Nova Scotia public school programs at the time were moving toward Whole Language, which encourages a range of reading materials centred around different themes. The advantage of that approach was that students could bring what they knew to the reading, and then the teachers could expand it with further research and questions. So a lot of our teaching to read in Mi'kmaq was done like a Whole Language program, preparing our own books, reading the books that we wrote, and that sort of thing. We drew especially on Elders in the community. We built on what we had.

GM What about other areas of the curriculum?

MB We stuck pretty closely to the math and science programs that were part of the provincial school system and we maintained a lot of other rudimentary things — the way you set up a classroom and all that. We wanted to maintain the basic content of the provincial curriculum but have the language base of instruction to be Mi'kmaq.

GM What about teaching to read in English?

MB Basically, we introduced English *as a second language*. We looked at the language as if the children really didn't know English, as if it was new to them, which for the most part it was, since even though they were English speakers, they spoke a *dialect* of English. We worked with that for about four or five years, and had a certain amount of success.

GM How did it turn out with Mi'kmaq?

MB We had varying successes with teaching kids how to read in Mi'kmaq. But I would have to say that it's not enough to give the students just a few years of reading experience and leave them, because now, four years later, they no longer have Mi'kmaq reading and they don't have any more Mi'kmaq teachers. And, their capacity to read and write in Mi'kmaq is slipping away.

GM Where are the students from the Mi'kmawey school now?

MB Some of them are still in the elementary system, while others have gone on to high school and junior high. The school only goes to up to grade six. At grade six you're out into a system that increasingly compartmentalizes education and gives highly specialized language for different subjects. We felt we had to prepare them for that kind of world. A lot of our efforts, especially in Grade 6, were to develop transitional skills for the world outside the community.

From Hieroglyphs to Roman Script

GM Can you tell me more about teaching the Mi'kmaq language?

MB As I said, we were using Whole Language approach for both teaching English reading and for developing Mi'kmaq literacy. I'm surprised at how quickly the students picked up the two languages, especially when we did hieroglyphic work. The students in Primary picked that up very readily.

About Grade 3 we began to work on the modern system for Mi'kmaq reading and writing. My son, who is now in Grade 8 and who went to this school when he was younger, still reads and writes Mi'kmaq, and he's got a very good handle on it. I've wondered sometimes whether it was because at that time he was primarily an English speaker, although he knew Mi'kmaq. He learned to read in the language he spoke — English — and then increasingly developed these skills in Mi'kmaq and just transferred them over. One thing I've noticed is that students who are English speakers and who begin reading in English can transfer readily to Mi'kmaq and are the better Mi'kmaq readers. Our Mi'kmaq speakers here at Eskasoni have a tougher time when we try to teach them to read in Mi'kmaq. I think this is because they were first taught to read in English, here in this school, instead of in their first language.

GM Tell me about teaching little kids hieroglyphics. A Whole Language approach generally begins with words that are part of students' daily lives. Why in Grade 1 would you not have begun with the words the kids used, rather than with hieroglyphics?

MB Well, hieroglyphics is a mnemonic system; it's designed to aid our memory. In teaching reading, Mi'kmaq hieroglyphics is very much preparatory. If you are going to teach kids to read, some of the first things to learn are the fundamentals of the reading process: showing that the writing goes from left to right, or that there is a one–to–one association of each word in print to words we use in talking, and that the words on a page are meaningful. Mi'kmaq hieroglyphics show these things; the hieroglyphics went from left to right and had a word-to-symbol association. But the hieroglyphic word was a big word, more like an idea or a concept than a word. It wasn't like the "John–cat–dog–boy" words of the regular readers. You can't do isolated words like that in Mi'kmaq.

So, starting with the hieroglyphics in Primary, we found we could teach kids pre–reading reading skills and word relationships, in the context of how Mi'kmaq is as a language. In addition, they very readily and easily picked up the chants that went with the hieroglyphics — in the prayers for example. But we decided that it wasn't good for them to chant it out if they didn't know what each part meant. So we decided we'd pull out each of the parts and we'd do visuals on it, and pretty soon they could see a hieroglyphic symbol and know exactly where it fit and what it was called. By using the hieroglyphics, we taught them *how to read Mi'kmaq* without having to teach them how to read in Roman script.

GM How did you move from hieroglyphics to print?

MB When we moved finally to print, we started to do things like putting the print words all over the room — on charts and on bulletin boards. We started teaching them through songs how to read Mik'maq in Roman script. We found that they could very readily pick it up with their own internal cues and rule-making. They synthesized the whole business without us teaching them the alphabet or the sounds of Mi'kmaq. We just *used* it. Eventually we could say, "OK, now we've been using print words in Mi'kmaq for the last six months, what's the alphabet in Mi'kmaq?" And they went around and could point to S and T and A and I and Q. And they just clicked into all the words they knew and found all the letters that were part of that and came up with the whole alphabet. We don't do the chant ABCDEFG, that sort of thing, but there are certain letters and signs, and they knew that. And so we said, "Let's find out what the values of these are. Give me a word that begins with this symbol." And they would give words. And pretty soon it was, "Okay, let's start writing with it." So they had internalized all the symbols, they had internalized all the sounds, and when we gave them words in Roman script, if we broke up the word very slowly for them, and let them think about what word they knew that started like that or ended like that, then they could pick it up.

GM Are there things that are difficult in teaching Mi'kmaq using Roman script?

MB Some letter–sound connections need to be taught explicitly because they're really close, like p/b, t/d, s/z, g/k. Especially the schwa symbol; it's such a short sound that if you linger on the letter you can make it into another word, depending on how long you linger on it. They had to be able to learn to hear it. So there were places where it was difficult for them.

GM So first there is the shift from hieroglyph to Roman print in learning to read in Mi'kmaq, and then there is the learning to read in English. How did you organize the English reading program in relation to the learning of Mi'kmaq?

MB We didn't limit them to Mi'kmaq, and we didn't limit them to English; we provided them with a whole score of things. We didn't want parents to be saying, "Well, they're not teaching them how to read." So we taught them English reading as well. We taught them the basic skills that were required with Primary, but at the same time we did them also in Mi'kmaq. And the children were cementing these things into their system by knowing them in both languages. And I felt that really helped them a lot more, and didn't inhibit them. I found that kids very readily picked things up.

The Erosion of a Language Community

GM But I get the sense you were unhappy about the capacity of many of your students to read and write Mi'kmaq by the time they hit Grade 6. It somehow hadn't gelled, particularly with your Mi'kmaq speakers.

MB I think we need to recognize that there is a social significance to language that is internalized early in children. The social significance and value that people place upon a language is evident in the way in which they use it and in the way it functions in their community. Things like this you don't have to *teach*; they are internalized by everybody around you. The reality for these kids is that the Mi'kmaq language was being seriously eroded in the community. Only the Elders

spoke the language. The next generation were doing a switching — half English, half Mi'kmaq. Of course, there were a few
parents who really wanted to make sure that their kids spoke
only Mi'kmaq. But, given the situation in the community, it
was difficult. Even if we speak Mi'kmaq correctly, here at the
school, the kids are not going to be able to get it unless there
is all kinds of motivation in their community that will enable
them to do so too.

GM When I was talking to people before I came, they said
that Mi'kmaq was in really great shape in these communities,
a "vital language" they said, "spoken as a first language by
almost everybody; not seriously damaged by an integration
with English."
    You're saying that's not true anymore?

MB That was true some years ago. But language systems can
erode, and very quickly sometimes, and most people don't
recognize how these changes occur. People need to sit down
and talk about how a language community changes; there are
steps, actual progressions that occur. Unless you understand
the progression of language use and change, and how those
deteriorate, you wouldn't recognize that anything is happening. Mi'kmaq *is* the language of this community, and it is the
home language for the majority of the people in Eskasoni. But
it is constantly under attack. At one time you wouldn't have
found more than one or two kids in kindergarten who spoke
English; those who started were Mi'kmaq speakers. That's
changed; a lot of kids now start with English.

GM What are some of the things that erode the language?

MB Well, the switching I mentioned is one thing. An example
I can think of centers around the English word 'ask.' One family
had kids that spoke half English and half Mi'kmaq. I heard a
father use the word *ask-awa'l*. I said to him, "Why do you do
that? Why do you use *ask-awa'l*?" I said, "Why don't you use

pipanim?" (That's the correct Mi'kmaq word, pipanim, instead of ask). And he said, "Well, it's easier for her to understand 'ask' than 'pipanim,' so I use the English word, and I put Mi'kmaq endings on it. Later on, when they understand it, then I will teach them the Mi'kmaq way to say it." And I said, "Why don't you just teach them good Mi'kmaq and let someone else teach them good English? For then they'll be able to use good Mi'kmaq when good Mi'kmaq is required, and good English when good English is required." "Well, no," he says, "they're too young to understand these things." And I said, "But if you give them the right Mi'kmaq word for 'ask,' they will remember it and use it because you've given them a context in which they would understand the word. They wouldn't have any more problem with that than with 'ask–awa'l,' which isn't a word at all." And so he said, "Well, I'll change it later." What happens with this sort of language switching is the deterioration of one language, and probably of the other as well. These children have had increasingly difficult times in school because of this.

GM What other things are going on that encourage language erosion?

MB Well, another process might be that Mi'kmaq communities have lost their language because a lot of them intermarry with other communities. Or it might be that the return into the community, since 1985, of Bill C–31 women with their children has created English–speaking pockets. And with children, you have to think about the playgroup. The playgroup plays a very important function in whether children learn Mi'kmaq or English. If the dominant language among the children is Mi'kmaq, and everyone follows the dominant child who has this language, then everyone will speak Mi'kmaq. If they have a dominant child who is English–speaking, then everyone will speak English, even children whose home language is Mi'kmaq. Child dominance is a very important factor in these changes in language.

GM What about the impact of television?

MB TV's been here a long time, and I don't think that it has that great a place in language breakdown. It's passive; there's no interaction, unless children repeat the play tactics of their heroes, like *Ninja Turtles*. They may pick up a few words, but basically unless there is an interactive play dialogue in which children use toys that build upon some kind of experience that they see on TV, the TV has no interactive value. Of course, the social experience of being a TV couch potato, can lead to less interaction with Mi'kmaq speakers and hurt the language that way.

But there are so many other things eroding language in our communities. In schools they're talking more English. And in business affairs, business terminology is in English; people talk English in meetings and functions. All of these things lead to breakdown of a language community. People begin to use English words in their Mi'kmaq dialect, and switch back and forth. They need to be caught in the switch, which is what we're trying to do in the school — to catch the switch by saying, "Let's be conscious of the words we use. If you don't know what a word is in Mi'kmaq, let's ask and find out, and we will use those words, and if we can't think of the word, then we might use the English word or find a new word for it." So, for example, even in things like studying about food, we learn the Mi'kmaq words. There's a Mi'kmaq word for carrots, there's a word for peas, there's a word for corn. Yet only a portion of these Mi'kmaq words are being used in daily dialogue with the children in their homes. So we want to provide them with the proper words.

GM How are you succeeding?

MB Well, I think that we are doing relatively well, although we haven't had an actual assessment of the language to determine where students were and are. My litmus is my own children. When I use a word, and they know what I am talking about, then I know they're picking this up from school. There are 13 Mi'kmaq teachers at the Eskasoni school. Kids like learning Mi'kmaq; they get along well with the teachers teaching it, it's a favourite thing and they are anxious for it. It 'clicks in' a lot of the words and concepts and thoughts and values and cultural tradition and history about themselves. It would be very helpful to them if they could have Mi'kmaq more than the two classes a week in a six–day cycle, which is all they get right now in this school.

GM Oh, I see. So they're not speaking Mi'kmaq in their regular classrooms? I thought this was a Mi'kmaq–speaking school you were talking about.

MB Oh no. Mi'kmawey School in Chapel Island Reserve was that. But when we came here to Eskasoni, we had to try to make the ball go the other way, towards teaching in Mi'kmaq. But it's been a very resistant ball to move. The most we can do is two class periods of Mi'kmaq each week. The justification for not teaching more in Mi'kmaq at Eskasoni was that students already speak Mi'kmaq here, so people argued that they wouldn't need any more than a couple of classes of Mi'kmaq a week.

GM So with 13 Mi'kmaq teachers, students have only a couple of Mi'kmaq classes a week and some Mi'kmaq culture. But, is there a spillover? Does even this limited attention to Mi'kmaq language and culture make a difference in terms of, say, how geography's taught, how history's taught, how English is taught?

MB It does, to the degree that we provide teachers with the background information for the Mi'kmaq content. I meet with teachers regularly; I'm their resource for whatever they need, for whatever theme they're working on, whatever concept they're building. So I get materials ready for them. I feed them the information. As much as you give them, they will use. Mi'kmaq teachers in particular will feed all that information back to the class. So, for example, when they did foods, I say to some of the Mi'kmaq teachers, "Do you do this in Mi'kmaq too, or do you do it just in English?" And they say, "Yeah, we do it in English, but you're right, I should do it in Mi'kmaq." So I say, "It will help us if you reinforce it in the classroom by utilizing the words." And they say, "But we don't know all the words." And I say, "Well, I'll give you all the words for things."

Culture and Politics

GM Alongside language learning I know you teach the broader culture and politics of the Mi'kmaq people. Can you tell me about that?

MB The way in which we teach is that we talk about the Nation first. We don't talk about our community, we talk about our Nation: what we are as a Nation, and who we are as a people, and how we all fit together under that one language and one culture. People may not all now have that language, but basically that's how we identify ourselves, by the language. And we connect with people from other districts in many different ways, through events like tournaments and games. Or, when people die we go to the funerals and wakes. And we share, we give; when someone gets hurt in Restigouche in Quebec, for example, there's fundraising in Eskasoni to help them, and so on. So we see ourselves as one greater community. But politically speaking these days, money creates the greatest divisions we've ever had. Which is why the Grand Council of Mi'kmaqs, which is our traditional government, has never gotten involved in having to give out money or decide who gets money. That's what federally organized Band Councils will do.

GM Tell me more about the differences between the Grand Council and the Band Councils.

MB Well, the Grand Council is our traditional form of government, while Band Councils are federally organized. As I said, deciding about money distribution is the Band Council's jurisdiction. But when we're talking about issues of family and communities and territories and treaties and rights, those are all under the Grand Council. We separate our awareness of things by knowing what each is and how each operates. And we try to build in our children a greater awareness of the Grand Council and how it makes us a spiritual community.

For a while the Grand Council lost a little of its strength, as federally organized Band Councils came into effect and sort of pushed the Grand Council to the side. But I'd say the Grand Council is growing in strength; it's in a stronger position now than it has been for a very long time. I think that we need to sort out the relationship of governments like Band Councils to the Grand Council. There's probably a better structure evolving. We need to bring these issues to the attention of the youth, to try to teach the youth, to try to help them to bridge the gap with the Elders and to know what is the right way of doing things.

Mi'kmaq Women In Politics

GM This shifting of structures away from the hierarchy of Band Councils to the workings of the Grand Council seems to be opening up deeper roots of the Mi'kmaq culture. In your piece on women in the *Canadian Women's Studies Journal* you touched on that, and I'm wondering if you could speak about the role of women in the Grand Councils and that political tradition.

MB I think that if there's anything that could be said about the ways in which Mi'kmaq women have talked about their roles, is that they are complementary to men's roles. Women today look at political structures and see hierarchy, which is based in feudal European thought. They see that if you are on top there is someone else on the bottom who is being oppressed. This continues to hold under modern liberal theory. But in aboriginal cultures (and I think this is true among other groups of people, not necessarily just Mi'kmaqs or Crees or Mohawks), there is a *complementary* attitude. There is a complementary notion of government that pervades aboriginal thought; that there is *no one on top*. Even in our own Grand Council, there is no one on top; they don't see themselves in a hierarchy or pyramid, but see themselves as a circle. Everyone in that circle is a Speaker, although someone is a designated First Speaker. Everyone has a right to come to the circle and speak, and no one's denied the right to speak and everyone has a right by his oratory talents to persuade others in any direction. And when debate is long and arduous and hard and they can't seem to get to a consensus, then the members of the Council will go to their women.

GM Are there any women on the Grand Council?

MB In the circle, no. But women are connected. So when consensus can't be developed, the Council member returns not to the men to discuss with the men what to do, but all around the community, including the children. They discuss in the community unit what's to be done. Everyone voices their opinion and has something to say. Here the women are very powerful. This is how it goes on today. When an issue comes up they all congregate in one corner or two in the community and talk and talk and wrestle out all the issues, one side or the other. And then someone is called to go into the Council meeting to bring the consensus of the group. So consensus is the means by which we operate. We don't just do a count and say majority rules. And sometimes, if there's just one dissenter, custom holds: we stop.

GM In your piece on gender, if I read it correctly, you say that women clearly were the spiritual core of the community, the people who were the most open to looking at the ordinary with awe, who continue to bring the flotsam and jetsam of the everyday world into a spiritual perspective, who continue to reinterpret the changing world so that some kind of future was possible. And yet your Grand Council's orators, those people who speak eventually to resolve the different opinions, are men. Can you help me understand that?

MB If you look at it from the point of view that "here are the men and only they can speak to the issue" — it's not that. The point is that women are essentially the ones who are going to have to live with whatever decisions are made, whether their son goes to war, or whether their family breaks up into various territorial hunting groups. These are very significant things to be decided upon. The cornerstone of a political family is the woman. The men are sort of given the role, the opportunity, to speak in Council to the community decisions.

GM You mean translate the family decisions?

MB Yes. There's always deference given to the central woman head of the family. And in every corner of discussion you'll find a woman head of the family. It might be a grandmother who is the core person, or it might be an aunt. The core person whom the group gathers around, that spiritual core in any home, any family, that centre is the woman. The men have had so many changing roles over time — they've been traders, they've been working in pulp, wherever. It's the women's role — the nurturing caretaker — that has remained fundamentally unchanged in the aboriginal family. And only the new feminist movement would speak against that. Wherever we find that female role breaking down, we see a lot of other breakdowns too. There's still got to be the core, the woman. The woman builds her strength over the years through her mother or her aunts who assume that position of great importance in decision-making. In this sense, then, it seems complementary to me — and in the Mi'kmaq consciousness — to have men be in the Council.

GM Let me ask this question. Would you envisage some future Mi'kmaq society in which these roles moved back and forth more? That men took more of the spiritual, nurturing side, and women took more of the speaking side?

MB There must be something that is deeply rooted in the whole thought to make me think, "Why couldn't that be?" But it just doesn't sound like it could be. And I would have to take some time to think about this. For example, birthing is such a *spiritual* thing. And death — you will find women moving around the dead person more than men, the women are always there to do the praying and to be part of the dying. You don't find men going to *do* this. The women are so much more a part of these spiritual ceremonies.

GM In my society I want to resist that separation.

MB I understand, but this is deep in our culture. I look back at history, I read Christian LeClerc writing about Mi'kmaqs in 1675, and I think, "That sounds just like the family I know." The people, their values, their attitudes, haven't changed. And even though there's been oppression and changes all their lives, some things don't change. And maybe it is some-thing that's embedded in Mi'kmaq thought and language and spirituality which keeps that continuum. But maybe some things sound very bizarre in the modern world.

GM This doesn't sound bizarre to me at all, it's just that I'm thinking, for example, of your role, as somebody who *speaks*. You don't speak at the Grand Council, yet I know a number of First Nations women, like yourself, who are very much at the forefront of speaking on behalf of their community to the world outside. So it struck me that some evolution of your society might see more of a back and forth in these roles. That evolution has certainly begun to happen, from quite a different perspective of course, within my own society.

MB But you always have to remember that in an egalitarian society, the power and prestige of its people are not by what they gain along the way — education, marriage into a family, money, the size of their car. None of these things will give them power and prestige. Power and prestige are intimately related in the Mi'kmaq context to lines of custom and tradition. And within these you become powerful by your way of life, by your history — and not just your own personal history but your family history — what your family was able to glean over a long period of time.

Consensual Politics and Schools

GM Could we shift for a moment and relate this back to schools? How does this world view of consensual politics, with its particular balance of men and women, get itself worked out in the school? How do you teach that in practice?

MB Well, it's important that people understand the values and customs and traditions of the people. You must have the core of that understood; harmony within the group can be achieved when you understand the relationship of individuality to collectiveness. Our collective values that have evolved include a place for individuals; individuality is nurtured. If there's anything that I would say about Mi'kmaqs, it is that each and every individual is allowed his individuality, to be as crazy and wild as he or she wants to be. But you must know that this individuality is part of *your* individuality and has nothing to do with what you pass on to whole generations of children within our society. The society of people has to know what the customs and traditions and values are of the people. And when you understand *that* you will understand that when you are banished, not allowed to participate, it is because you are not acting the appropriate way.

GM Is banishment the worst punishment?

MB Yes, it is. But it is not practised frequently. When you are no longer connected to the community — no longer connected or allowed to be a participant in the society — it's quite a big thing, because where do you go? How do you live? How do you survive until you make your way back? People do get back; it's not the end. People often express their individuality by going and living in Boston, Toronto, Halifax, where individuality is the core of modern society. That's fine, as long as you're not *here* doing that. This whole aspect of collective thought and individual thought has a very predominant place in the Mi'kmaq thought.

GM I'm wondering how you actually work that out among the kids in school.

MB OK. It's very difficult unless you have the right kind of system that allows you to do those things and to practice your traditions and customs in school. What I can say about *this* school is that basically we've been running under a white system for a very long time and that that system is still entrenched in our schools. So we are not at a place where we can practice Mi'kmaq thought and philosophy as a basis for school operation. It's *possible*, but you have to give up some things in order to yield to the other.

GM What about the Chapel Island school?

MB I tried not to use rules and regulations. We had some, but we didn't yield to them, we yielded to consensus of thought. There were teachers, there were teacher assistants, there was me, there was a janitor. When everyone in the group accepts that consensual judgement will be made, then you defer, you put everything into the centre, just like you would do in Grand Council. Everything goes to the centre, and then judgements are made around that until everyone agrees that that's what we should do, whether it was calling off school, or having a meeting. I never set up staff meetings every third Wednesday of the month. It would be, "Do we need one?" And somebody would say, "Well, I think we need to have a staff meeting", and I'd say "Okay, after school at three o'clock we're having a staff meeting." We also brought the community, through the Elders, into events in the school. I felt that we operated under a Mi'kmaq system.

GM What about with the kids themselves? For example, how does discipline work?

MB We had our share of discipline problems. We cared for those children like we were their parents, a mother, an auntie, a grandmother. Each one of us assumed that these were our extended family and our extended family required us to go and spend time with them. We had an open school. Every day parents came in the morning, and it was social. They had tea with us, and if kids wanted to have tea they had tea with us. We had breakfast in the morning with our kids, we had lunch with them, we had people in the community volunteering to help us with cooking and cleaning and getting lunch ready. They brought their babies and toddlers in. We said, "If you help with school, then come on, bring your families in." So, when you conduct yourself as a family like that, then you can operate under the same family rules.

GM What are those rules?

MB The most important thing was to try to keep a consensus about what needed to be done in order for this classroom to operate. And when our students had that, then they were also able to accept that when anybody went beyond this, and didn't do something right, then we would talk about it as a group, make some decisions together as a group about what to do about it. Sometimes it would require that we would ask students to leave. If you were having difficulty with behaviour, we might ask you to remove yourself, to get yourself together. If you're angry, which everyone is at some time or another, what you do when you are angry is that you leave the group. That's what everyone does. If you are angry, you get up and walk out. It's the same with kids. But they could only walk out of the class, they weren't allowed to walk out of the school. And if they walked out of the building, then there were consequences for that. The key is that students have to have knowledge of what are the consequences for particular kinds of actions. For example, one consequence might be suspension. If you're suspended, we involve your parent; your parent has to come back with you and has to sit in the classroom with you. Another consequence might be that you'd have certain privileges taken away from you, like working on the computer. If you did something inappropriate, you couldn't use it for a day. If you did it again, then it would be for a week. The computer was the big thing, everybody wanted to play the computer.

GM What other ways does the Mi'kmaq way of being get integrated into the schools?

MB Classrooms can operate in the Mi'kmaq way. We find that Mi'kmaq teachers who have children of their own operate in the same framework as they would in their own home. The chastising is not direct; it's done by means of teasing and often that is all that's required. That's a means that is used in the community. Another approach is to call upon a third person. Third-person calling-upon is a frequent means by which we do any kind of reprimanding. Just as in a family oftentimes a parent doesn't reprimand directly. Direct reprimand means you will lose the contact and relationship — damage something. So a parent will call upon someone else to do it. And usually it's a godparent, an uncle, an aunt, so that the direct relationships are guarded.

GM So would it be very unusual for a teacher to directly rebuke a child?

MB Well, it's not usual, I would say. It happens certainly, but the best means to handle a discipline problem is to not direct your anger and the other person's anger at each other. We then have to wait until the anger's cooled, before we can start talking about the issue at stake. The better way I have found is not to let that happen, but to work through a third party. That's why the principal is so key. You let the principal handle the mediating. As you can imagine, when kids who are used to dealing with problems in this fashion get to high school, outside the community, they tend to reject the imposed authority of the teacher. They don't like to be told what to do. No Mi'kmaq likes to be told what to do. *But* you can tease him into doing it, you can make everyone go along with it and get everyone to do it so that by doing group collective activities then you've got that happening. Or you go through another person.

GM Would that be true in adult relations, when people have something to say to one another and they're angry? Do they say it straight or do they use mediators?

MB Most times mediators are used. Mi'kmaqs aren't great for confrontation. If I'm mad at you I'll go tell that guy and he'll tell you. Very rarely will I come and give you hell. That kind of direct confrontational style is not valued in our community; people prefer to tell somebody through somebody else.

GM Are there other things that teachers do that are more the Mi'kmaq way?

MB Yes. There are some things that teachers have come to realize about Mi'kmaq kids. For example, when someone gets wild and angry, then that is not the time to deal with the problem. But always you try to bring that person back in, you speak kindly to them, try to get their angriness away by complimenting them. You know, Mi'kmaqs have a way of doing things. We compliment somebody to the point that we can get them to do something. Mi'kmaq teachers tend to do this sort of thing and non–native teachers don't. They don't compliment, compliment, compliment, praise, praise, praise. Occasional praise is dished out in white society, but in Mi'kmaq, it's much more effusive. As a people we are 'naqitpat,' (I can't think of an English equivalent, it's sort of that we have a propensity toward being easily manipulated), and we know that about each other, and we work with it, with this cultural trait.

GM It's a social response to a discipline issue rather than a individual one.

MB Yes. And you can do that so well in Mi'kmaq. In English so much praising and complimenting doesn't sound real, it sounds so fake. But in Mi'kmaq it's such a natural part of the way in which people are socialized. You can correct anybody's behaviour by praising another person and how *they* do things. And the other person begins to listen and is drawn into it. So there are ways to manipulate children. And working within a family you know those things, you begin to utilize some of those same manipulative processes. Actually, 'manipulative' sounds too negative for the context in which I mean it; for us, it's a loving manipulation and it's a utilization of custom and tradition to achieve your end, which is the way we have always been able to operate in our culture, through utilizing these cultural traditions and values.

And when we are in school we teach specifically what these values are and what they mean, and we utilize them in the classroom as a mode of operating, a mode of discipline. Kids are disciplined in their community in particular ways. But if they go to school in a non–Mi'kmaq setting it's different. They don't encounter the same kind of strategies. And they respond differently to the different strategies. But as soon as the language clicks in, they click into the network again, and begin to respond appropriately. It's a response built around the social customs and traditions that are part of the people. We have many strategies that are part of social/cultural socialization and those are the ones that Mi'kmaq teachers use, and use very effectively.

The Church

GM You mentioned it was early in the seventeenth century that the Mi'kmaq nation became Catholic. How does the Church integrate with Mi'kmaq culture, with these ways of dealing with children, for example? The Church is a deeply hierarchical organization. How does it fit in, or how does the community fit with it?

MB In 1610 Grand Chief Membertou was baptized with 150 of his clan members. One could say by his baptism he became Catholic. But we would say more that the rituals entered him into not a spritiual but a political relationship with France as a Catholic State. At the time he probably understood very little if any of the rudiments of theology. So theologically speaking he did not become Catholic; he only became allied with France through the institution of the Church. We've had this long historical relationship since then with them. But the Church has really not done much more than be a spiritual presence in our community. I don't feel that they have greatly influenced the internal structures of things.

Basically Mi'kmaqs have been Mi'kmaq Catholic over the years. And this is different from being Catholic, because if you go to the centre of the Mi'kmaq beliefs, you'll find a lot of the same rituals as in the Church, but the Mi'kmaq belief system in the deep core is very different from that of the Church. So you could say that the Mi'kmaq continued to hold on to their spiritual beliefs and have adopted its more public rituals around Catholicism. It has worked very well. And in some cases we simply shared symbols. Our people believe, for example, that in dreams and visions before the missionaries arrived, the Mi'kmaq had been given the cross, which in our vision appeared as the source of Mi'kmaq survival. The cross is seen as symbolic of the strength of thought that's in the medicine wheel and is seen as symbolic of the Grand Council, which is a circle with a cross in it. So we feel that we have had a basis of our spirituality that grew from things that are aboriginal, things that are traditional to us.

The Purposes of Schooling

GM In all of what you've been telling me, what you do in school is linked to a larger sense of community and its meaning. How do you tell children about this? What do you say to them about why this language is important, why this culture makes a difference?

MB I guess I need to start off this way. There are some key people in this community who have been in a ten-to-twenty-year movement to correct the oppressive imperialism that we've been under, to assert Mi'kmaq culture as a valued, important and beneficial way of living, which will not only survive, but will flourish in the future. This vision has been undermined by boarding schools, by English-language instructional schools, and by those "pull yourself up by the bootstraps" educational philosophies. Poverty, abuse and violence have set barriers and have worked hand in hand with the worst parts of oppressive thought against us.

GM To what extent is your view — that the revival of the language is key to the survival and flourishing of the Mi'kmaq way of living — shared by people in the community?

MB Well, people are certainly glad they speak Mi'kmaq; they realize the importance of Mi'kmaq to their friends, to their family. But they don't always see it beyond that. They don't see it on a broader political level. There's this notion that if you want your children to get ahead, then they have to learn what is in the school, the English way.

There are people in the community — the Grand Captain Alex Denny, Professor Murdena Marshall at the College of Cape Breton, her husband Councillor Albert Marshall, our Chief here, Leonard Paul — who are all trying to change this mindset to the idea that Mi'kmaq is good, that it is good to be Mi'kmaq, that you don't need to change yourself, that what we have to do is improve the instruction for our kids so that they retain both languages. But we're still a long way from changing the community and nation perspective toward this. We have everything running against us, and only a few things going for us. We have our treaty of 1752, and there's the United Nations who support our efforts. We've been working with the United Nations in doing some global things that can affect our situation right here. We have key people — Sa'ke'j Henderson and Russell Barsh — who are working to correct all kinds of legal issues that prevent us from asserting our Aboriginal and Treaty rights. So there are a good number of key people who have made a great difference here. By myself, if I were the only key person, it wouldn't work, because they would say, "Well, you're coming in with your doctorate, you speak good English, that's what we want our kids to have."

GM You mean that it's all very well for you to talk, you've made it?

MB Yes. People don't see that my fancy English education has been at a cost to my identity, to my language, my culture, my connectedness, my belongingness; they see these as not important in relation to the other things that I do have. On the other hand, people don't want to move out of that community belongingness, they don't want to do what I have had to do. And they're right not to want to. So I say, "Well you don't have to, you don't have to. Just do it another way." But it's difficult for the people here to believe that. But when they get to university, under the Mi'kmaq Studies at the College of Cape Breton and working with Murdena Marshall and Sa'ke'j Henderson and other professors and teachers who are there, they begin to realize the importance of these things on a political/social level, and try to bring that home in their own community with the education of their own kids. It's had a tremendous impact. We're beginning to see people really wanting, accepting, advocating, thinking "this is right."

Chapter Ten

BLACK HISTORY MONTH
A Multicultural Myth *or* "Have-Black-History-Month-Kit-Will-Travel"

Althea Prince

Many self-respecting African Canadian educators, artists, parents — children, many of US — have participated in it: The 'Great Canadian Multicultural Myth' called "Black History Week"; then later, "Black History Month." We do it in the name of community and history, for our children, for ourselves, for our society. We want to see our faces, hear our voices, read our words, speak them. We want our children to do those things too.

We seize opportunities to share who we are, explore where we came from, discuss where we are going. Black History Week was such a time when such a space would be opened. Black History Month showed progress, some people thought: twenty–eight whole days (and twenty–nine in each leap year), even though it is the coldest and shortest month of the year.

So, during this shortest, coldest month of the year, many of us educators and artists traverse the land bringing "Black

History Month" to schools, libraries, community centres, churches, universities — anywhere and everywhere.

How do we transport Black history with such agility? It's sort of "Have–Black–History–Month–Kit–Will–Travel"; and travel we do. One February, I wore out a whole pair of boots and a whole pair of running shoes. But we press on, because it's all we've got; and didn't our parents teach us not to fly in the face of our good?

What's in a Black History Month Kit? "Everything!" the customers think. Once, it was suggested that instead of reading from my children's book, that I read a story from a collection of Anansi stories collected in Haiti(!) by someone with an eastern–European–sort–of–name. The woman (librarian) who thrust the book at me, mumbled something about none of the children being Black and that all children were able to understand Anansi.[1] She also mumbled that they were going to have "difficulty" with my children's book.

I did not reach out my hand for the questionable Anansi collection. I had been brought to the school as a children's author and was ready to read from one of my books, which was set in nineteenth century Antigua. As had been pre-arranged with the principal, the children had already read the book. From somewhere in the depths of my soul, I found my mother's Bolans-Village-Antigua-power. I opened my briefcase, took out my own books and asked politely, "Where shall I sit for the storytelling session?"

I won the unspoken battle. I list it in my personal struggle for a more inclusive cultural vision. I should add that the storytelling session went extremely well. Not only did the children have no trouble with the book, they asked if I could tell them another story. Their teachers also invited me to come back for the next year's Black–History–Month. I agreed, smiling. Inside, my weary heart thought, "When will it end?"

I tell this little tale to dramatise the point that the Black-History-Month-Kit demands great flexibility. Given the oppurtunity, teachers and librarians can, at will, dictate their own vision of Black History Month.

✦ ✦ ✦

Clearly, the history of African Canadian peoples needs to be dealt with within the schools. A month is not the way. An inclusive curriculum is not only desirable, but clamours to be developed. It feels sometimes as if we are in a bind. For if we continue to enable the ghettoised version of our history as a people, allowing it to be relegated to one month, then we are complicit in the perpetuation of a hegemony that denies our existence. Yet if we do not take this Black History Month crumb that is offered, we may find that our children, and all children, for that matter, have no access to even this ghettoised version of the history of African peoples.

Antonio Gramsci (1971), an Italian political activist and theorist, writing of Italy while in prison between 1929 and 1935, used the term *egemonia* (hegemony) to describe the pervasive cultural domination exerted by a ruling power bloc. In Gramsci's view, domination is exercised through popular consensus building as well as by physical coercion (or threat of it), especially in advanced capitalist countries where education, the media, law, mass culture etc. take on this role. Gramsci also argued that in order to challenge existing power relations, oppressed groups need to struggle on the cultural level as well as on the economic and political level. The dominant "consensus" needs to be challenged by the building of an inclusive counter-hegemonic ideology, which reflects more honestly the experiences of the majority. African–Canadians' historical reality then would surface and would be included in the overall hegemony that determines the history curriculum.

The fact that the history of African peoples is not included in the school's curriculum is an example of how cultural hegemony operates in the Canadian school system. I say these things in as bold a way as I can, for I observe that to be heard we sometimes have to be blunt, and sometimes we have to be bold, as if these things about which we speak are *a given*.

I would like to illustrate the notion of cultural hegemony

by using the metaphor of a giant umbrella which reaches over us. We languish under the guise of this "multicultural" umbrella and actually, we suffer. For multiculturalism suggests equality in the plurality of cultures that exist in Canada and thus serves as the mechanism under which some groups in the society are denied access to real power. In this case, we are looking at the unequal distribution of power as it manifests in that most important social institution: The School. The umbrella, disguised as shelter, is actually a control mechanism. Nothing is exempt. All the way through the school system, up to and including O.A.C., our children do not find themselves and their people in the curriculum.

The weave of the umbrella clearly displays that the fabric does not contain representation of certain racial and ethnic groups. Yet all groups are made to stand under the umbrella. When it rains, it is the position of the umbrella that determines where all groups may seek shelter. Any attempt to deviate from the weave of the fabric of the umbrella creates quite a stir in the hands that control the umbrella. Groups desperately seeking shelter under this kind of oppressive umbrella, soon find that there is no shelter. What is to be had under the seeming 'shelter' of the umbrella, is in fact, oppressive cultural hegemony. History = *their* history; that is, the historical interpretation of the dominant group. In the context of our discussion, Black history = Have–Black–History–Month–Kits–Will–Travel.

If we accept Gramsci's notion of 'hegemony' we recognise that there is a meaningful distinction to be made between 'hegemony' and 'direct domination.' Subordinate groups can be oppressed through cultural policies and practices just as effectively as by such coercive state mechanisms as the police and the army. To challenge the dominant order, oppressed groups need to come to an understanding of themselves, their past and their social and political rights. They need to do this by creating an inclusive, counter–hegemonic culture. In other words, a struggle has to be waged in the cultural arena as well as in the political arena.

In my view, the Gramscian concept of hegemony is useful for us African people living in Canada. I want to suggest that we challenge the hegemonic "umbrella" by constructing a counter-hegemonic culture in The School. We can do this, in part, through insisting on the creation and utilisation of an inclusive curriculum which enables US to read about US, speak about US, hear our own words in what is taught to children; not just *our* children, but all children. Again, here is a point made by Gramsci about the emergence of a new trans-formative cultural vision, a new potential "hegemony"created from below, which is useful for our discussion. He writes:

> ... it must be stressed that the political development of the concept of hegemony represents a great philosophical advance as well as a politico-practical one. For it necessarily supposes an intellectual unity and an ethic in conformity with a conception of reality that has gone beyond common sense and has become, if only within narrow limits, a critical conception (Gramsci: 1971:334).

I am, of course, suggesting a marriage between theory and praxis: a step taken theoretically that has a matching step made in the practical realm of 'the real,' in this case, The School. We understand, theoretically and philosophically, the need to have wholeness in The School's curriculum. It is not only African Canadian children who get cheated by a curriculum in which they are not included. All children suffer from this distorted interpretation of history. Clearly, a curriculum which adequately includes African peoples would enhance the intellectual understanding of all children who participate in the educational process. This is simple common sense, requiring no large-scale treatise. However, with the umbrella principle in full operation, it is necessary for us, as African Canadian intellectuals, to spell out the problems for our children and for all children that are created by a one-dimensional curriculum. I am speaking here of history, but there is a need to look at the entire school curriculum with this eye.

Children are in the process of 'becoming.' If we accept this, we understand that to facilitate that process, education and educators have a responsibility to provide whole concepts and not partial concepts, whole 'stories' and not one-dimensional 'stories,' whole history and not partial history. Again, I refer to Gramsci:

> ... man's nature is 'history' (and in this sense, history equals spirit, the nature of man is the spirit), if history is given the meaning of 'becoming' in a *concordia discors* which does not destroy unity but contains within itself grounds for a possible unity . Therefore 'human nature' is not to be found in any one particular man but in the whole history of mankind (and the fact that we naturally use the word 'kind' is significant), while in each single individual are found characteristics made distinct through their difference from the characteristics of other individuals. The concept of 'spirit' in traditional philosophy and the concept of 'human nature' in biology also, should be defined as scientific utopias which are substitutes for the greater utopia 'human nature' sought for in God (and in man, the son of God), and which indicate the travail of history, rational and emotional hopes, etc. It is true, of course, that the religions which preached the equality of men as the sons of God, as well as those philosophies which affirmed man's equality on the basis of his reasoning faculty, were the expressions of complex revolutionary movements (the transformation of the classical world, the transformation of the medieval world), and that these forged the strongest links in the chain of historical development (Gramsci:1987:80).

We must forgive Gramsci for his use of the words "man" and "men" to signify human beings, writing as he was, in the times that he lived. We move beyond that, however, to hear the ways in which his words resonate with the business of history and epistemology and pedagogy. The historical development of peoples of the world, their differences, their similarities, their relationships with each other over time, are important conceptual understandings to which all children need access.

To break this down into what my Antiguan language calls "common-a-garden talk": in order not to repeat historical mistakes, historical atrocities, historical oppression, historical

crimes of peoples' inhumanity to other peoples, it is important for children to understand the rhythm of world historical
events. It is necessary therefore, for children to understand
why Europe carved up Africa. The spread and greed of European capitalism, driving Europeans to employ that inevitable
tentacle: imperialism, complete with the criminal activity of
annexing others' land, people and resources — all of this will
be understood by children if it is taught with an enlightened,
humanistic commitment to historical truth.

It is necessary also, for children to know that Africans
resisted their domination, spawning several generals onto the
world stage, embodied in persons like Queen Nzinga of
Angola, who spearheaded her army against the invading
Portuguese; the market women of Nigeria who waged 'The
Women's War' against British colonial government agents
(Prince and Taylor, forthcoming); and Chaka, king of the
Zulu, who received the British with outrage, coupled with
brilliant and effective tactics of war and resistance against his
people's domination. It is similarly important for children in
Canada to know that African people's resistance to their
enslavement in Jamaica brought the first large numbers of
Africans to Nova Scotia (James, 1996).

The list is never-ending. So much truth is clouded in the
umbrella's smothering hegemonic weave, that to redefine it,
to re-weave it, requires the skill and dexterity of an Antiguan
patchwork-maker. I speak here, not of multi-cultural 'ethnic'
demonstrations, but rather, of a conscious, conscientious
inclusive curriculum. The Antiguan patchwork does not ghet-
toise any piece of fabric, relegating it to an obscure corner,
but rather, ensures that all pieces of fabric have full display,
because they are all parts of the whole design.

This kind of story-making, this kind of wholeness of history, would, in fact, be liberating for all of us in Canadian society. For we would see ourselves adequately portrayed in the
fabric of society. The careful logic with which the Antiguan
patchwork is created, would be represented by the epistemo-
logical underpinnings of the curriculum. The pedagogical

method is the enabling mechanism, much like the thread and the border which hold the patchwork together.

Sometimes, the Black–History–Month–Kit makes me shake with 'fear and trembling,' afraid for us all as human beings. I have listened to distortions of Martin Luther King as an icon of all that we need to do, hear and say. I watch Malcolm X ignored by the status quo, because of his early rhetoric, taken out of its historical context and detached from his later and much more dangerous political theory that understood class consciousness to be an all–race issue. The "danger" in this latter theoretical position is that it has the capacity of uniting the under–classes of American (and Canadian) society. The children need to be taught about King, Malcolm, Mahatma Ghandi, Fidel Castro and Che Geuvara in the same breath, representing as they do, different responses to the same oppression. Understanding these political theorists and political actors, could have far-reaching implications for all children. The decision about what constitutes a hero or heroine and how he or she is interpreted and presented to children, is again made through the lens of the dominant group, operating out of the powerful position of having control over the fabric of the umbrella. Hence, the librarian could dare to suggest that an Anansi story would be more acceptable to the children than a story set in nineteenth century Antigua. Even Black History Month receives censor-ship, for its truth is not always palatable to the dominant group. Martin Luther King is presented as a hero and Malcolm X is not. Taken to its logical conclusion, this makes a parody of the whole notion of "Black History."

Under the umbrella, groups of people who get to be called "minorities" experience the 'rain' of life with damp shoulders, soaking wet feet and straw hats which leak water onto their faces. Still struggling to understand why they should open their mouths and sing "Oh Canada," members of these groups find themselves vilified for daring to say that they have difficulty singing the song.

One day, I overheard a white child sing "Oh Canada, we stand on God for thee" instead of "We stand on guard for thee." I smiled inwardly. I have never forgotten that childish voice, raised in a high-pitched treble, reaffirming what we, springing as we do, from Fanon's hordes of hungry masses, experience as reality (Fanon:1963). For to deny people their real place in historical recounting, in story-making, is indeed to "stand on God" in the name of country.

I am reminded of the child's voice, too, whenever I hear adult voices saying, "If you don't like it here, then leave." Usually, these voices are suggesting that if what people see in the weave of the umbrella is not to their liking, they ought to go back to "wherever they came from." For history = the history of the dominant group and African Canadian people ought to be grateful for the twenty-eight day crumbs. Historical distortion and exclusion are responsible for some people thinking that "here" is their preserve. I have never heard First Nations peoples ask anyone to leave; not even their oppressors, let alone other oppressed groups in the society.

Sometimes, the "crumbs" (Black History Month activities) are so confusing that the children themselves question their authenticity. Once as I was being introduced and waited for my turn to speak, a white teacher explained that Black people were taking this time to praise their kings and queens, their heroes and heroines. "They want their children to have a sense of Black pride," she said.

One bright little, Black girl raised her hand and asked, "What is Black Pride?" I was so glad that she had asked the question that I wanted to give her what Antiguans call "a big hug-up." She had given me an opening with which to dispense with my introduction without insulting the teacher. I had no intention of speaking about Black pride. In fact, I was going to tell the children an Anansi story from Bolans Village, Antigua. This particular story had been one of my early lessons in fractions, on being fair, about having integrity and a whole host of things. None of these things were, however, about 'Black pride.' I introduced to those little children, epistemology, African cosmology — their way of seeing. But at no point and at no time did I speak of this nebulous thing called 'Black pride.'

I do not by any means, wish to deny kings and queens their place in history. We have indeed had our share of these high-ranking people. But they were unlikely to have been the source from which we all sprung. Further, what kind of class consciousness is it to teach children that to be somebody, one had to have been descended from a king and/or a queen?

These things need to be taught, not as isolated incidents in Black Heritage classes and Black History Months, distorted as icons of something called 'Black pride.' Rather, they need to be taught as parts of a whole, parts of world history. In Gramscian terms, "links in the chain of historical development." For that is what they are indeed: "links in the chain of historical development." When my daughter dared to ask for this interpretation of her people to be included for intellectual balance, her OAC history teacher referred to historians who wrote of such things as "a few quacks." The African experience as one of the "links in the chain of historical development" was not, in his view, a historical truth. This truth will never surface in ghettoised Black-History-Month-Kits, just as it will not surface in the kind of curriculum which refers to Africans in the New World simply as 'the slaves.'

This brings me to a discussion of how the teaching of distorted history, or history isolated into a series of interpreted pieces of information can effectively distort a peoples' whole existence. I refer to that notion of 'the slaves.' It is the non-inclusive curriculum which relegates African peoples in the New World to the category of 'the slaves.' Gone is their Africanness, gone is their cultural persona, gone is their rootedness in African soil and African race definition. Gone. All gone into the great void of 'the slaves.' For without a world historical perspective, the definition of these uprooted people is left to the interpreted piece of information that describes them only in terms of their relation to their oppressors. They were enslaved by the white planter class in the New World, and thus they are defined as 'the slaves.' Saying that they had been the children of kings and queens does not wipe out the words: 'the slaves.' Historical truth alone will do that. An inclusive curriculum, dedicated to exploring the broad spectrum of world events, would of necessity, continuously refer to African peoples as what and who they were and are: African peoples. It was only to their oppressors that they were 'the slaves.' To themselves, they were and are people, from whence they had come, Africa.

I refer often in my work and in my public speaking, to my Bolans–Village–Antigua–ancestry. It is my closest ancestral memory, my *particular*, although Africa is a strong part of my collective memory. I mention it now in order to enhance and enliven the discussion of this business of 'the slaves' versus African peoples. For I recall that Bolans villagers refer to their ancestors as '(their) generation' and to the period of the enslavement of African peoples as 'slavery days.' Never have I heard them speak of 'the slaves.' This is 'agency' taken to an incredible, empowering degree.

Black–History–Month–kits simply cannot redress these historical distortions in one fell swoop. Twenty–eight days is not sufficient time to rewrite history. Hence, psychological band-aids of stories of kings and queens and stories of the slaves' journey on the Underground Railroad to freedom in Canada will fail every time to empower our children. Pretending that Black History Month is able to redress historical atrocities and provide succor for the souls of African Canadians, is an act that The School can no longer be allowed to practice. This is simply another multicultural myth which gives validity to the hegemony represented by the dominant weave of the umbrella. I am reminded always that the Act For The Preservation and Enhancement of Multiculturalism in Canada, passed in 1988 contains within it, a clause which states:

encourage and assist the social, cultural, economic, and

political institutions of Canada to be both respectful and inclusive of Canada's multicultural character.

We are not, after all, asking for anything extraordinary. It is our due. It is also common sense and wisdom.

Frantz Fanon made this point in *The Wretched of The Earth* in 1963. Like Gramsci, Fanon uses male-biased language, but his political analysis has significance for us. He reminded us that the way forward is merely a question of

> ... starting a new history of Man, a history which will have regard to the sometimes prodigious theses which Europe has put forward, but which will also not forget Europe's crimes, of which the most horrible was committed in the heart of man, and consisted of the pathological tearing apart of his functions and the crumbling away of his unity. And in the framework of the collectivity there were the differentiations, the stratification, and the blood-thirsty tensions fed by classes; and finally, on the immense scale of humanity, there were racial hatreds, slavery, exploitation, and above all the bloodless genocide which consisted in the setting aside of fifteen thousand millions of men. (Fanon:1963:313)

It is a fitting note on which to end.

FOOTNOTE:

1 Anansi is a trickster spider who is the centre of stories which African people brought to the Caribbean with them from West Africa. There is much irony for me therefore, in an African person being offered a collection of Anansi stories, collected by someone who is European. The issue of appropriation of culture, coupled with the underlying insult of denying the validity of my children's books, makes this incident stand out in my personal struggle for a more inclusive cultural vision.

REFERENCES

Gramsci, Antonio (1971). *Selections from the Prison Notebooks.* International Publishers, New York.

Gramsci, Antonio (1987). *The Modern Prince & Other Writings.* International Publishers, New York.

James, Carl E. (1996). "Challenging the Distorted Images: The Case of African Canadian Youth." In C. Green: *The Urban Challenge and the Black Diaspora.* New York State University Press, New York.

Fanon, Franz (1963). *The Wretched of the Earth.* Grove Press Inc., New York.

Chapter Eleven

KEEPING WATCH OVER OUR CHILDREN
The Role of African Canadian Parents on the Education Team

Keren Brathwaite

Whenever African Canadian[1] parents speak, in public forums or in personal conversations, one major topic that engages us is the education of African Canadian students. This topic is discussed beyond the parameters of personal interest in the accomplishments of one's own children; focus is more often on the performance of the African Canadian student collectivity — a group which has developed the profile of academic under-achievement in school systems which generally do not support their psychological well being nor their aspirations.

The various studies and research documents on African Canadian students, as well as their lived experiences in the classrooms of the nation, confirm that the education system is a problem for our students. Time and time again, Black parents have been publicly voicing their dissatisfaction with the outcomes of their children's schooling, most recently to Ontario's

Royal Commission on Learning (1994) and to George Dei in his research study of drop–outs (October 1995). It is reasonable to assume, therefore, that African Canadian parents would wish to be involved in their children's education, and many have done so in a variety of formal and informal ways for a very long time.

That the value of parent involvement in education is now gaining more recognition among parents, educators and governments in Canada is significant,[2] but for African Canadian parents and community, educational involvement has now assumed the status of an imperative which we must obey if we hope to improve our students' school experiences and counter the trend of poor performance among them. If the drop–out rate from school of African Canadian students is to decline and their achievement levels increase, if the practice of streaming them (by whatever name) into dead–end programmes and futures is to be arrested, if we believe that their potential is unlimited (which we do believe), then African Canadian parents must become active, serious and recognised participants in their education. African Canadian parents must be a welcome partner on the education team and must continue to push for deep systemic change in education. The experience of many parents, however, is that schools are unwelcoming and problematic institutions which tend to keep parents at a distance rather than include them as partners, in spite of the current rhetoric of parent involvement. Many parents have penetrated the pretences of the system, uncovering what has historically been beneath it: unequal education and unequal results for African Canadian students.

I will argue in this chapter that for the majority of African Canadian students to achieve success in the schools (and also in the colleges and universities), their parents, families and community will have to provide a strong support system for them. They will have to advocate on their behalf on the education team and at a political level for an education that is of good quality, relevant, inclusive of our local and global reality and anti–racist. Many parents and organizations in the

Black community have already been deeply involved in providing this support to our students, but our role has not been fully appreciated by education institutions and professional educators, nor has it produced the results our students need. It is important therefore that the African Canadian presence is felt on the education team. We need to serve as "guardian angels" for our children and to keep watch over them. Who is better placed than parents (in a moral sense) to assume this role?

Two stories which stand out among the many I have heard or witnessed will help to advance my argument of the importance of parent involvement in education as it relates to African Canadians.

A teacher in 1983 recounted to me her experience with a Black student and her mother from the Caribbean. The teacher assessed the student in her Grade 5 class as unable to read and reported this perceived deficiency to the mother of the student. The mother was astounded at the teacher's assessment. How could this be so? The girl read fluently at home and the mother would prove this to the teacher. So she brought a Bible to the school, and to the amazement of the teacher, the student read fluently from it. The teacher recalled later that she learned a very important lesson that day about the role of parents in education. She told me that parent and teacher often see students from different perspectives, and I confided to her that with Black children in Canada there was often a gap (and sometimes a chasm) between the teacher's and the parent's perception and understanding of them.

The second story I heard on the CBC Metro Morning on October 18, 1995 when Andy Barrie, host of this radio show, played a recorded message of a woman's reaction to the Million Man March on Washington on October 16, 1995. On tape this parent spoke about her experience on a school trip with her child's class to Pioneer Village, Ontario. When she commented to the teacher that "it was a shame no Black pioneers were included," the teacher responded, "Why the hell should there be? There were no Black pioneers."

The parent held her ground, arguing that "Blacks had made a contribution to Canada but this is not taught in schools." The teacher retorted that "what Blacks did was so minimal it was not worth mentioning." The parent ended her taped message with the words: "It is ignorant teachers like this who are teaching our children." The host of CBC Metro Morning expressed shock at the behaviour and views of this teacher and advised him to take a journey into areas of Black history.

These two stories among the many that Black parents tell indicate a problem in the education of African Canadian students which has been long studied and discussed in the Black community and among educators and institutions.[3] However, the amelioration of this critical condition has been moving at a slow pace, to the extent that many students and members of the Black community have been losing their patience with the status quo. The public institutions in which our students study in preparation for their future have not up to this time made the significant changes which are necessary for nurturing their success. Numerous recommendations have been made to educational institutions in Ontario over many years but they have not borne much fruit in the daily experiences of Black students. It is mainly in community programmes (Saturday schools, parent organisations, tutoring programmes, Black Heritage classes, etc.) that there is direct intervention/action aimed at improving the quality of Black students' educational experiences and their academic performance as well.

As Ron Edmonds has said, "We know more than we need to know" about Black students.[4] This educator was commenting on Black students in the United States, where the National Association of Black School Educators (NABSE) has pronounced that this body of students is in a state of danger from which they need to be saved. Ron Edmonds' words are true for Canada as well. However, knowledge has not provided the necessary cure for what ails Black students — and also their parents and community. And one needs to emphasise that the malady is in the system rather than in the students who have to develop a variety of techniques for survival.[5]

The above stories (among the many Black parents tell and live) are at the heart of my argument. They underline the urgent need for a defined place for African Canadian parents on the education team — *a vantage point from which we can keep watch over our children* and fill in the blanks and correct the distortions resulting from bias, racial prejudice and stereotyping which are often present on the institutional education team. African Canadian parents need to become vocal members of their children's education team to help neutralise the low expectations and negative stereotypes which some educators hold of Black students and to help place on the agenda of the schools an appreciation of the history, culture, experience and complex global reality of Black people.

In *keeping watch over our children*, the *voice* of African Canadian parents *must* be listened to and we must be recognised as advocates of Black students and their need of a good education built on foundations of anti-racism and justice. And, most importantly, there must be a full acknowledgement by professional educators that parents are the *first educators* of their children. This is not an empty cliché. As parents, we teach our children in the home and community before they enter formal schooling. Several Black parents I know taught their children to read before they registered them in school. For some of these children, their progress in reading was arrested on their entry to a Canadian Kindergarten. Further, parents continue to be *co-educators* of their children, and in this area, many Black parents are making a creditable but often unacknowledged contribution.

The education team might therefore be viewed as having both a formal and an informal component. On the informal level, parents in general and Black parents in particular, assume their role by nurturing, guiding and teaching their children. However, on the formal side of education Black parents as well as other parents also need to assume a stronger role as acknowledged, respected and consulted partners. For

Black parents, this presence is critical due to the documented common problems many Black students face in the school system. In another article I have referred to these problems as a "Canadian dilemma,"[6] and George Dei has used the word "crisis" for this phenomenon.[7]

On the formal team, therefore, Black parents should be considered *advocates* for their children, but for effective advocacy, training and support are essential. Some of this necessary training has been provided in the Black community in many forums and workshops which are sponsored by groups such as the Canadian Alliance of Black Educators (CABE), the Black Secretariat, the African Heritage Educators' Network (AHEN), the Organisation of Parents of Black Children (OPBC) and others. OPBC, for example, runs workshops on various aspects of parent education, including developing skills to assist children in the home and preparation for successful parent–teacher interviews. Its monthly programmes since 1980 have provided parents with information and advice on new policies and directions in education. In October 1995, to give an example, the topic of discussion was A Curriculum for All Students and reporting to parents.

Our Presence on the Education Team: Personal Reflections

The role African Canadian parents ought to assume in education has engaged my attention for many years — ever since I enrolled my two children in Kindergarten in Toronto in the mid–1970s. This experience has taught me more than academic research could that our involvement as parents is essential to our students' *success* in Canadian schools, by whatever yard-stick *success* is measured. For me, success would include the students' academic achievement, preparation for their future careers, participation in various aspects of the life of the school and also participation in their community, assumption of leadership in the student body, retention of pride in their racial and cultural identity, development of confidence and a healthy self–concept, nurturing their aspirations for the future with the expectation of reaching their goals, and most importantly, inculcating in them a sense of hope and belonging.

These ingredients of success will have to be pursued in another context, but it is necessary to mention them here as one parent/educator's measures of success which needed to be expressed to those who had the institutional responsibility for educating her children. In general, "success" for an African Canadian parent would require an anti-racist, inclusive curriculum, a teacher with high and non-stereotypical expectations of a Black student, and a willingness to communicate with the student and the home in a manner that would inspire trust and confidence and help motivate the student to perform to the unlimited level of his/her potential. This notion of success would assume that the education system cares about educating all of the students entrusted to its care, including Black students.

Our presence on the education team is therefore a requisite for raising such issues and expectations concerning our students. Furthermore, since the student is central to the education process and the reason for its existence, our discussions should also include the student as an active participant. Lamentably, African Canadian students as a group, have been pushed in large numbers to the sidelines of education, as they themselves complained to Stephen Lewis in 1992 and to the Consultative Committee on the Education of Black Students in 1988. They have also expressed this in the various Black Students' Conferences in the Toronto Board of Education from 1989–1995. The "sidelining" has been confirmed by Carl James' (1990) research and most recently in George Dei's (1995) study: *Drop Out or Push Out? The Dynamics of Black Students' Disengagement From School.* Dei shows that African Canadian students are well represented in the drop-out statistics of schools. Their disproportionate number is a troubling reminder of how education institutions have failed our people and confirms the necessity that we constantly monitor them in the interest of the group of children for whom we are personally, collectively and morally responsible.

My experience of guiding my children through Ontario's education system (which I once described as a *maze*) demonstrated to me how powerless parents are generally made to feel in their relationship with the schools. I am a witness to the confusion the system generates about the parents' role. This confusion has been experienced by most parents (of different races and social classes) with whom I have interacted over many years of working in local school PTAs, Area Parent Councils, Heritage Programmes, Parent Liaison Committees, Parent Conference Planning Committees, School Staffing Committees, Principal Hiring Committees and in the Organisation of Parents of Black Children which we established in May 1980 in the Black community to be an advocacy group for Black parents and our students.

My experience has been that when parents organize to change the power relations between the educators and institutions versus the parents and community, there is more often than not much tension generated between the home and school. Dehli in her study on *Parent Activism and School Reform in Toronto* (1994) examines some of the challenges of school — community relations with "attention to the politics of parental participation in schools."[8] The causes of the tension, however, have not been sufficiently studied to date, probably because its impact has not been fully appreciated in the troubling relations between school and home/parents/ community. Further investigation is needed in this area.

The power dynamics of parent/community–school relations is strongly felt, but its impact has not to date been fully assessed in the schooling experiences of African Canadian students. In many workshops over the years, Black parents have spoken of some attitudes and practices in the schools which tend to limit their involvement: unwelcoming attitudes among some personnel, as well as patronising or condescending ways. Some Black parents have decided not to become members of their local school P.T.A.s, since they feel their presence and their concerns are not sufficiently recognised by not only the school administration, but also by other parents who may consider themselves to be in a position of privilege. Many Black parents, however, have sustained interest in their local groups for the good of their own children. Others involve themselves in organisations like Organisation of Parents of Black Children (OPBC) which they feel provide a more comfortable environment in which to discuss troubling education issues. My experience, however, is that parents across class and racial lines generally experience some difficulty when they question the system about policy and practices. Some of these frustrations Dehli analyses in her work.

African Canadian Parents' Brand of Educational Engagement: Historical and Contemporary

African Canadian parents and community have been addressing the theme of this chapter for many decades, dating back to the nineteenth century and earlier. Historically, we have not been silent spectators to the drama of Black students' education which has invariably been a challenge to mainstream institutions in Canada, as well as in England and the United States.[9]

Before Confederation in Canada, Black people had good reason to be concerned about racist practices in education. The Confederation in 1867 changed nothing in this respect. Education has continued to be a dilemma for us as a people. There is now a significant body of research documents and other writings about the schooling experiences of Black students, which indicate much agreement between researcher and researcher, study and study, between what Black parents and students tell in the many education forums inside and outside the Black community in Toronto and other urban centres. There is a disturbing similar resonance in the voices of Black parents, students, and community in Cole Harbour, Nova Scotia, and the voices of Black parents, students and community in Scarborough, Ontario and Côte des Neiges, Quebec. The resonance is also similar in Hamilton, Ontario, and in the voices of past generations and the present generation of Black parents, a few of whom now mistakenly believe that their complaints and their fears are new.

I have observed over 15 years in the Organisation of Parents of Black Children (OPBC) that some African Canadian parents who at one time were embarrassed to disclose their or their children's difficulties in the system became more comfortable in the company of other parents in voicing their displeasure with the school system. Some parents have confessed that until they had the good sense to communicate with others and join an organisation working for educational improvements for Black students, they were isolated in their local school, believing that it was only their child who was experiencing racial discrimination; it was only they who had a *problem*. Little wonder that in Black community organising, focus on education is a centrepiece and has been so for a long time. In the Black community, there are more workshops, conferences, forums, discussions of education than any other topic, including the justice system and Black youth which is another subject of much concern; this pre-occupation with education has remained with us as a people for a very long time.

Ever since I have been involved in education in Canada, as a parent and as an educator for more than two decades, the Black community and parents have been vocal critics of the formal education system represented by various boards of education, separate and public, and by the Ministry of Education and the schools under their jurisdiction. The universities and colleges have also come under our scrutiny, and have been found deficient, but more research into the inequities affecting our students at this level needs to be carried out.

It must be noted, however, that we have been much more than critics of the system. The documentation referred to earlier demonstrates that the Black community, Black parents, students and educators included, has made a major contribution to critical pedagogy and other education themes over many years: anti-racism and equity in education, streaming and de-streaming, inclusive curriculum, the Heritage/International Languages Programme, teacher education, development of anti-violence policies by the Ministry of Education and school boards, Black-focused schools, and, very importantly, the role of parents and community in education.

Black people have worked not only in their own community for educational change, but have also worked in collaboration with educational institutions, governments and other groups of parents, hoping to realise benefits for our collective group of students. The Black Educators' Working Group in Ontario, chaired by Councillor Bev Salmon, is an example of a lobby group of educators which is currently doing collaborative work with the Ministry of Education and Training while being at the same time critical of the system's delivery of education to Black students. This group contains parent/educator/community membership.

The Black Liaison Committee also worked in collaboration with the Toronto Board in the 1970s with the goal of improving Black students' schooling; their work maintained a critical approach to the system. The Black Education Project of the late 1960s and 70s, however, took a more distant approach to the system, administering its own programmes of education in tutoring and counselling to supplement that of the school. These are examples of different approaches to working for needed change in the lives and schooling of Black students, but they attest to my conclusion that the Black community, including parents, has been one of the communities most vigorously engaged in education activism — and for good reason.[10] Since the level of our students' alienation is very intense — from Kindergarten to Graduate School — then keeping watch over them is one way of protecting them from perils to which many of them will fall victim.

The foregoing considerations lead to the questions: What have been the results of Black parents and community long-standing engagement in education? And why is there a myth that Black parents are not involved in education still circulating among some teachers and school administrators, and disturbingly among some Black educators as well (as I have heard some express in Black forums)? And who has benefitted from our work in education? The answer to the last question is critical, for we need to know why Black students' school experiences and academic performance have not improved significantly over many years to reflect the great mass of time, energy and ideas their parents and community have given to the formal education system.

If we cannot achieve the *change* for which we have struggled and worked, lobbied and generated new ideas, then we need to re-evaluate our past approaches to education institutions. It would seem to me that it is time to reflect again on the role African Canadian parents (and community) should assume in education. What is our place? What is our role? And with due consideration to the fact that education is both formal and informal, community-based as well as school-based, and that the formal system is the one which is wreaking havoc in our students' lives, then it would seem that we need a new definition of the place African Canadian parents ought to occupy on the school's education team.

This chapter proposes, in the light of all we know and agonise about in Black students' education, that we as *Black parents will need to keep watch over our children* from the close range of the education team, on which our presence is essential for protecting them from the malady that is troubling the group: the fall-out from racism and racist foundations of education. Since the education system has thus far proved itself (as a system) as incapable of knowing, nurturing and instructing our collectivity of students, we have to make new demands. We should insist on having input on the school's *formal team*, making it a precondition for our participation in the system. By *participation* I mean our continuing to register our own children in the public school system. We should participate under the terms of a *partner*, not as a *customer*, the term Ontario's new Minister of Education and Training, Mr. Snobelen, recently assigned to parents (*The Toronto Star*, Sept.

13, 1995). The terms of our involvement should be drawn up by us, with the proviso that we will withdraw if our students' needs are not met within the system.

Too long have we operated under terms we knew would be obstacles to our children's success. It is time we propose to design a partnership which will either truly draw us in, or allow us the choice to develop schools that will embrace our students' total being — their total complexity within a rational context that makes good sense to us. The development of such schools is under much discussion in the Black community at the present time, and is supported by George Dei (1995), Vernon Farrell (1994) and other educators who view the "African–centred" alternative as one which should yield good benefits for many of our students.

The active participation of African Canadians in education, to which I have been alluding, is strongly supported by Agnes Calliste's research (see footnote 9). Enid Lee, myself and others who presented on education in the Association of African Studies Conference in Toronto, November, 1994 focused on this community connection as a cornerstone in Black students' development. The community forums on education at this conference, organised by George Dei and others, were considered by many as the *soul* of the conference. Lee's paper "On Any Given Saturday" analysed the active work of the Black community, including parents, in programmes to support Black students: tutoring, counselling and teaching material which was not part of the regular school curriculum, etc. She made reference to CABE's (Canadian Alliance of Black Educators) Saturday Tutorial Programme, the African Heritage Educators' Network (North York) Saturday Classes, the programme of OPBC and the Scarborough Black Education Committee, etc. The Black Education Project of the 1960s and 70s as well as the work of the Black Secretariat were part of the discussion of these workshops. The model of *Black Focused Schools* surfaced in many deliberations at that conference. In addition, it was the topic of one of the community workshops where the meaning and relevance of these schools and the fears they generate were aired with the passion this topic invariably stirs up among Black people.

The work of the Organisation of Parents of Black Children (OPBC) and the Black Secretariat received much attention in these workshops. If we focus on the life of OPBC since its inception in 1980, those of us who are founding members of this organisation and have been active in it since, are witness to the persistence of Black parents' disenchantment with the education system. It was our disillusionment which made necessary the formation of this organisation in the first place, and it is our critical voices which continue to enliven it and sustain it as the group struggles for real change in education. (OPBC Tenth Anniversary document, June 9, 1990).

The work of OPBC can serve to illustrate the timbre of the voice of parents advocating on behalf of their children. A review of the various submissions by this organisation to the Toronto Board of Education, 1979–1995, Ontario Ministry of Education and the recent Royal Commission on Learning, 1994, should help us locate the persistent themes in Black parents' discussion of the education system and our children's place in it. Many of these themes have become identified with the voice of Black parents and community advocates for change. To reiterate, Black parents and community have been engaged in a struggle for educational change since the nineteenth century and earlier, but the struggle though of long duration has not produced results which we anticipated. However, the point cannot be over–emphasized that we have been active participants. Let us consider two of the submissions from OPBC as examples of the critical work of Black parents: one to the Toronto Board of Education in November, 1985, and the second to the Royal Commission on Learning June, 1994.

On November 28, 1985, a group of parents from the OPBC met with the Associate Director of Programs of Toronto Board of Education to discuss our continuing concerns about the education our children receive. This discussion later became part of an internal report which the Board reviewed on March 6, 1986. OPBC's statement of complaints included the following:

- the high drop–out rate [among Black students]
- lack of Black teachers as role models in the system
- the persistent 'invisibility' of Black Studies and Black History within the curriculum
- the present ignorance of teachers about Black culture and the history of Blacks in Canada
- the over–representation of Black students in non–academic schools
- the low level of teacher expectations of Black student achievement
- the crucial question of curriculum implementation
- *the incomprehensible school system* [Italics mine][11]

The Board Minutes in which the above statement was reported continued: "these wide–ranging concerns indicate the need for a review of the current policy and practice as they affect the education of Black children, in order that the Director of Education and the Board take effective action to deal with these concerns"[12]

It is important to note that this Toronto Board internal report for discussion at a meeting of the elected trustees of the Board was precipitated by a *motion* placed by a member of OPBC, Keren Brathwaite, the writer of this chapter, before the Board's Heritage Languages and Concurrent Programmes Consultative Committee (HELACON). The motion stated:

That the Director of Education establish a consultative committee on the education of Black students in Toronto schools with the following terms of reference:

(1) To examine, in the light of current Board policy and practice, the concerns expressed by HELACON and the Organisation of Parents of Black Children about the education of Black students in Toronto schools.

(2) To recommend to the Director and to the Board appropriate action.[13]

The above is one of many of our proposals to a Board of Education, but it is significant that this proposal to the Toronto Board to establish a consultative committee bore fruit in the *Report on the Education of Black Students in Toronto Schools*, 1988, a study which contains 58 recommendations aimed at improving education experiences and outcomes for our students. However, from 1988 to 1995 not enough measurable improvement has taken place among our students as a group.[14] It is apparent from the research that the collective condition of our students has deteriorated rather than improved in recent years, though individual Black students have excelled beyond expectations, as is often reported in our community newspapers. Individual successes of our students are laudable, but when the group continues to lag behind, we believe it is a sign of deep systemic problems which have been troubling both the parents and the students. Many parents have been at the centre of questioning and challenging the education system over these systemic conditions which have a negative influence on Black students' schooling. Often parents whose children are performing well in school who express their views in OPBC meetings, will almost apologise out of empathy with the many who expose their children's education scars. "But for the grace of God, there go I" is a sentiment not restricted to the Church.

It is important to stress that the critical themes which Black parents frequently discuss in groups such as OPBC, the Scarborough Black Education Organisation, in community forums and in one–on–one conversations I have been party to, have remained virtually the same for the past 15 years and also bear much resemblance to many of the concerns of Black people in Upper Canada (Ontario) more than a century ago.[15] The concerns about racism, equity, drop–outs, representation in curriculum and staffing, teacher expectations, setting up our own institutions and the role of parents and community in education remain persistent. OPBC's oral and written submissions to the Royal Commission on Learning (Ontario, 1994) is another echo of the concerns which parents presented nearly a decade earlier to the Toronto Board of Education.

In its June 6, 1994 written submission, OPBC drew the attention of the Royal Commission on Learning (1994) to the following:

> The school system is a reflection of the larger society in which we live with persistent problems of racism, stereotyping and the lack of equity in all areas. These problems have been discussed and documented over the past several years. It must therefore be emphasised that racism is endemic within the system of education and for us it is the major obstacle. Thus new reports, however well-meaning, will not bring about change without firm and decisive action.[16]

Here OPBC was focusing the attention of the Commission on the impact of race on the schooling of African Canadian students and pleading for *action* rather than recommendations to arrest the situation that was well known and well studied.

OPBC's written submission was preceded by an oral presentation given by 5 members representing the organisation which was invited to meet with the Commission on October 13, 1993. It is noteworthy that there was much harmony between OPBC's presentation and those of the Black Educators' Working Group, the Canadian Alliance of Black Educators and the Jamaican Canadian Association which also made their submissions on the same evening. The verbal response which was reported to me as coming from a member of the Commission was a comment on the *passion* of the parents. But *passion* indeed there should be when one's children — (one's future) have been habitually floundering in the school system, many dropping out of it or barely surviving in it. *Passion* pushes the African Canadian community to action vis-à-vis the school system, which this chapter has shown to be a hostile, unwelcoming place for many Black parents and our students. *Passion* sustains our struggle, which for some parents is carried out with almost religious fervour as we confront the burden of failure weighing down the group of children we are parenting. Which other group in Canada would have accepted the unjust conditions that have been impacting on our children's future for so long?

The reference to *new reports* in OPBC's submission is a reminder of the numerous documents, reports and recommendations which have resulted from the study of Black students' alienation at all levels of the education system that have remained ignored and unimplemented — "gathering dust on shelves," as the expression goes in the Black community. The reference to new reports alludes to what the system has failed to deliver to our students. *Implementation* is a word which often punctuates our discussion of education. *Implementation* and *accountability* we use as measures for the *progress* some educators and boards have attempted to lure us into believing has taken place — because some *words/recommendations* are written on paper about our cause.

The 22 pages of submission from OPBC comments on areas which are troubling in Black students' education:

- Effects of racism, labelling and stereotyping
- Curriculum Concerns
- Parent Involvement in Education
- Education Governance–Accountability
- Our Vision and Conclusion.

Our discussion is followed by 34 recommendations, 9 of which deal with School/Parent/Community Partnerships. They are:

- Schools should hold regular open forums for students to discuss their problems with school staff and parent groups.
- *Schools must include and involve parents in meaningful ways. Parents must be involved in the decision-making processes at the local school level, the Board of Education level and the Ministry of Education.*
- One member of the teaching staff in every school should

be appointed as a community liaison person.

- *Parents must be involved in the evaluation of what is good quality education in the schools.*
- *Clearly defined school procedures should be instituted to allow parents and students input in the evaluation of teachers/administrators.*[17] [Italics mine].

The place for parents which our recommendations delineated gained some profile in the Report of the Royal Commission (1994) where the role of the community and parents as partners in education is seen as an essential alliance referred to as the first engine "to drive the momentum of large-scale reform."[18] The Commission went on to recommend the formation of School Community Councils, which would include parent participation, "responsible for bringing appropriate resources into the school to assume some of the obligations teachers now bear alone."[19] Recommendations 108–111 formulate the function and design of the Councils which would assume an administration function in the school.

For African Canadian parents and educators, there is now much concern over the formation of these Councils, (by whatever name). The concept has been discussed by some parents and educators in our community who see accountability in education and lack of implementation of equity policies as a major hurdle to achieving our goals. Who will sit on these Councils? How will they be selected? How representative will these Councils be of the student body, parents and community of the school? What powers will they have to influence the direction of the schools: What is taught? What are the priorities? These questions some of us have been discussing with the lone African Canadian representative on Ontario's Parent Council who conveyed our concern about representation to those charged with drawing up the guide-lines for the operation of School-community Councils which should have a role in the schools from 1996.

These questions could lead to critical examination of the design and mandate of the council. The legislation of Ontario's first Parent Council in September 1993 was considered a bold, political act by some, but for many of us who had been involved in the vibrant parent movement of the 1980s, it seemed a measure long overdue, that had already been pre-empted by the Toronto Board, for example, whose Parent Council was established earlier in 1992.

What Ought We to do Now, After the Dialogue and the Struggle?

This chapter has cited and commented on examples of African Canadian parents' engagement with the school system, as well as their central place in the historical struggle that Black people in Canada have carried out in the name of education reform for the *saving* of African Canadian students. Ours has been a righteous cause fired by our indignation over a condition which has festered for an unacceptable length of time. When our offsprings do not receive their nurturing in public institutions which we support with our dollars, then if we do not cry out, the stones will.

I have established that as a people we have not been idle, but have expended much energy and hard work on improving the academic performance of African Canadian students. Parents have put commendable effort in the pursuit of our goal of just and equitable treatment for our students. Many Black parents have participated in their children's formal education, even when schools are unwelcoming of our presence (which many are); even when Parent Teacher Associations (PTAs), Area Education Councils and Parent Involvement Committees disregard our agenda items (as many Black parents have complained over the years), or placed our concerns on the low priority list. And if some Black parents stay away from the schools, then so do many other parents from different racial, ethnic and socio-economic groups, yet the results of their general student population are far stronger than our students as the Grade Nine Student Surveys (Toronto Board) have shown over many years.[20]

Yet despite the barriers and the disappointments, the African Canadian community has made and continues to make a remarkable contribution to educational thought and critical pedagogy in Canada, probably because our concerns and fears about education have been so strong that we constantly raise the issues, ask the questions, and make suggestions to institutions in Ontario, Nova Scotia, Quebec and other provinces for arresting a condition that has produced in us a group headache.

Our work has been in the form of projects, interventions, innovations, proposals to education institutions, and much research. We have established independent or co-sponsored tutorial programmes, Saturday schools, parent education seminars, mentoring programmes, Black Education Projects, Each One Teach One support groups, etc., and in our community, some independent private schools have been attracting parents who can afford to pay for a service or who make the necessary sacrifice for what they hope will be academic success for their own children. Private institutions such as Higher Marks, Centre for Achievement, C.A.R.E., and the counselling provided by Goodall's Counselling Service and others have also been well utilised in our community's goal of higher educational attainment for our children. These have been used by many parents to fill the gaps in the offerings of the schools. *Innovations in Black Education* (1994) has analysed the purposes and results of some of the community efforts as well as the institutional initiatives which were designed to enhance Black students' success. Further work is needed on the variety of these programmes and their impact on our students of African heritage. Many believe that our community projects have served as a life-line for many Black youth *disengaged* from school — to use George Dei's term.

What has been our aim in this work which some have pursued with missionary zeal? What has motivated us to remain engaged? Our aim has been to bring about a *change* in formal education systems so that principles like *equity* and *justice* and *anti-racism* in which we believe will be put into practice; that our students' alienation will be lessened and their sense of belonging will be strengthened. We have been pursuing a *change* that we hoped would accomplish for our students more satisfaction than they have had up to this point in their schooling. However, this *change* requires a change in the manner in which the system views our children, how it relates to them and how much it is really interested in educating them. I have been part of this movement for change for over 20 years and the movement is now reflecting on *where we need to go and what we need to do at this time*. What is the next move we should make? Should we be tentative and careful now, or is this perhaps the time to try some bold measures to arrest a chronic condition? We need to ponder seriously these questions and seek answers to them, for the *change* we have been pursuing with much intensity has been eluding us — like a firefly whose glimmer we sometimes see, but it soon disappears.

One of the reasons why the theme of African Canadian parent education engagement has been so important to me is that I have over the years become a constant listener to narratives of frustration, disappointment or despair with the public system which is charged with educating our children. Very few Black parents are satisfied — at least among the many with whom I have been communicating over the years. Few of us are able to share narratives of *success* of our own children, not even among friends and colleagues from the professional class who expected their children to exceed their accomplishments. Some parents I know are so disappointed in their own children's performance that they are embarrassed to disclose what their true situation is. Several educators have confided to me their regret that they did not school their children outside of Canada. In an age when many parents across race, class, language and gender are experiencing various levels of disenchantment with education, the voices of Black people can be distinguished from many other voices in the clarity of our conviction of what is wrong in the system for our students.

To the African Canadian parent who made an appointment with the principal of his son's Grade Six class to complain about the unruly atmosphere in his classroom and his son's need for more challenging work, the principal's response was: "If you don't like things here, why don't you return to Barbados?" Return to *Barbados*, when the majority of these youth were born in Canada! Another parent experienced the humiliation so many have experienced when her son's principal stifled her complaints with his words, "This is my school and I run it the way I like," words with which many of us are familiar, even when they are unspoken.

Such episodes, which are myriad, confirm there is a need for improvement in the school's manner of relating to and communicating with parents in general, and very importantly with African Canadian parents. What are we to do now?

I submit that it is time for us to seriously invoke some alternative ways of educating our children, so that they will be filled not only with knowledge, some of which means mis–education, but that they will truly be *filled*. As parents, it is our duty to help our children remain whole and integrated persons, just as they were when we lovingly held their hands and walked with them to Kindergarten on the first day of school.

If we are not allowed a space on their formal education team from which space we can participate as respected and consulted partners, *then we need to pursue some alternative models of education, including the model of African-centred schools*[21] *in our community* — at least for a time — until the education system demonstrates its capability of dealing justly with our collectivity of African Canadian students. Thus far, our research studies prove that the current system does not know how to educate a significant number of our students — and for these students we are also morally responsible, as I stated earlier. Either we remain on the fringes of the traditional education team with little power to effect change or we locate ourselves where we can make a difference. Either we have a substantial role on the team in the formal education system, or we concentrate more on using the resources in our various communities to help educate those who need a more wholesome, nurturing environment for survival.

It is obvious to me that we now need some Marva Collins Schools[22] and more African–centred pedagogy as Abena Walker[23] employs in Washington, D.C. to help arrest the conditions I have critiqued in this paper. We need to transform some of our *Saturday Schools* into *All Week Schools* and our church basements into *African Canadian Centres of Learning*, for herein might lie some of our children's educational salvation.

DEDICATION

I dedicate this chapter to the memory of the late Lilly Snider, friend and former teacher at McMurrich Public School, with whom in the 1970s and early 80s, I often discussed the education of African Canadian students.

FOOTNOTES:

1. The terms "African Canadians" and "Blacks" are interchangeable in this chapter.

2. See Toronto Board *Final Report of the Work Group on Parental Involvement*. November 1991; Report of the Royal Commission on Learning. *For the Love of Learning*, 1994; *Rethinking Schools*, Spring 1993. Vol. 7, No. 3; The Ontario Parent Council Application Statement, Ontario Ministry of Education, 1993.

3. See A. Calliste "Blacks' Struggle for Education Equity in Nova Scotia." In V. D'Oyley (ed.) *Innovations in Black Education in Canada*. Toronto: Umbrella Press, 1994; W. W. Anderson and R. W. Grant *The New New-comers*. Toronto: Canadian Scholars Press, 1987. First published 1975; G. Dei *Drop Out or Push Out? The Dynamics of Black Students Disengagement from School*. Final report to the Ministry of Education, Toronto, 1995; Toronto Board. *Education of Black Students in Toronto Schools*, 1988; BLAC Report on Education. *Redressing Inequity – Empowering Black Learners*, December 1994. C. E. James "I Don't Want to Talk About It." *Orbit 25*(2). 1994. pp. 26–29.

4. The Ronald Edmonds Summer Academy Document, 1995.

5. P. Solomon *Black Resistance in High School*. New York: State University of New York Press, 1992; Panel discussion with Carl James and Black students at African Studies Association Conference,

Toronto, November 1994.

6. K. Brathwaite "The Black Student and the School: A Canadian Dilemma." In S. W. Chilungu and S. Niang (eds.). *African Continuities/L'Heritage Africain*. Toronto: Terebi 1989, pp. 195–216.

7. G. Dei. Presentation to OPBC on his research on African Canadian Students, May 1995.

8. K. Dehli with Ilda Januario. *Parent Activism and School Reform in Toronto*. October 1994. p. 4.

9. See A. Calliste. "Blacks' Struggle for Education Equity in Nova Scotia." In V. D'Oyley (ed.). *Innovations in Black Education in Canada*. Toronto: Umbrella Press, 1994; F. Case *Racism and National Consciousness*. Toronto: Plowshare Press, 1977; A. Cooper – Presentation to OPBC on The African Canadian Historical Struggles in Education, Feb. 1994; R. W. Winks *The Blacks in Canada: A History*. Yale University Press, 1971; OPBC Papers 1980–1995.

10. See K. Dehli and Ilda Januario *Parent Activisim and School Reform in Toronto* 1994; A Cooper's presentation to OPBC, Feb. 1994 also discussed the Black community's education activism.

11. Toronto Board. *Education of Black Students in Toronto Schools* 1988, pp. 6–7.

12. —— p. 7

13. —— p. 5

14. See Toronto Board of Education *The 1991 Every Student Survey*, Parts 1, 2, 3. Research Services; also Stephen Lewis *Letter to the Premier*, Toronto, 1992; Complaints brought to the Consultative Committee on the Education of Black Students. Toronto Board, 1988–1995.

15. See K. Brathwaite, A. Calliste, R. Winks.

16. OPBC Submission to the Royal Commission on Learning. Toronto, June 6, 1994. p. 3.

17. —— p. 19–20.

18. Report of the Royal Commission on Learning 1994. A Short Version. p. 10.

19. —— p. 11.

20. See Toronto Board of Education. *Every Student Survey*, Parts 1, 2, 3. Research Services. 1991.

21. In my view of African–centred education, I place emphasis on

the African Canadian student being the centre of the education process and I believe their education must include them, motivate them and develop in them a variety of skills and knowledge. African–centred pedagogy must also utilize the complex global context in which Black people operate and interact with others, and should not be defined so narrowly that the fuller picture is missing. It should engage students in a range of challenging cours-es, including Language, Mathematics, Science, Culture, History and Philosophy, the Arts, Business, Physical Education, Design and Information Technology. See also George Dei "Rethinking 'African–Centred Schools' in Euro–Canadian Contexts" (1995), in this book.

22. Marva Collins' Schools in Chicago have been documented as being successful in educating African–American students who were failing in the regular system.

23. Abena Walker is an African–American educator who runs an African–centred school in Washington, D.C., supported by the State.

Part IV

Science Teaching:
On Having Wonderful
Ideas

"IN MY ENTIRE LIFE as a student, I remember only twice being given the opportunity to come up with my own ideas," recalls Harvard education professor, Canadian-born Eleanor Duckworth. Both she and teacher Elaine MacIntosh describe an approach to teaching science to elementary school children which encourages learning by observing, asking questions, trying things out, sharing information and following your own "wonderful ideas."

Elaine MacIntosh in "Bears and Collective Learning" is interviewed by George Martell about a science program on bears she developed in her Grade 2–3 classroom in a working class neighbourhood in Scarborough, Ontario. She stresses the role the students had in both choosing the topic and in sharing information and insights with each other, as the project developed over several months. She tells the interviewer that she wanted the students to act as much as possible as "real scientists," figuring out what the real world — in this case the world of bears — is all about. The important thing for her was to put the children into the centre of the program, open them up for a lot of solid information on bears, and then let them sift through it and decide for themselves what was important to remember, write about and illustrate. The interview is documented with samples of the children's writing and drawings, which amply demonstrate the fruitfulness of taking this approach.

Eleanor Duckworth, who has studied with Piaget and worked on developing elementary school science curriculum, discusses in "Twenty-four, Forty-two, and I Love You: Keep It

Complex" her own experiences as a learner, teacher and researcher. She argues that a good science program — and any education program, for that matter — has to be based on allowing each child to test out ideas she or he finds significant. This process of testing out ideas is also critical to a child's intellectual development in general. Teachers can assist this development primarily by accepting the child's perspective as a legitimate framework for generating ideas and by allowing children to work out their own questions and answers. The primary task of the teacher, she argues, is to provide varied settings and materials which will suggest ideas to children.

She offers many concrete examples, such as working with balances, gasses, liquids and numbers in an open–ended fashion. Duckworth urges teachers not to oversimplify their subject. "There is a parallel between a poet and a teacher: the universe is complex: science is complex: the poet's thoughts and feelings are complex," she writes. Science, like Shakespeare, should not be condensed to a few pointers or formulas.

Chapter Twelve

BEARS AND COLLECTIVE LEARNING
Elaine MacIntosh interviewed by George Martell

This interview with Elaine MacIntosh deals with a science program on bears she developed with her Grade 2-3 class in Scarborough, Ontario. Many of her Grade 3's had been in her classroom
the year before and were already accustomed to a program which
demanded a good deal of committed writing. Her school was situated in
a working class area of south Scarborough. Her children's parents, she
says, "we're quite feisty, very interested in their kids' work at school, very
much involved. They weren't a bit like your stereotyped working class
parents, who think teacher always knows best and are ultra strict at
home. Many of the kids had a lot of freedom in their lives, even indul-
gence, and they had an extraordinary level of energy." The interview
focusses on what it means to do science — and any kind of real learning
— with elementary kids and how you deal with issues of quality and
standards.

George Martell

GM As I looked around your classroom during this work on
bears there must have been at least fifty or sixty books and
articles on the subject available for student research. That's a

The Brown Bear.

lot of information for little kids to take in. What do you say to people who think you're asking too much of your students or overwhelming them with too much information?

EM It's a long answer, I'm afraid.

The first thing I'd say is that this kind of science program isn't simply laid on by me. I did suggest, though, earlier in the year, that animals might be a topic for study. In this I always get 100% support; kids of this age love investigating animals. Around November I talked with them about a number of animals they might look at and left a wide variety of materials on different animals on shelves and tables, which they could leaf through at any time during the day. I also suggested they go to the zoo and think about the animal they'd like to study, which a number of them did. The Chinese pandas were there at the time, and they made a big impression. After a month or so it became pretty clear that bears were on the agenda, and in January, when we took a vote, bears won hands down. So from the beginning there was a sense among the kids that they had some ownership of this project.

The second thing I'd say, and which is more difficult to find words for, is that we then began a process that had very little laying on by me of information (though it had some of that). What was learned was much more by way of research and discussion — a process in which the kids and I and the kids among themselves got hold of this subject together. We were honestly curious about the subject. (I certainly didn't know much about the details of the various bears when I started). In this, I think, there was some real science going on. Not the awful stuff that high school students often have to suffer — filling in physics' formulas by rote or getting the "right answer" in chemistry lab. My Grade 2's and 3's really thought about this subect — how bears lived and what their physical beings were like.

GM How about telling us a little about the research first.

EM Ok. As you mentioned I had all these books and articles around. I got many of them from the library — it was very well stocked — and some from my own collection. I read to them the most interesting material I knew about bears — from novels and science books. And I laid out the rest of the books on the science table, along the blackboard, on various

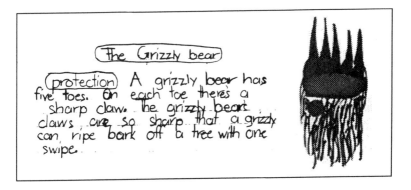

Kevin (The grizzly Bear)

shelves and display counters and let the kids browse. In this context you don't have to worry about overloading them with information. They take what they want — what really captures their imagination. They'd be drawn, for example, to pictures of little bear babies and descriptions of how they were born. Or, because they'd seen the pandas at the zoo, they'd be especially interested in looking at pictures of pandas and reading about them. Or they'd be a bit scared by the ferociousness of the grizzly. They were very interested in the grizzly's claws.

As we browsed, we got into discussions with each other. Which was the biggest or meanest or scariest bear? What were different kinds of foods that bears ate? How did they protect themselves? What did you think of the polar bear making a nest for her babies in the snow? We compared cubs of different animals. Whether they stayed for one year or two.

Whether they had one or more babies. How did the parents protect their cubs? What were the differences between the panda, the polar bear and the Alaska brown bear? We looked at different footprints for different kinds of bears. We thought about different sizes and weights. We measured how far up the classroom wall the grizzly would stand. Way above the blackboard, it turned out, which we all thought was really tall. (Our classroom was built 60 years ago and has a high ceiling.) Jennifer found out that pandas weighted 4 oz. at birth, and we approximated this on the balance scales. We learned that panda cub eyes don't open until they're 40 days old and that they can't crawl until they are three or four months old. So we could compare them with kittens, which most of us knew about. In this discussion you could see how so many kids, even if they had never seen a bear, had thought about bears or dreamed about them, and were now grateful to see them for what they really were. Scary, alright, but not so frightening as when they were unknown dark creatures of the woods.

You can see in some of the pictures how the kids took in the qualities of the bears they wanted to know about and used materials and approaches appropriate for these qualities. Brian, as you can see in the first illustration, used pastels to show a sweet and soft panda. Kevin, on the other hand,

used a hard–edged magic marker to draw his ferocious griz-zly, with blood dripping from the fish in his mouth.

They were gripped by the details of bears' lives. They wanted to get them right. Here's Kevin's picture of a bear sleeping during the winter. The kids had all been told, as I had been told, that bears hibernate during the winter. In our reading we found out that wasn't true. They don't really hibernate; they just sleep. A true hibernation occurs when an animal's temperature goes much further down. They espe-cially wanted to get the physical qualities right. Here's Kevin's picture where he tries to show that the hump on the grizzly's shoulder is unique to it and that it isn't the same with the polar bear.

GM I think to some people this process of student choosing might sound like a liberal smorgasbord approach to science, rather than something solid and systematic. What do you say to that?

EM My answer is that I think this is real science. The kids are acting like scientists, trying to figure out what the real world — in this case the world of bears — is all about. If there is technique involved here, it's the process that puts kids into the centre of this real thing, opens them to a lot of solid infor-mation about bears, and then lets them sift through it to judge what's important to recover and eventually to write about. The real world — whether it's nature or human rela-tions — is exciting and kids want to respond to it seriously. They don't need gimmicks or cutesy materials.

Let me tell you about Brian.

Brian was the youngest kid in the class — at a Grade 1 level in a Grade 2–3. His previous year's teacher thought it best to keep him back for another year, but his grandmother, a very caring and hardworking person who was raising him, didn't want it. She'd had bad experiences of Special Education with her own son, and didn't want Brian to go through anything like that. She was especially concerned that he not lose the friends with whom he had been going to school with.

I was worried about Brian being able to connect to this project. But, it turned out, he was really interested in pandas. He had been to the zoo and seen them there. Like many of the other kids, he was especially interested in the fact that pandas play, just like children do. He was delighted that pandas like to slide down hills, and are willing to walk up a hill just to slide down it. Just wanting to play. That's what the panda is doing in his drawing.

Brian was also a very feisty little kid. If everyone else was going to produce a book on bears, he was determined he would too, even though writing was very difficult for him. Brian went through some very discouraging times, and sometimes he got turned off and didn't work as hard as the others. Nobody just sat down and wrote one of these books, you know. They spent hours and hours writing out information in the most scrawled way and then they would set about organizing it (in conferences with other kids and with me) and that took all sorts of time and energy. And after they wrote it out in final draft, they had to write it out again for publishing. (In the past, parents had sometimes typed out their final drafts, but this time they had to print out the final

version themselves.) In all of this I was afraid Brian would get really discourged and give up. But he was terrific about it. He had to re-write many times, but he very cheerfully stuck to it. He really ground away. I'd drop by and give him encouragement and so would the other kids, who had strong opinions about everyone's stuff and were glad to comment and make suggestions. It was really tough for Brian to eke out information from the material in class. He'd go to the books I'd read — sometimes books I'd read more than once — or to sections I had read to other students who needed more information, and pour over pictures and maybe get a line or two. I'd read to him directly sometimes and so would some of the other kids. He never really stopped hanging in and, in the end, was very excited by his production, Later, he would often go and re-read his book. At the time his reading was quite limited, and it gave him a big boost.

GM You've touched on some of the "discussion" part of this "scientific" process, and I was wondering if you could tell us a bit more about it in detail.

EM Perhaps I should say first that the reading and the discussion and the writing all go on at the same time, which is how it is in real life. There's no neat sequence. Of course, you have to have some initial discussion and research before the kids can get down to any writing, but after that it goes back and forth in many different ways. Let me try to get at it from a couple of directions.

There was a pretty wide spread in the different kinds of bears the kids decided to write about — pandas, brown bears, grizzlies, polar bears, etc. — and when one of them hit a book that was really tough or a difficult problem in thinking through something or writing about it, I would have a discussion with them or read from one of the books for them. But, often, I wouldn't just focus on just one kid. I'd gather everyone around for the reading or the discussion even though for many it would be about a bear they weren't doing. But they didn't mind at all. In fact, they'd often take off with this new conversation themselves in different corners of the room. They were very interested in each other's work, and very interested in discussing it.

Throughout this process I never imagined that I should give the kids a research task and then let them get on with it themselves on an individual basis. We must have spent a month and a half reading about bears (of course we did other subjects as well), and only a small amount of this reading was done before they started writing. I'd make suggestions for books, read from books they might want to read, and the kids would make suggestions for each other. All the time individual kids kept adding to the information they had in conversation with us all. I read to the whole class on bears almost every day. It might be a fairly simple book on polar bears or quite a technical discussion from an encyclopedia. By the end I was reading pretty difficult material and encouraging them to do the same. We also saw films in which they could see bears in the wild.

One film was fantastic in showing how a polar bear would float flat down on a piece of ice to get close to a seal. The kids were really impressed that an animal could think so cunningly.

Throughout this period the kids were teaching each other, and not always about a bear they were working on in common. They got excited about each other's work. In conferences one kid would begin

to talk about the food his or her bear ate, and then another kid would say, yeah, but you should see what my bear eats. They were all excited, for example, about the word "omnivorous," which one boy came up with when finding out that his bear ate both plants and other animals and fish. It was great fun to have this long word they really knew the meaning of. They were fascinated by the panda's thumb not being a thumb, but rather a wrist bone. We all felt our wrist bones and thought about it growing out and becoming a thumb. In her book Jennifer (Grade 2) made sure to call it "a radial sesamoid bone."

GM Where do the kids go from here? What develops from this plunging into nature — the world of bears in this instance? What kind of thinking?

EM Well, they do learn about categories and not in a boring, mechanical top–down way. The categories come out of the material they're dealing with and help structure it for them.

We had discussions about organizing the material they were writing. I started by giving them some suggested section titles, so they'd have some handles on the material, somewhere to put it. You can't throw kids out there and say find whatever information you can, when they have never done anything like this before. We talked about what they would like to know about and categories like "appearance" would emerge or "babies"/"cubs"/"family," which they could use to cover material about children or infants and their parents. "Interesting facts" emerged as a category for what got stuck in their heads when it was all over, something that was outstanding but didn't fit anywhere else — like grizzlies having a wide range of colours from creamy white to black, which Kevin learned, or that the word "grizzly" had to do with a quality of fur rather than ferociousness.

They also learned to think more generally about the subject they were studying. Environmental issues came to the fore pretty quickly. They talked over and over again how the Panda was endangered and what should be done about it. They had good hard facts to build on. They also got into hunting — how humans are so careless and thoughtless and selfish. They talked about the seal hunt and fur coats, how it seemed cruel and unnecessary, and how the natives and the fishermen needed it.

The thing that made me most excited was that after we had done all this research and writing about bears, they wanted to go off and do other animals. To be scientists on their own. But, I should add, always in the context of having buddies around to discuss their explorations and newly acquired information.

GM How did that happen?

EM It seemed so natural.

Look, for example, at this section of Jennifer's book, where she is linking the giant and red panda with the racoon family. You can see her delight in these different animals and with her knowledge of them. Kids like Jennifer just want to go on with it. It's fascinating for them.

After completing their books on bears a number of the grade 3 kids were so excited at being able to do this work that they insisted I go off and get them a bunch of books from the library. (They could only take out two each on their own.) So I got them a whole bucket of books on birds or lions or whatever. Here is an example of their research in Adam and Robin's The Praying Mantis.

Maybe I should tell you about Derick's lion book. Derick joined the class a year before in the middle of Grade 2. He seemed very soft and sweet, but really had some very strong leadership qualities about him. At the time he was struggling with a lot of difficult changes in his life, but his new dad seemed a very caring person and his mom was solidly on his side and very loving. When he came he had no confidence in his reading ability and was, in fact, a very poor reader. But he worked very hard, and by Grade 3 was a good confident student. He'd also become a classroom leader and carried a lot of respect. I could say to kids doing badly in Grade 2, look at Derick, he had more difficulties with reading than you and look what he's done. You can do it too. And they knew I wasn't talking about a sucky kid. He was respected. Because the work was collective and serious, doing it well didn't make you a teacher's pet.

Anyway, Derick decided he wanted to do a lion. He came up with his own headings and changed them as he went along. And he read as much as he could. I didn't help him at

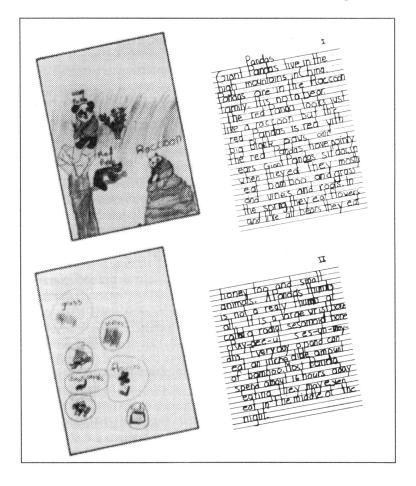

all on this. Of course, he consulted his buddies, three or four of them in Grade 3, who talked about it with him just as he talked about their work. They would hash everything over. They even decided how many days they wanted to work on their projects. How much information they wanted. But each did their own work. And Derick worked long and hard in the time they set for themselves.

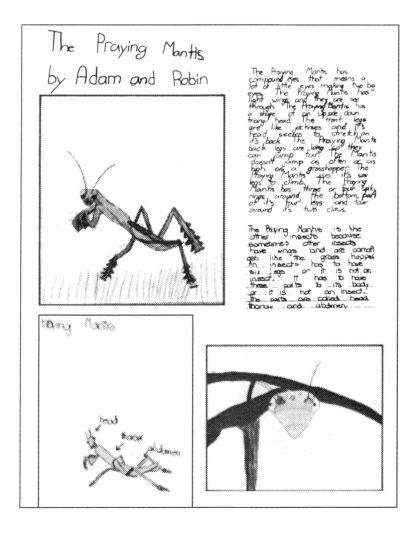

GM What are the standards operating here? How do you know your kids are really doing good work? How do you tell others that?

EM My standards are inside.

GM You don't mean they're just subjective? You think other people will agree with you, don't you? You think Brian's sliding panda is just great, for example, and you expect me to say the same.

EM Sure, but you also know that standards are sliding things. You can't forget where the kid is starting from. A drawing from one kid may be exceptional, while the same level of skill may be just so so from someone else. The first kid may have really sweated over it and the second didn't need to try that hard. I'll be critical of the second and push for a higher standard.

GM But you have a direction for your pushing, an idea of where the kid end up, an idea where most of the kids should end up.

EM I do, but I'd be hard pressed to find the right words for it. One way into it is to understand how the collective of all the kids helps make your standards. When, for example, Brian finishes something that's good, everybody rushes over to look, they tell him it's great, and they are inspired to do better themselves. Standards are collective in that way. We had, for example, a native kid in class. He was way behind in school, but he was cool and gained an increasing amount of respect as the year went on. Discussions with Lance got us started talking about racism in the world, how Indians had been put down, and how American movie makers had made them look like such nasties. There was a lot of straight talk. Lance had a strong character and became something of a hero to the other kids. At the same time, they all knew that

The Lion
By DEREK

Interesting facts
The lion is about 10 cm long.
Most male cubs when they are
3 or 4 years old hunt whenever
there is prey. The home of the
Pried of lions is 100 square miles
That is a lot A lion roars to warn
the other lions that the place
that the lion is in is already
taken for a home. Most people
think that the lion is the king
of wild animals. He is but he
has a rough time being the king
of animals. He has to struggle and
fight to live and survive. When the
lion roars it can mean another start
of a new nap

writing was a struggle for him. There was no pretence about
this. Most everything about each child, after a while, was
accepted as an ok truth. It wasn't dwelled on, though. It's like
a family. There's an accepted understanding of how things
are, the good and the bad. So Lance wasn't humiliated by his
writing problem, and he didn't have to hide it. Gradually, he
started to do much better work, and that was understood by
everyone, who got in on the judgement. But some days he
was right out of it, and I'd have to kick his butt. "You do this
fabulous work," I'd say, "and then, all of a sudden, you're sitting around on your thumbs. What is this? You can do much
better than this." Lance didn't think I was unjust and neither
did anyone else. The same thing happened to other kids. We
all knew what was true and built our standards together.
And we moved together to a more solid grasp of the material, more insight, better expression. What else is there?

GM Do the parents believe you? How do you convince them this isn't mindless liberalism? How do you show their kids are coming away with something solid?

EM I think it's right there in the production. The writing is there, the books are there. And so is their ability to read. The kids can sit down and read books to their parents. And, in case you're wondering, they do alright on mechanical reading tests like the Gates McGinitie, which I don't think test very much. There is a lot of phoniness to these tests; they're tricky in ways kids don't expect. Kids aren't looking out for tests to be tricking them; they expect tests to be finding out what they know. But relative to other classes this class did fine on the Gates, and some kids actually jumped quite a lot. I should add that if you want your kids to do really well on these mechanical tests, you have to teach to them, especially about the tricks. And in the "reading for comprehension" sections, they have to be taught to pay attention to banal stories and answer mindless questions about them. So doing well on the Gates doesn't mean much to me. What I know about these kids is that they have a much stronger base of literacy than that which is reflected in the Gates; it's something they can really move forward on. It's linked to their human desire to really know about the world.

Chapter Thirteen

TWENTY-FOUR, FORTY-TWO, AND I LOVE YOU
Keeping It Complex

Eleanor Duckworth

In my entire life as a student, I remember only twice being given the opportunity to come up with my own ideas, a fact that I consider typical and terrible. I would like to start this chapter by telling how I came to realize that schooling could be different from what I had experienced.

Figuring Out My Own Ideas

After my university studies, I joined in the 1960s the Elementary Science Study, a national non–profit curriculum development project located in the Boston area. I had been hired because of my background with Piaget, studying how science and math ideas develop in children, and had no formal training in either education or science. While the first of these lacks was probably a liability, the second turned out to be a great boon. I was with a highly imaginative bunch of scientists and teachers of science, all trying to put together their favourite kinds of experience to entice children. Because I was innocent in science, I made a great "sample child" for my colleagues, and I spent a lot of time exploring the materials and the issues that they came up with. Of the many areas I explored, three seemingly unrelated ones came together in a way that showed me what learning could be like. I got hooked and have been an educator ever since, trying to develop learning experiences of that sort for every child and every teacher. It was the first time — with two exceptions mentioned in the opening sentence — that I got excited about my own ideas. I had been excited by ideas before, but they had always been somebody else's ideas. My struggle had always been to get in on what I thought somebody else knew and knew to be important. This was the first time that I had a sense of what it was like to pay attention to my own ideas.

It is, of course, exhilarating to find that your own ideas can lead you somewhere. Few feelings are more effective in getting you to keep on thinking on your own. I would like to focus here, though, not so much on my feelings as on the nature of my understanding.

One team of colleagues was developing ways to study balances. They posed problems with a simple balance consisting of a strip of pegboard resting on a rounded support with metal washers as weights. They started with the balance in equilibrium, horizontal. Then holding the balance, they moved one or more weights and asked me to adjust other weights so that when they let go, the balance arm would remain horizontal (see Elementary Science Study, 1967b).

For example, they set up a relatively easy problem with the balance as shown here:

Balanced
(a)

Their move
(b)

Where should I add one washer, so the board stays balanced? My solution was as follows:

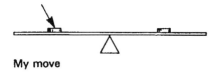

My move

302

They then gave me a problem that I found more difficult: they presented me with the board balanced with one washer on one side and two washers stacked on the other side, but closer to the middle. If they moved the single washer a certain distance to the right, how could I move *just one* of the other two washers, so the board would still balance?

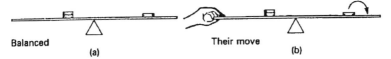

Balanced

(a)

Their move

(b)

I found a solution that worked:

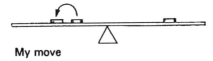

My move

Through this example and others similar to it I found that it did not seem to matter where the washers started; I just had to move one of them the same distance the original had been moved on the other side, but in the opposite direction.

My grand triumph was the following problem. To start with, they put three washers in a pile on one side so as to balance one on the other:

Then they moved the single one a long way — practically to the center. Again, how could I move just one of the others so it would still balance?

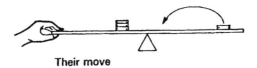

Their move

Well, I knew by now that I should try to move it just as far in the opposite direction. But there was no room. I ran into the middle almost right away. So what should I do? Move it in the *same* direction? That didn't seem right. Move it as far as

I could towards the middle — just barely short of the middle? I thought I might try that. But the one I decided to try was my first idea — moving the washer in the opposite direction, even though it meant crossing the middle.

My move

It felt to me like a very daring move. And it worked! That rule worked, even across the middle. I remember saying to my colleagues at the time that I felt like Helen Keller.

I did not stop then. Among other things, I tried designing balances myself, and eventually even figured out what the differences were between a balance like the one in this example and a seesaw, that accounted for the fact that the balance with nothing on it is horizontal, while a seesaw with nobody on it always has one end up in the air.

A second group was working on a study of what they called "Gases and 'Airs'" (Elementary Science Study, 1967a). The tight sequence of reasoning demanded by this unit turned out not to work very well with elementary school children, but the unit did entail a wonderful variety of experiences that, for me, gave substance to what gases and airs are. It started from a close and critical look at the classic school science lab demonstration of burning a candle in a tube inverted over water: the water rises, the candle goes out, and one has "proven" that the atmosphere is 20 percent oxygen. But there are basic problems, as my colleagues pointed out. For one thing, the water doesn't rise gradually as the candle burns; it rises suddenly after the flame is out. If it were gradually using up the oxygen, wouldn't it gradually rise? Another problem: the amount that it rises may indeed average about 20 percent, but it varies widely; in contrast, when wet steel wool is wedged into a tube above water and left to rust overnight, the water rises exactly the same amount in each tube.

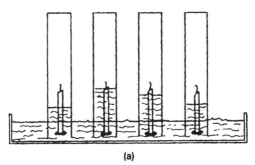

(a)
Water rise after 4 candles burned

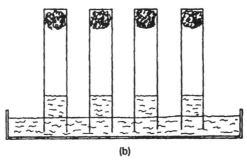

(b)
Water rise with steelwool overnight

The "demonstration" with a burning candle turns out to be a hoax, based on a totally different phenomenon. The candle actually goes out long before all the oxygen is used up (for various reasons). While the candle burns, it heats the air so that the air expands; some of it leaves the tube, bubbling out through the water in the dish. While the remaining air cools, the water rises to take the place of the air that bubbles out. As one who had been taken in by that demonstration in my own schooling, I was fascinated to explore the more complex relationships that had been covered up by it. To begin with, I was intrigued by the idea of different kinds of "airs" easily available to us; air that a candle had burned in; air that steel wool had rusted in; lung air; room air; air that seeds had sprouted in. Could a candle burn in the steel wool air? Would another rusting steel wool ball pull up the same amount of water in steel wool air? Would seeds sprout in candle air?

I became very good at putting into a tube whatever kind of air I wanted to. Using a syringe, I could take air from any tube and put it into another tube that had no air in it (by virtue of being full of water). Bubbles came to be real things filled with some kind of air — room air, lung air, steel wool air, or other. Putting an Alka Seltzer tablet under the lip of a water-filled tube, for example, did this:

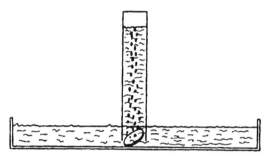

and I had a tube full of Alka Seltzer air.

I came to imagine the inverse of filling any container with liquid. As long as your container has no other liquid in it already, you can put it straight under the dripping liquid, and you'll capture all that is falling right over the opening. In the inverse, as in the case of some escaping Alka Seltzer air, you could think of it this way:

In a bucket of water, move a water–filled jar over the bubbles, and you will collect the escaping Alka Seltzer air.

This is not, I hasten to point out, intended as a practical example. I've never happened to be holding a water–jar upside down in a bucket of water when an Alka Seltzer tablet dropped into the bucket. But conceptually it helped me a lot: an "air" was for me as real as a liquid.

A third area that I explored originated in my attempts to build on my Piaget background. I thought of trying to find some situations for young children in which a certain order was maintained in spite of some striking change. It occurred to me to use the constant ordering of liquids floating on each other in a tube. Though the idea had less mileage in it for little children than I had thought it might, it did have some value (See Duckworth, 1964). More importantly for my education, however, it led me into a long series of explorations with liquids, starting with trying to make as many floating layers as I could in a tube. If I did not shake the tube, I could manage about six layers, and I experimented with dyes to keep them distinguishable. I expanded my horizons to include solid pieces — seeds, bits of plastic, bits of wood, bits of food. I don't recall any of these specifics, but a radish seed, say, would fall through three layers and sit on the fourth — and *every* radish seed would do that. One kind of plastic would sit on the second layer, another kind would fall through four, and so on. Some material, (I do not now remember what, and it took me a long time to find this material), stopped at the top of the top surface, and floated there.

I also tried to mix alcohol and water so that the resulting liquid would have exactly the same density as the salad oil I was working with — to see what would happen when neither liquid would necessarily float on top of the other. Would I be able to make stripes with them then? Or would they stand side by side, with a vertical separation? Or what? I found that the oil always formed itself into a single enormous sphere in the middle of the water–alcohol liquid; and that this sphere *always* moved slowly either to the top or to the bottom of the water–alcohol liquid. No matter how delicately I added one drop of water or of alcohol, I could never get the sphere of oil to float right in the middle — it was always either *just* heavier or *just* lighter. (These explorations came back in my own teaching more than 10 years later; see Duckworth, 1986.)

Six or eight months after I started learning science like this, someone presented a puzzle that happened to draw on the three areas I had been exploring, and I think I was the only person around at the time who put together the right prediction.

On the left-hand side of this balance is a plastic bag, sealed air–tight, an Alka Seltzer tablet stuck in a piece of plasticene, near the top, and some water in the bottom. On the right-hand side is just enough weight to keep the balance horizontal. The question is, what will happen to the balance of the arm if the bag is shaken, and the tablet falls into the water?

Most of the people present knew that when the tablet fell into the water a lot of "Alka Seltzer air" would be formed, and the bag would fill out. Some people thought the balance would remain level, because the same matter that was in the bag to start with was still in it at the end, even if in a different form, so the weight would not change at all. Others thought the left side would go down, because Alka Seltzer air (being, so they knew, carbon dioxide) is heavier than room air. My prediction, which turned out in fact to be the case, was that the left side would go *up*, because the filled–out bag

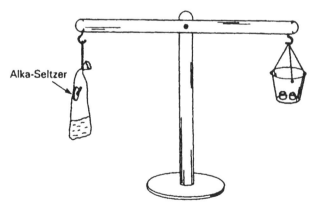

Alka-Seltzer

would take up more space, while adding no more weight, thus being more buoyant in the surrounding sea of air.

I believe that it was because I started from my own ideas and found my own ways into these parts of the world, that my understanding belonged so thoroughly to me. Notice the difference between what usually happens in formal education — presenting the simplest, neatest explanation of "the law of moments," "the composition of the atmosphere," "density," "buoyancy," or whatever — and my experience of being enticed with the funny, frustrating, intriguing, unpredictable complexities of the world around me. Instead of disassociating myself from my own interests in my struggle to find out what whoever was supposed to "know" might have understood by the word "buoyancy," my learning was based on my own connections, within the idiosyncrasies of my own system of thoughts. The very complexities of the subject matters enabled me to connect with them, made them accessible, and the integrity of my own ideas enabled me to retrieve those connections when they could help me understand a new situation.

Lisa Schneier (1990) has put it this way, the relationship between complexity and accessibility:

> [W]e organize subject matter into a neat series of steps which assumes a profound uniformity among students. We sand away at the interesting edges of subject matter until it is so free from its natural complexities, so neat, that there is not a crevice left as an opening. All that is left is to hand it to them, scrubbed and smooth, so that they can view it as outsiders. (p. 4)

The Universe in a Sentence

My favourite radio show is "A Hitchhiker's Guide to the Galaxy." In one episode, a computer is built expressly for the purpose of answering the question, "What is the meaning of life, the universe, and everything?" When it is ready, they ask it if it can answer that question. It says, yes, it can. But that it will take, as I recall, seven million years. They say, "Well, OK, go to it." Seven million years later, whoever is around goes to learn the answer. It says that it does have the answer, but that they might be a little disappointed. "No, no," they say, "go ahead, what is it?" "Forty-two," it says.

Who knows? Maybe forty-two *is* the answer. But such an answer is of no more help to us than no answer at all. It does not speak to our level of interaction with the mysteries of our existence.

Note the parallels with the following story from Lisa Schneier's class in an urban high school:

> It had been a lively class, with the various Juliets taking turns standing on a table and the Romeos making elaborate and often comical gestures as they stood below…. A group of ninth graders and I were working on a scene from *Romeo and Juliet*. They had chosen to read the balcony scene aloud and were acting it out, taking turns with the parts. They took the difficult language and its foreign style into stride, at times staying true to the text and at others replacing or skipping words and phrases. It was clear as they spoke that at points the words held meaning for them and at others they hadn't a clue as to what it was that they were reading. But we didn't stop much for discussion; the students were enjoying this kind of involvement with each other, and there was a momentum in the reading that I didn't want to interrupt.
>
> But our last Romeo of the day finally did interrupt it. We had started the scene again to give more readers a turn, and he had begun to wade through his first speech. In the midst of it, he broke off, shook his head impatiently, and turned to me. "He loves her. *That's* what he's saying. So why all that other stuff? Why not just say it? I love you! (to the current Juliet). There!" And then in a memorable tone, a mixture of humor, frustration, and honest confusion: "Why can't he just say what he means?" (Schneier 1990, pp. 1–2)

Why doesn't Shakespeare just say what he means? Of course that's what the poet *is* doing. "What he means" is complex. The words he chooses are the best he can choose to say what he wants to say. Poems and stories and paintings and dance and music are not just fancy ways of saying what could be said in a sentence. "I love you" does not quite express everything that Shakespeare meant, just as "forty-two" does not quite substitute for living our lives. There is a parallel here between a poet and a teacher: the universe is complex; science is complex; the poet's thoughts and feelings are complex. "Forty-two" doesn't do the trick. Nor does "buoyancy." Nor, in this case, does "I love you."

In this spirit, when studying a poem with a class, I start by asking students what they notice — an invitation to keep every complexity of the poem under consideration. People notice very different things, and almost each thing noticed leads to a question or another thought. Putting together what everyone notices and returning to the poem to try to look for answers to the questions leads to an understanding of the poem that is greatly expanded for each of us. Take, for instance, this Frost poem:

Design
I found a dimpled spider, fat and white,
On a white heal-all, holding up a moth
Like a white piece of rigid satin cloth—
Assorted characters of death and blight
Mixed ready to begin the morning right,
Like the ingredients of a witches' broth—
A snow-drop spider, a flower like froth,
and dead wings carried like a paper kite.

What had that flower to do with being white,
The wayside blue and innocent heal-all?
What brought the kindred spider to that height,
Then steered the white moth thither in the night?
What but design of darkness to appall?—
If design govern in a thing so small.

(Frost, 1969, p.302)

Somebody will notice that there is a lot of white. Somebody will mention the rhyme scheme, or will imitate the rhythm. Somebody will mention that the first part of the poem seems to present a picture, and the second half seems to ask questions about it. Different people point out different possible plays on words: kindred and dreadful kin; appall and a funeral pall; a paper kite and a bird kite; morning right and morning rite; morning and mourning. Different people have different thoughts about whether the darkness is that which appalls, or that which is appalled. Arguments develop about why the flower is described as white in the first line, and blue in the ninth. This is a bare beginning. A group of adults can easily go on for more than an hour, with increasing interest, and everybody's initial understanding is expanded by hearing from others.*

I have always been frightened by being asked: "What is the meaning of this poem?" My reaction is, "How could I know? I'm no good with poems! " But it is easy for me to point out something that I notice about it, and in turn listen to what other people notice about it, and to figure out whether I think what they say makes sense, and why, and what other thoughts their ideas provoke in me. Many students have feelings similar to these. One in particular said that she had determined when we started discussing the poem that she would not say a word, knowing nothing about poems, and feeling scared by them. But as she heard the various things that people were saying, her own thoughts developed, and she finally couldn't contain herself, so much did she have to say, and so strongly did she feel about it. One student referred to himself as a "poem–phobe," which prompted another student to say, "If Frost had been able to put what he had to say into a sentence, he would have, so don't worry that you can't."

I recognized that this was the same thought I have had about the accessibility of science. It is in acknowledging the complexity of the poem, not "sand[ing] away at the interesting edges," to use Schneier's words, that we render it accessible. Our understanding seeks to do justice to the complexity that the poet sought to render, and by the same token it belongs to us. Just as the poet seeks to present his thoughts

---

* For an analysis of one high school student's developing understanding of this poem, see Schneier, 1990.

and feelings in all their complexity, and in so doing opens a multiplicity of paths into his meaning, likewise a teacher who presents a subject matter in all its complexity makes it more accessible by opening a multiplicity of paths into it.

"I Know there are Twenty-Four"

I ask students to do the following: Take a fistful of four different kinds of markers (four colours of paperclips, or four kinds of dried beans, for example) to represent four children who are going to the movies. Lay out the different arrangements in which they can sit in four adjacent seats. Some students ask, "Do I really have to do this, I know there are twenty-four." And I say, yes, you really have to; the question isn't how many arrangements, the question is *what are* the arrangements — each of them. (It happens, not infrequently, that someone who has impatiently affirmed that there will be twenty-four, because he knows a formula, has trouble generating the actual arrangements — which strikes me as not too different from knowing that the meaning of life is forty-two.) And the question behind that is, when you think you have laid out all the arrangements, how could you convince yourself or anybody else that you don't have any repeats, and that you are not missing any? I urge the reader to try this before continuing, and to see what system she or he comes up with.

Most people who are not yet comfortable with math start this exercise more or less randomly, but many systems emerge when they think about whether they have generated all the possible arrangements. In what follows I will present some of these systems.

Some people make diagonals, such as the P in the following arrangements:

P	B	L	M
M	P	B	L
L	M	P	B
B	L	M	P

This could be called the "revolving" system, where the last letter to the right revolves around to appear on the left and everything moves over one. This looks systematic and promising. But when they follow this rule to a fifth step, it turns out to be a repeat of the first (PBLM). So they have to side-step, and think about how to find the various different possible starting points.

Another system which keeps P on the diagonal is the "squeeze between" system:

P	B	L	M
B	P	L	M
B	L	P	M
B	L	M	P

Move P to the right by squeezing in between the next two letters. Again, the question arises about what to do after the fourth.

You could reinterpret that system to be, not "squeeze between," but "exchange": Keep P moving on the diagonal by exchanging it with whatever letter is in the place where it will be moving. That explains the four above, and allows you to keep going:

P	L	M	B
L	P	M	B
L	M	P	B
L	M	B	P
P	M	B	L
M	P	B	L
M	B	P	L
M	B	L	P

At this point, after twelve arrangements we get back to the starting point. Is that, then, all there are? Is there a reason to think that this system would have generated all we could possibly get? Or is there a reason to think it is inadequate? Or can't we tell anything about it at all?

Not all approaches use diagonals. For the next ones, I will limit the discussion to three children, in three seats, in order to write out fewer arrangements.

Many people, as a system starts to emerge, lay out something like this:

```
L   M   B
L   B   M
M   L   B
```

By this time they have an idea about what comes next. And most of them think that their idea is the only sensible, systematic possibility. The first surprise is that there are two different, almost equally popular, next moves:

```
M   B   L   or   B   L   M
```

And the two completed lists would look like this:

I	L	M	B		II	L	M	B
	L	B	M			L	B	M
	M	L	B			M	L	B
	M	B	L			B	L	M
	B	L	M			M	B	L
	B	M	L			B	M	L

The system on the left started with the two L's in the first position, then put the two M's in the first position, and then the two B's. The system on the right started with the L's in the first position, then moved the L's to the second position, and then to the last position. In both cases, people can say, "Once I have one position filled, there are only two ways to fill the other two, so these are the only possible six ways for three children to sit." They are two very different systems, and yet they end up with the same exact arrangements.

Playing this out with four children and four seats, using, for example, the first system, would give this result:

```
P   L   M   B
P   L   B   M
P   M   L   B
P   M   B   L
P   B   L   M
P   B   M   L
```

There would be six different arrangements with P in the first position. There would, therefore, be six ways to put each of the four lettters in the first position, that is, four times six ways altogether. (Playing out the system II above, P would end up in each position six times — again four times six ways altogether.)

One nine-year-old — no math whiz, he — after placing a few arrangements according to no system that I could see, started to make new ones by reversing pairs in the ones he already had. (From PLBM, say, he might make PBLM; or from MLPB he might make LMPB.) He worked slowly, and for a long time he would make a new arrangement and then check to see whether he had already had it rather than generate a new one from some over-all system he had in mind. After a long time though (he worked at this for close to an hour) and as he explained to me what he was doing, a system emerged; he started to know how to look for ones that were missing and to fill in the gaps. It was a system that was totally new to me. He never articulated it as clearly as I am about to here, but essentially his system was this: Start with one block, let's say P, and pair it up with each of the other blocks in turn. Let's start with PL.

Put them in the middle, and put the two remaining blocks at either end. Then reverse the two on the ends. Then reverse the originals (PL becomes LP) and repeat: then put the end-ones in the middle and the middle-ones at the ends and start over.

B	P	L	M
M	P	L	B
B	L	P	M
M	L	P	B
P	B	M	L
L	B	M	P
P	M	B	L
L	M	B	P

Now we have eight. Starting with PM gives us another eight and starting with PB gives us eight more. This way you get three times eight instead of four times six. And is there any

316

reason that this system is a convincing one? When you've started with P and each of the other letters, and done all the rearrangements as described, is there any reason to think that you would necessarily hit all the possibilities?

I could go on. Looking for relationships among the systems enhances our understanding even more: what is the relationship between a system which has four variations of 6 positions, and a system which has 3 variations of 8 positions? The point is that the more you look at this question, the more ways there are to see it. "Twenty-four" is a sadly impoverished version of all that can be understood about it. Just as with the poem, each different way of thinking about it illuminates all of the others — a wonderful pay-off for allowing for the complexities of the matter. Note that in this math problem *as with the poem* individuals tend to think that their way is the one way to look at it, unless they are in a social context where other possibilities are presented; then it is not a matter of replacing their point of view, but of enhancing it.

Of course, many people raise for themselves the question of arrangements of five children, and work out a formula that applies to any number — a formula which, then, represents their understanding, instead of substituting for it.

One further comment: Another nine-year-old pointed out to me that, once he had laid out all the arrangements (and he came up with twenty-four), if he removed the first item from all of them, the twenty-four arrangements of *three* items are still all different from each other. After some thought, I can more or less understand that this must be so. But it certainly brought me up short when he raised the idea.

Extended Clinical Interviewing

Now I want to move, with one last example, to develop the idea of a kind of research that such a view of teaching and learning leads to and calls for: extended clinical interviewing. Early in my work in education I found that the Piagetian methods I used to investigate learners' understanding — that is, having them take their own understanding seriously, pursue their own questions, struggle through their own conflicts — was at the same time a way of engaging people in pursuing their own learning. People became avid learners, even in fields which had not interested them before, and my ways of trying to follow their thoughts were, in fact, excellent ways to help them learn.

Later I came to realize that the circle is full: this way of helping people learn is at the same time an important form of educational research about how people's ideas develop. It really amounts to Piaget's clinical interviewing, extended in two ways: It can be extended over time, and it can be carried out with more than one person at a time.

This approach requires, however, more than just an interviewer's questions. Many of the interviews in Piaget's early books used only the interviewee's previous experience as the basis for discussion (what makes the wind; where are thoughts located). In contrast, the questions I found most often engaged interviewees in the pursuit of their own learning grew from his later work, where children tried to explain or predict or describe relationships in something which they had before them and could transform or otherwise keep returning to (the last example above is based on an investigation in Piaget and Inhelder, 1951/1975). The more surprises people encountered, and the more possibilities they became aware of, the more they wanted to continue to do and to think.

Extended clinical interviewing as a research approach requires just as much resourcefulness in finding appropriate materials, questions, and activities as any good curriculum development does. Whether it be poems, mathematical situations, historical documents, liquids, or music, our offerings must provide accessible entry points, must present the subject matter from different angles, elicit different responses from different learners, open up a variety of paths for exploration, engender conflicts, and provide surprises; we must encourage learners to open up beyond themselves, and help them realize that there are other points of view yet to be uncovered — that they have not yet exhausted the thoughts they might have about this matter.

Only if people *are* interested in expanding their views does one learn anything about how people's ideas actually develop. Curriculum development goes hand in hand with following the intricacies of the development of ideas. (This intertwined relationship led me first to refer to this research as "teaching–research.")

Once we are willing to accept the real complexities of subject matter, we find that they lurk even in the most unlikely places. One of the abilities I seek to develop in teachers is the ability to recognize when there are unsuspected complexities in what seems like straightforward, even elementary, material. (David Hawkins, 1978, has pointed out how mistaken it is to think that "elementary" ideas are necessarily simple.) It is always in confronting such complexities that one develops real understanding.

"And That's How They Did The Latitude Lines" ... *"It Makes Me Dizzy"*

I want to close with one detailed example of extended clinical interviewing that shows what can happen when learners confront, rather than cover, complexities. I want to show the process as it actually takes place in a group over time. I hope to be able to convey the relationships — both interpersonal and ideational — that this approach entails. I hope to reveal the interplay of thoughts and feelings, the tantalizing confusions, the tortuous development of new insights, and the crowning accomplishment possible when people struggle honestly with their own ideas. I think it is a rare picture of minds at work.

The account here comes from some of the teachers from the MIT Experimental Teacher Development Project (Bamberger et al., 1981). After the official end of the two–year project , about ten of the original fifteen teachers wanted to keep going. We met periodically through a third year, as we tried to decide what strands of our work together we wanted to continue. For six of the teachers, the original moon–watching was really the most passionate interest. This was the experience which they

319

felt had given them the greatest insights into themselves and their students as learners, and thus themselves as teachers. (For more on moon-watching, see DiSchino, 1987.) So for thirteen more years, seven of us* continued to meet with a focus on moon-watching. For some time now I have been a learner like everybody else. This, in fact, does not change my role very much. In all of my extended clinical interviewing I keep asking people to say what they mean again, please, more clearly. In this group I have no special standing in asking for such clari-fication.

I did not set up the conflict described below. It emerged on its own as we continued to try to understand the motions of the bodies in our solar system. I may have played a role in keeping the conflict on the floor as an issue worth trying to resolve, and in refusing to believe too readily that we had resolved it. The discussion presented here is about what "east" means, which at first blush seems like a pretty simple idea. Let me first try to present two different views, and then give some sense of the discussion that took place.

Both views put east in the general direction of the rising sun. ("Orient"ing literally means taking a bearing to the east, heading for the rising sun.) The first view is relatively simple: east is along a latitude, in the general direction of where the sun rises. The second is more difficult to convey, and for us it came from two different sets of thoughts. The simpler of *these* is the following. East lies 90 degrees from north, in the gener-al direction of the rising sun. If you look at the North Star, (or to the earth underneath the North Star), and put your right arm out at a right angle, you'll point east. If you cut a 90-degree L-shape from a piece of paper, and lay it on a globe so one tip of it is at the North Pole and the bend in the L is at Boston, say, then the arm that is heading east does *not* go along a latitude; it goes on a gentle slant from the latitude, so it ends up crossing the equator.

---

* The members of the group besides myself are: Virginia Chalmers, Joanne Cleary, Mary DiSchino, Fern Fisher, Wendy Postlethwaite, and Mary Rizzuto.

Our second way of getting to this view is the following. In September you may find the sun rising in a certain position, relative to your house, for instance, or the end of your street. As the months go by, the sunrise point changes, moving to the right along the horizon, until by Christmas, it is very much further to the right. By mid-January, it has started to move back, until some time in March it is again where it was in September, and it then continues to move left for a couple of months. In June it begins to move right again, and by September it is back where it started. So where, in all this, is east? This group thought that the one in the middle of those extremes is a reasonable candidate – the place where it started in September and reached again in March. That is also the time when the sunrise and sunset divide the twenty-four hour period into exactly half. Everywhere in the world, that day, the twenty-four hour period is going to be divided exactly in half. Everyone in the world, that day, will look to sunrise to find where the exact east is. And here's what that led us to think. If everyone on one north-south line from the North Pole to the South Pole is looking toward the sun at the same sunrise moment, they are all looking at the same place at the same moment. On that day, the sun is actually rising so as to keep going directly overhead *at the equator*, which means that we

321

must all be looking, not directly along a latitude, but in a direction gently sloping towards the equator.

We had two reasons to think of east as tending toward the equator, rather than along a latitude parallel to the equator. And, of course, we also had very good common sense and pragmatic reason to think of east as heading along a latitude. In order to proceed with an investigation that we were engaged in we needed to know which of these easts to deal with.

This discussion lasted three long sessions, which are the essence of this account. The first took place at a summer retreat in June, 1987. It refers back to a conversation at a retreat three years earlier, when one central idea first emerged and left us perplexed. The second session took place in December, at an all-day meeting, and then there is a follow-up to that. *Much* material is cut, but I still hope to convey a sense of the nature of what can happen when complexity is accepted as a peda-gogical resource, rather than avoided.

> **Fern** [one major protagonist in this discussion; always willing to take on an unlikely-seeming idea if it expands her/our understanding].... [T]here's always east, even if the sun isn't rising there. There's still due east ... it's down there, because it's towards the equator.

> **Wendy** [another major protagonist] No. I'm not happy with that sentence, I'm sorry. Due east is *not* towards the equator....

> **Fern** Where is due east, even if the sun isn't there? It's towards where the sun rises on the equinox, which is ... towards the equator....

> **Wendy** What makes you think that it tips towards the equator?...

> **Eleanor** [altogether quite unsure of myself in the discus-sion] It's the 90 degree thing [the L-shape, which we had discussed earlier] — the latitudes are not 90 degrees to the longitudes....

> **Wendy** I think I see what you're saying. You're saying

that if I look due east eventually my eyes will … touch the equator … if I could look around the corner.

Fern You know what it is? There's always due east. Whether or not the sun rises there. And what due east is, the definition of it is, where the sun rises on the equinox.

Wendy I think of it very differently. I think of due east as, I drew a line from the North Pole to the South Pole and then went 90 degrees off … from that.

Eleanor OK, that would come to the same thing.

Wendy But I don't like it … I don't like it ending up on the equator…. It really makes me nervous.

Wendy [Taking a styrofoam ball] Well if I draw a line from there [the North Pole] to there [Boston] and go at a right angle [she starts to draw a line like a latitude]

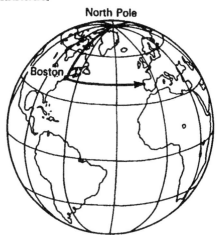

North Pole

Boston

Fern Nope, that's not a right angle, your right angle's going to go like that [tending toward the equator].

Wendy Yeah, but I don't like that right angle. I'm having serious problems with that right angle…. Well how come the latitudes don't tilt down? How come they don't bump into the equator?

Fern Latitudes are latitudes, they're not east.

Wendy You say Spain is due east from of us, and….

Eleanor That's a good point….

Wendy If I get into a boat and I drive due east and I keep the compass on due east, I bump into Spain.

Fern [stretching things a bit] You say Spain is on the same latitude, you don't say Spain is due east.

Eleanor [quite uncertain] Although we do say that….

Fern They're not east–west lines, they're latitudes. If they were east–west lines we wouldn't need latitudes.

Eleanor Huh?

Mary R. Why? Why [then] do you have longitudes? They're [after all] north–south lines.

Jinny [Laughing] That *was* a little — cryptic! Go on!

Mary R. Go on, we need to hear this. [We all recognized that she had made a far–out comment, but had confidence that Fern would say something interesting about it.]

Fern Ok, here we go. [Fern thought silently for a while, but, to our great disappointment, she decided she did not, after all, have something clear to say.] No….

Wendy Alright, hang on. You're saying that if I got a compass, and I started walking in California, and I followed that compass wherever it said east, I would end up on the equator.

Fern Right….

Wendy You're saying that if I were a sailor, and my compass told me to sail due east, I would end up on the equator no matter what I did.

Fern Right….

Mary R. So which way would you have to go to get to Spain?

Jinny You'd have to go....

Mary D. North of east ... [with hilarity] So north isn't north and east isn't east.... So if you want to stay in the Northern Hemisphere you have to keep going north....

Wendy [arm around Fern's shoulder] This is the first time in eight years that I don't understand what you're saying. In eight years you're the only person who I've always, always understood.... If I'm driving [east] ... am I driving [on a latitude]?

Jinny Probably if it's short enough. Because, right? it's going to take you a long time to get down to the equator. [This was the first inkling of a resolution — but nobody noticed.]

Mary R. It's incredible. Well it's interesting, one of the kids last year in mapping asked me why there was an Eastern and a Western Hemisphere. Why did one get named one and the other one get named something else [given that they each get their turn at sunrise] [She laughs] I said, " I have no idea. " I had no idea. I mean, why?...

Mary D. What would happen if we took the crust off the earth and then started walking due east?... Lie it flat.... It would be like the orange peels [another reference to an earlier session].

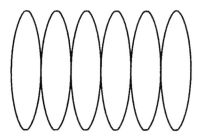

Wendy Do you mean to say you don't believe that com-passes tell you where due east is?

Fern No, I do.

Wendy So you think that if I were a sailor and I sailed whatever number of degrees due east is, 90 or whatever, that I would end up on the equator? [we acknowledge the need to adjust a compass for magnetic north, and proceed on the assumption that that is done.]...

Fern I think you'd go due east.

Wendy And would you end up on the equator?

Fern Yeah.

Eleanor Instead of Spain.

Wendy Instead of Spain. If Kevin who has sailed and navigated said that doesn't happen, would you say your due east is different from the compass due east? I don't know what he's gonna say, he might say, yes, you have to correct....

Fern This is the thing. This is the thing. I *think* maybe this is the thing. If you *start* — [Now here, Fern *is* able to articulate her insight, and it is related to Jinny's partially formed thought above. She comes to it, however, alas, just as the men and children arrive back for lunch, so the tape is stopped! I wrote down the following, in which Fern refers to an example we had used of walking along the 49th parallel.]

Fern If you *walk* east, you walk along the [US–Canadian] border; if you *look* east, you look into the United States.
[We get a brief respite from the children, to finish our discussion, and the tape is back on. I had not understood what Fern had said, and Jinny tried to recapture it for me.]

Jinny ... Where were we. We were on the border. If you're going to walk, umm, if they, if you continue to adjust ... 90 degrees, so you stay consistently 90 degrees east of north, you know, 90 degrees in relationship to north, you'll stay on that border, and…. [A new thought she has here now] And that's the definition of a latitude….

Eleanor But I want to know, I just want to know the thing you said, about it keeps pushing up, could you say that part again.

Mary R. Well it, it keeps, if you're just walking, [**Eleanor**: yeah] then you're just, you're constantly straying down. [**Eleanor**: yeah] But if, if you, if you keep yourself on the compass, and you constantly push the compass, then you're constantly keep-ing yourself at 90 degrees….

Eleanor And what's the pushing up?…

Jinny You have to adjust. You have to keep the adjust-ment happening. Because of … the sphere. That's what the pushing up is….

Eleanor Yeah. I haven't quite got that. I'll keep thinking about it.

[In December, we started by watching some of the summer's videotape, and the conversation went this way.]

Joanne [who was running the video camera in the sum-mer session] The last thing you said there, [on the tape] do you know what it is? "There's always due east." [laughter]….

Fern [reflecting her insight at the end of the last ses-sion] I think where we ended up was if you nav-igate, if you're a sailor and you navigate and you're heading due east you don't go to the equator. You go to Spain or whatever….

Eleanor Any step is headed toward the equator, but the next step….

Mary D. It's due east from that step. Due east is due east from each step that you take. That's how you get across [to Spain]. As opposed to due east from your starting point. [**Jinny**: Mmhmm] If you look at a compass when you begin, and you go due

327

east, if that compass froze there at that moment, then you'd get to the equator, but the compass is heading due east even when you're ten steps ahead of where you started....

Mary R. It corrects it sort of.

[I still do not follow the line of argument, and keep asking for more clarification.] ...

[Fern starts drawing a picture]

Fern's drawing

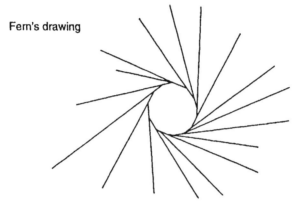

Wendy If you were walking around a circle, around the top of the globe.... It's telling you to go, like, due east is this way [she steps slightly outside the circle]. But really it's saying take a step this way and then it says, OK, now, north is over there. [Wendy essentially outlines the argument that I finally understood a little later. I shall present it more clearly at that point.]

Jinny It's like making a circle in Logo....

Wendy East is pointing off the circle, down.

Eleanor Yeah

Wendy But I don't believe it.

Eleanor I believe it but I don't get it. You get it and you don't believe it....

Jinny Well the only thing I said just when Wendy just did that, is it's like making a circle in Logo....

Mary R. With straight lines. You make a circle with straight lines.

Wendy That's lovely.
[I try and fail to understand this analogy.]….

Mary D. … [Y]ou keep moving, also. That's part of it.

Fern [Fern finishes her drawing] Something like that picture….

Eleanor How come I go there [around the circle] when the compass says to go off into space, I don't know. How come I go there, that's my question. [Jinny and Eleanor laugh.]

Wendy 'Cause the circle is big enough that you can take a step this w— I mean, if you think of, like, octagons, but with, like hundredsagons…. You walk a little bit this way, and then you look and say, oh, north has moved from here to here, cause I've gone a little bit around….

Eleanor 'Cause *north* moves.

Mary R. It doesn't

Eleanor No, it does, with respect to *me*.

Wendy Perhaps you move with respect to it.

Mary R. Yeah.

Eleanor Yeah. [I start walking with my left arm out to the side, supposedly pointing at the North Pole, and my right arm straight ahead of me, supposedly in the direction that my compass would indicate is east.] So I take this step now [*top figure* p. 328] [ahead of me, essentially down one of Fern's lines] but I can't have … kept my hands like that, … cause I have to stay like this [*bottom figure*, p. 328] [I shift slightly left, so my left arm still points to a supposed North Pole.] So then I take this step here, [down another of Fern's lines] and then I have to move back [to the left] like that, [**Mary R.**: Right, right] and then I take this step here [down another line]. [The others break out in applause.]…. And then I follow that one [another line], but if I take my left arm with me, it's left the North Pole, and it has to correct back again....

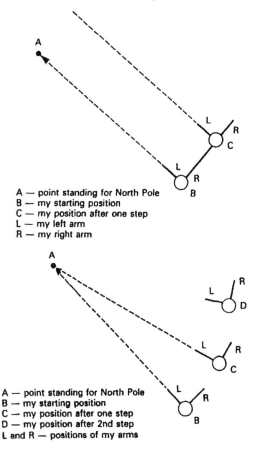

A — point standing for North Pole
B — my starting position
C — my position after one step
L — my left arm
R — my right arm

A — point standing for North Pole
B — my starting position
C — my position after one step
D — my position after 2nd step
L and R — positions of my arms

Mary R. It keeps adjusting you. It's really neat....

Wendy But if you are glued, if you could clamp the compass so it wouldn't move when you walk a little bit, suddenly north would be in a totally different place....

Fern ... [T]his line that you're going around here is a latitude ... that would bring you to Spain, as opposed to down there [down one of the lines], to the equator.... This shape, when you put this shape onto the globe [her drawing, with the North Pole at the center], this line [the circle] would set at a certain latitude....

Mary R. Everything else would go down....

    Fern 'Course then they would keep going past the equator, I don't know about that.

        [This introduces the third idea of east, which we did not resolve with the other two. The going-to-the-equator view of what east is had, as you recall, two sources. The L–shape *crosses* the equator, while in the other version, Fern's lines would wrap around the equator. I include a short bit of discussion of that idea.]....

    Fern [T]here's something wrong about the L, maybe ... maybe it's not really an L....

Eleanor Wouldn't it stay on the equator once it got to the equator?...

Mary D. Because then if you're in the Southern Hemisphere, you'd do the opposite....

  Joanne What kind of a shape is that?

Eleanor That is an amazing shape, though ... a spiral that then reaches a circle, and stops getting bigger....

Fern The only way you'd get this line [the one that would wrap around the equator] is if you had a laser beam, and you shot your laser beam from where you were standing, due east, and in an instant, the laser beam burns a trail on that line....

Joanne This line is a continuation of one of those lines up there [in Fern's drawing], which eventually reaches the equator....

Wendy If you could stand on the earth, on the equinox, and shoot one of those pistols that has a string with a sucker, and you could shoot it right at the sun ... and have it "blip" on the sun, so you had this lovely string from you to the sun. And then the earth began to turn, that day, and the string would be wound....

Mary D. You could be putting this dot on the earth, as every point on the earth passes through sunrise. This is sunrise. As it passes through sunrise, if there were something spitting at the planet, making points on it, ... when you went through, when the day was over, you'd have an equator on your planet ... I see how the equator is made. Now the equator has a different meaning for me. [We return to a discussion of our other two easts.]....

Wendy I will not agree that that's due east, toward the equator.... I want another word than due east for that....

Wendy [If Fern's east is east] how can you say Spain is east of us? Spain is north of us [since the compass reading is corrected to the north].

Mary R. No it's not!...

Wendy But you have to constantly correct, after each step.

Mary R. You don't have to correct, because your constant corrects for you. Either the North Star, or the compass — one of those change for you. They keep you going in the direction, and that's how you, and that's how they did the latitude lines.

Wendy But then, why— Then there are two easts.

Mary D. Yes! We said that. There's Fern's east, and there's the latitude east.

Wendy Right. But I don't—, I can't—, I don't feel comfortable with it ... it makes me dizzy....

Wendy What I would like to do is ... I'd like to present that kind of information to somebody who deals with east and west....

Fern I'm thinking, if he came in here right now, and said, you're right and I'm wrong, I would think he hadn't thought about this problem long enough....

Wendy ... Now we have two different words for east.

Eleanor Different meanings for east.

Wendy Right. And one word.

Jinny In two different lang— I mean it's like two different worlds, it's a flat world and a spherical world....

Eleanor You'd like a map–maker.

Wendy Yeah, or somebody who sails....

Fern I don't think any of those people would have had to resolve this issue in order to be able to do what they do....

Wendy ... What I understood today doesn't fit with what I've understood from all of that learning and all the things that I understand about east so far. Or believe about east, have read about east, hold about east ... I'm trying to think if there's another way to resolve it that wouldn't have two easts....

Fern The two views that we have right now are not, one, that east is Spain and the other one that east is something else. We have two views. One is that east is Spain. And the other is that east is both Spain and something else.... They're not two conflicting things. One is part of the other.... Do you know what I mean? Like one has more parts to the explanation....

Wendy I don't think that anyone will agree....

Mary D. Then why aren't we the experts?

We did go off to see Philip and Phylis Morrison, creators of PBS's *The Ring of Truth*, which included one episode on map-making. And there we learned, to our extraordinary satisfaction, how Charles Mason, astronomer, and Jeremiah Dixon, mathematician and surveyor, laid out the Mason–Dixon line. At night they fixed north, by the stars. By day they cut through the trees at 90 degrees from north. At night, they fixed north again, and when they started each new day, returning, in Jinny's terms, to the "flat world," they had to adjust their continuing swath slightly to the north. It was just like Wendy's walking circle. As Mary R. had said, "And that's how they did the latitude lines."

Conclusion

This is an exceptional group, admittedly; not in its make-up at the onset, but in its history of learning together. This is one reason I wanted to present an impression of their work together. They know it pays off to stick with a complex issue. They know the value to each person of starting from her own set of ideas and points of engagement and relating new ideas to that base — Piaget's fundamental point, but so rarely acted on in formal education. And they know the value of paying attention to each other's ideas, to see how they can expand their own through making the accommodations necessary to assimilate other points of view — classic Piaget again.

Any one of us in this group might have dismissed the discussion by saying that, of course, Spain is east, so let's get on with it. Or, well, we know that east is where the sun rises, so let's get on with it. Instead, by recognizing that this was a complex issue, we pushed our ideas into a construction of a fairly sophisticated understanding of relationships between a flat world and a round world. This took us into map–making, surveying, history, geography (as we talked about this issue with various people we learned that the east–west highways in the Canadian prairies have periodic small–angle turns — like Wendy's hundredsagons — having been set out in a fashion similar to the Mason–Dixon line), and math (what is the mathematical nature of that third version of east, a curve which approaches the equator and wraps around it?)

Our delving into these areas grew out of the simple question of what east is, which itself grew out of the simple question of what can we see the moon do in the sky — a question that had engaged this group for fifteen years. This exaggerated example is the strongest way to make my point: most areas of study that are at all worth our attention entail far more complexity than is acknowledged in our curriculum; and further, people's intellectual engagement, when they are given the chance to pursue these complexities according to their own lights, is extraordinary. Our challenge as curriculum developers is to find the ways to engage learners, young and old, in the complexities of the area we think is important for them to know about. As researchers who are interested in how ideas actually develop, I think we have exactly the same challenge. I hope I have made clear how intertwined these challenges are.

I am under no illusion that, in the current climate of over–simplification, curriculum that celebrates the complexities of subject matter will be readily received. The point of this article is to rail against that climate, and to offer an idea of what our schools, our teachers, and our students may be missing by being subjected to that oversimplified view of the nature of teaching and learning.

I would like to end, though, with some high school students' points of view, that poignantly express their awareness of how they are short–changed by current curriculum. With

Candace Julyan (1988), they studied trees changing colour in the fall. They were studying the trees themselves, in all their complexity, and trying to relate what they saw to their text-book course on chlorophyll and photosynthesis. The quotes exemplify their feelings about details which make a complex study accessible; about being able to figure out complex things in their own ways; and about the futility of trying to over-simplify curriculum.

> "It took me a while to get it … [to get] my ideas together and see what I think. Once I got it was good…. This is fun. I like it. It's neat that I figured all this out."
>
> "I was thinking how the wind takes the tree and the leaves … and when the tree bends, it stops feeding the leaves. Did you ever think of that?"
>
> "I love this project … I can never come up with ideas like this during labs…. But *this*, it seems like I can come up with ideas really well. I don't know. I like this so much. I love it…."
>
> "You have to think. I don't think a lot of people like to think…. [This study takes] a lot of figuring out. It's fun, but it's hard."
>
> "They throw something new at me and I can't stand it, and I have to do it their way. That's what I don't like about science, everything has already been figured out ahead of time. But if you find something different it's wrong."
>
> "I don't know why we *read* about trees in science class. It seems stupid not to come outside and really study 'em, don'tcha think?"

References:

Bamberger, Jeanne, Duckworth, Eleanor, and Lampert, Mag-dalene, (1981). *An experiment in teacher development: Final report* (Contract No. G–81–0042). Washington, D.C.: National Institute of Education.

DiSchino, Mary (1987). "The Many Phases of Growth." *Journal of Teaching and Learning*, 1(3), 12–28.

Duckworth, Eleanor (1964). "Floating color tubes." *Nature and*

Children. 1(2), 6–7.

Duckworth, Eleanor (1986). "Teaching as Research," *Harvard Educational Review*, 56, 4.

Elementary Science Study. (1967a). *Gases and "Airs."* St. Louis: McGraw–Hill.

Elementary Science Study. (1976). *Senior balancing.* St. Louis: McGraw–Hill.

Frost, Robert (1969). *The Poetry of Robert Frost* (E. C. Lathern, Ed.). New York: Holt, Rinehart & Winston.

Hawkins, David (1978). "Critical barriers to science learning," *Outlook*, 29, 3–23.

Julyan, Candace. (1988). "Understanding trees: Four Case Studies," Unpublished doctoral dissertation. Harvard University.

Piaget, J., & Inhelder, B. (1975). *The origin of the idea of chance in children* (L. Leake, Jr., P. Burrell, & H. Fishbein, Trans.). New York: W.W. Norton. (original work published in 1951.)

Schneier, Lisa (1990). "Why not just say it?" Unpublished manuscript, Harvard University, Graduate School of Education.

Contributors

Marie Battiste teaches in the Faculty of Education at the University of Saskatchewan in Saskatoon.

Bill Bigelow is an editorial associate of *Rethinking Schools* and a teacher at Jefferson High School in Portland, Oregon.

Keren Brathwaite is a founding faculty member of the Transitional Year Programme, University of Toronto, where she teaches and co–ordinates the English programme. She is also a founding member and former chair of the Organization of Black Children which she helped to establish in 1980 as an advocacy group for African Canadian parents and students. She is on the Editorial Board of *Our Schools/Our Selves* .

Bob Davis teaches social science at Atkinson College, York University. He has taught history at Stephen Leacock Collegiate Institute in Toronto.

Eleanor Duckworth is associate professor of education in the Graduate School of Education, Harvard University, and director of the Harvard Teachers' Network.

Dick Holland teaches at Ursula Franklin Academy in Toronto.

Michael Kaufman, a founder of the White Ribbon campaign, is a writer and public speaker, and works with teachers and students on issues concerning men and masculinity, violence and sexism.

Elaine MacIntosh teaches a JK–SK–1 class at Dundas Street Public School in downtown Toronto.

Anne Manicom teaches in the Education Department at Mount Saint Vincent University in Halifax, Nova Scotia.

George Martell chairs the Social Science Department at Atkinson College, York University. He is also the chair of the *Our Schools/Our Selves* Editorial Board.

Robin Mathews teaches in the Centre for Canadian Studies at Simon Fraser University. He lives in Vancouver, B.C.

Myra Novogrodsky is the Co-ordinator of the Equity Studies Centre at the Toronto District Board of Education.

Ken Osborne has recently retired from the Faculty of Education at the University of Manitoba.

Bob Peterson is an editor of *Rethinking Schools* and a bilingual fifth-grade teacher at La Escuela Fratney in Milwaukee, Wisconsin.

Althea Prince is a writer of adult fiction and children's stories. A sociologist by training, she teaches in the Faculty of Arts, and is academic advisor in Calumet College, York University.

Chris Searle teaches in a comprehensive school in Sheffield, England.

Margaret Wells teaches in the Faculty of Education at York University.

John Willinsky teaches in the Faculty of Education at the University of British Columbia.

Reprint Permissions

Grateful acknowledgement is made for the permission to reprint the following material.

"Getting Off the Track: Stories from an Untracked Classroom" by Bill Bigelow. Reprinted with permission from *Rethinking Schools: Agenda for Change*, Rethinking Schools, 1001 E. Keefe Ave., Milwaukee, WI 53212; 414-964-9646.

"Teaching for Social Justice" by Bob Peterson. Reprinted with permission from *Rethinking Schools* Vol. 8 Number 3, Rethinking Schools, 1001 E. Keefe Ave., Milwaukee, WI 53212; 414-964-9646.

"Twenty-four, Forty-two, and I Love You: Keeping It Complex" by Eleanor Duckworth. *Harvard Educational Review*, 61:1 (February 1991), pp. 1–24, Copyright (c) 1991 by the President and Fellows of Harvard College. All rights reserved. Also in Eleanor Duckworth *"The Having of Wonderful Ideas" and Other Essays on Teaching and Learning*, second edition, New York, Teachers College Press, 1996, pp. 122–149.

"The Gulf Between: a School and a War" by Chris Searle. *Race & Class*, April–June 1992. The Institute of Race Relations, 2–6 Leeke Street, King's Cross Road, London WCIX 9HS.

The Our Schools/Our Selves Series

James Lorimer & Company is now distributing and
marketing the Our Schools/Our Selves book series.
New titles will be published as series titles.
The backlist of titles is now available to the trade
through James Lorimer & Company.
Our Schools/Our Selves subscribers will continue
to receive copies of these titles as they are published,
as part of their *OS/OS* subscription.
Libraries and bookstores can order *Our Schools/
Our Selves* from James Lorimer & Company
through its distributor:

Formac Distributing Limited
5502 Atlantic Street
Halifax B3H 1G4
Toll free order line 1-800-565-1975
Fax orders (902) 425-0166

In the U.S.:
Formac Distributing Limited
121 Mount Vernon Street
Boston MA 02108
1-800-565-1975

*Contact the order desk to be sure to receive your copy of the
1997 Lorimer university catalogue*

Subscribe & Save

Please enter my subscription for 6 issues of OUR SCHOOLS/OUR SELVES starting with issue number_____. Please check one:

INDIVIDUAL

____ Regular rate $38.00
____ Student/Unemployed/
     Pensioner rate $32.00
____ Outside Canada   Cdn $50.00

ORGANIZATION

____ In Canada $50.00
____ Outside Canada   Cdn $60.00

SUSTAINING

____ $100   ____ $200   Other $____

OR send me issue number(s) _____ at $9.00 per single and $16.00 per double issue

To subscribe please phone our toll-free number at 1-800-565-1975 or mail form to *Our Schools/Our Selves*, 5502 Atlantic Street, Halifax, NS B3H 9Z9

Name _____

Address _____

City _____ Prov _____ Code _____

Occupation _____

     ❏ Cheque enclosed   ❏ VISA/Mastercard

Card No._____ Expiry Date _____

Signature _____

- -

Pass to a Friend

Please enter my subscription for 6 issues of OUR SCHOOLS/OUR SELVES starting with issue number_____. Please check one:

INDIVIDUAL

____ Regular rate $38.00
____ Student/Unemployed/
     Pensioner rate $32.00
____ Outside Canada   Cdn $50.00

ORGANIZATION

____ In Canada $50.00
____ Outside Canada   Cdn $60.00

SUSTAINING

____ $100   ____ $200   Other $____

OR send me issue number(s) _____ at $9.00 per single and $16.00 per double issue

To subscribe please phone our toll-free number at 1-800-565-1975 or mail form to *Our Schools/Our Selves*, 5502 Atlantic Street, Halifax, NS B3H 9Z9

Name _____

Address _____

City _____ Prov _____ Code _____

Occupation _____

     ❏ Cheque enclosed   ❏ VISA/Mastercard

Card No._____ Expiry Date _____

Signature _____